THE REVOLUTIONARY ARMIES

THE REVOLUTIONARY ARMIES

The Historical Development of the Soviet and the Chinese People's Liberation Armies

JONATHAN R. ADELMAN

Contributions in Political Science, Number 38

GREENWOOD PRESS

WESTPORT, CONNECTICUT • LONDON, ENGLAND

UA
837
A62
c.2

D 8052

Lamont Library
Harvard University

Library of Congress Cataloging in Publication Data

Adelman, Jonathan R
  The revolutionary armies.

  (Contributions in political science; no. 38
ISSN 0147-1066)
  Bibliography: p.
  1. China (People's Republic of China, 1949-   )
Chung-kuo jên min chieh fang chün—History.   2. Russia
(1923-   U.S.S.R.) Armiiâ—History.   3. Sociology,
Military—China.   4. Sociology, Military—Russia.
5. China—History—1945-   6. Russia—History—
1917-   I. Title.   II. Series.
UA837.A62   322'.5'091717   79-7728
ISBN 0-313-22026-3

Library of Congress Catalog Card Number: 79-7728
ISBN: 0-313-22026-3
ISSN: 0147-1066

First published in 1980

Greenwood Press
A division of Congressional Information Service, Inc.
51 Riverside Avenue, Westport, Connecticut 06880

Printed in the United States of America

10 9 8 7 6 5 4 3 2 1

In memory of my grandfather,
David R. Sandler (1888-1962),
a true *maskil*

CONTENTS

TABLES

ACKNOWLEDGMENTS

Like many students of Soviet politics, I am deeply indebted to Professor Seweryn Bialer. From my junior year in college to the completion of my doctoral dissertation at Columbia, he was always a patient advisor and generous intellectual mentor. Much of whatever value this work possesses is owed to his influence. In addition, I wish to thank Professors Thomas Bernstein and Steven Levine for their frequently helpful advice in the course of writing this work.

On a personal level I would like to thank my parents for their constant encouragement in the pursuit of what seemed to be, at times, almost ethereal goals.

THE
REVOLUTIONARY
ARMIES

INTRODUCTION

The role of the military in developing countries has been extensively explored in the last fifteen years. Considerable attention has been focused on the structure of the military, the military in power, and the military as a modernizing force. Various taxonomies of civilian-military relations have been developed. Although the Soviet Union (at least for much of its existence) and the People's Republic of China have been developing countries, their civilian-military relations have not been adequately explained. The role of the Communist army in relation to a party and society undergoing revolutionary transformation has been relatively ignored.

This work tries to rectify this situation. It examines in detail the sharp differences that have existed between the Red Army and the People's Liberation Army (PLA) in their roles in party and societal affairs in the two decades after the end of the civil wars. The manuscript further explores the sources of these differences, with particular emphasis on the civil war period and the nature of revolutionary change in the two countries, and shows the remarkably formative influence of the civil wars and the impact of different modes of revolutionary development on the role of the army in Russia and China.

The overall comparison of Russia and China in the two decades after the end of the civil wars is validated by the numerous similarities which existed between the two countries in this period. Paul Shoup has argued that Communist states should be considered comparable among themselves if "they have adopted the Marxist ideology, if they have experienced a revolution which has destroyed the power structure of the earlier system and if the Party has acquired a monopoly in the decision-making processes of the societies in question, exercising decisive control over all major political, economic,

3

and cultural organizations."[1] Both Russia and China meet this definition. Indeed, Treadgold has stated in an introduction to a collection of articles read at a 1965 Lake Tahoe conference of Russian and Chinese specialists,

> Probably the majority of contributors would agree that the two societies have much in common; that the two great Communist parties in power were more like each other than like organizations existing anywhere else on the planet (the parties of the smaller Communist-ruled states differing at least in scale); and that the leaders had similar concepts of the nature of power and the function of ideology, purposes of controls, the objectives of economic planning, the goals of cultural management.[2]

Furthermore, key similarities existed in the two countries at the end of their civil wars. By 1950 in China and 1921 in Russia, both parties had created multimillion man armies, composed largely of poorly educated peasants. These armies operated at relatively primitive levels of military technology. Both the Russian and the Chinese Communist parties, lacking significant roots in key areas of the country (Russia countryside, south China), were faced with major tasks of economic reconstruction and socialist construction. Both countries possessed powerful external enemies openly hostile to their very existence.

Given these important similarities between the two countries, it is especially interesting that the roles of the Red Army and the People's Liberation Army diverged so sharply in the two decades after the end of the civil wars. The greater influence of the Chinese army relative to party and society has been manifested in several ways. In 1956, for example, seven of ten PLA marshals were elected members of the Chinese Politburo. During and immediately after the Cultural Revolution the army exercised decisive political power in the restoration of public order and the conduct of policy.[3] In 1969 at the Ninth Party Congress twelve of the twenty-five Politburo members served in the army. Defense Minister Lin Piao was Mao's officially designated heir apparent from 1966 until his death in 1971. The Chinese army participated actively in political leadership and economic production functions in society in the 1950-71 period, and in the 1960s it was hailed in "Learn from the PLA" campaigns as a proper model for a future socialist society. Mao seemed to view the army in the 1960s as a repository of revolutionary virtues.

By contrast, the Russian army played a relatively minimal role in the policymaking process. No professional military man joined the Politburo during the 1921-40 period.[4] The lone army man on the Politburo during this period was usually the war commissar, the party's representative in the army. The Russian army played no significant role in society, whether in economic production or political leadership, and during this period it was never acclaimed as a proper role model for society.

Although its involvement in party and society affairs has fluctuated sharply over time, the Chinese army has consistently played a considerably greater role in society and possessed greater power in party affairs than the Russian army. The available literature on the role of the military in developing countries does little to explain either the general role of Communist armies or the specific differences between the Russian and Chinese armies. Most of the literature is oriented toward the role of the military in poorly integrated new nations. These nations, unlike Russia and China with their Communist parties, lacked any vehicle to direct a massive revolutionary transformation of society.

Communist armies are given relatively little attention in the literature. Those studies that do try to account for their political role often have placed them in inappropriate categories. Finer, for example, has placed the Soviet Union in the developed political category together with Weimar Germany, interwar Japan, and Gaullist France. Under his schema, the military in a country of developed political culture is capable of a role of influence or blackmail in relation to the government.[7] However, the power of the Soviet army, especially in the interwar period, was far more circumscribed by the party than the power of the German army during the Weimar Republic or the power of the Japanese army in interwar Japan. Another tendency of the literature has been to create a single unitary category for all Communist armies. Thus, in their analyses of civilian-military relations, Janowitz and Speier have created a "totalitarian" category while Huntington has created a "Communist" category.[8] Such categories do not account for the great differences that have existed between the Russian and Chinese armies in their roles in party and society affairs.

The literature also possesses a static bias. Whether in the Shils and Janowitz taxonomies of civilian-military relations or in the Huntington and Finer schemata relating level of development to the role of the army in politics, the literature takes little account of the revolutionary transformations that have occurred in Russia and China.[9] The literature also contains a further ahistorical quality in tending to ignore the importance of such formative events as the civil wars in shaping army relations to party and society.

From the literature, we can also adduce certain factors—level of military technology, international political environment, political culture, and level of development—that help explain the differences between the Russian and Chinese armies. While each of these factors is of some value in explaining the differences, none of them, either separately or in combination, is able to provide a totally satisfactory explanation of the differences.

It would seem logical that as an army became significantly more technologically advanced, it would dispose of more resources and would increase its role in the policymaking process. The great increase in the power and strength of the American armed forces after World War II was paralleled by the rise of a supportive military-industrial complex that greatly strengthened the role of the army in the policymaking process.[10] Gordon Craig, in linking the level of military technology to the role of the army in the policymaking process, has declared,

It is perhaps an inevitable concomitant of technical progress that military influence in the directions of foreign affairs should have increased sharply in all countries since 1870. The progressive mechanization of warfare has, for instance, made it essential for policymakers, in time of international tension, to solicit and weigh the advice of army and navy staffs concerning foreign capabilities. In the democratic states it has always been recognized, however, that the broadening of the sphere of military activity is inherently dangerous and that, unless the right of ultimate decision rests with the civilian authorities, foreign policy will tend to be dictated by military expediency.[11]

However, the shortcomings of level of technology as an explanatory variable are readily apparent. During the 1930s the Red Army vastly improved its technological capabilities. Yet, despite this change, the army's role in the policymaking process—especially during the Great Purges—actually shrank rather than expanded. In the case of the Chinese army one could argue that there existed possibly even a certain negative correlation between the level of technology and the army's role in party and society affairs. To the extent that the "red" and "expert" dichotomy was meaningful for the PLA, any gravitation toward the "expert" model would imply a withdrawal from the broader policymaking process and from societal affairs.[12] It would also imply both a diminution of the army's role as an independent politicized actor and a withdrawal from functions, such as economic production and political leadership, performed in society. Thus, in neither country could changes in the level of technology explain differences in army/party and army/society relations.

A second possible explanatory variable would be the international political environment. The role of armies generally has risen in times of international crises. This view has attained its fullest expression in Lasswell's "garrison-state thesis," which attempts to explain the role of the army in the policymaking process by reference to the international political environment and the threats it might pose to the security of a nation.[13] These threats in turn might necessitate a strengthened military posture and concurrent rise in the power and influence of the army.

However, both Russia and China, as Communist countries, existed in very hostile international environments which seemed to threaten their very existence. During the 1920s, in the aftermath of the Allied intervention in the civil war, the Bolshevik leaders felt that, in the words of the Tenth Party Congress in 1921, "The capitalist countries surrounded us in a dense ring."[14] In the 1930s the "drawing near of military menace" in the form of the rise of German fascism and Japanese militarism further strengthened the sense of "capitalist encirclement."[15] As Dinerstein has concluded, "the feeling of extreme vulnerability ... pervaded Soviet life for a third of a century after the October Revolution. ... The constant Communist fear of the outside world was no product of a disordered imagination."[16]

From 1950 to 1971, the Chinese existed in an equally hostile international political environment. During the entire period they faced the strong and enduring hostility of the world's leading superpower, the United States. Its animosity was manifested in military pacts, intervention in the Korean and Vietnam Wars, and the disposition of its troops between China and Taiwan. For the Chinese Communists, there always remained the serious possibility of invasion ("unleashing") by the Nationalist troops of Taiwan.[17] A *Jen Min Jih Pao* editorial in February 1954, for example, spoke in terms redolent of statements made in the Soviet Union in the 1921-40 period, "However, our country is still surrounded by capitalism and the threat of a new war of aggression which American imperialism tries to unleash has not been removed, while the possibility for remnant forces of bandit Chiang in Taiwan to disturb the coast also exists."[18] Furthermore, as demonstrated by Sino-Soviet border clashes on the Ussuri River in 1969, the Chinese in the 1960s also were threatened by the world's other superpower, the Soviet Union.[19] Thus, as both countries operated to a large extent in relatively similar international environments, this variable lacks the ability to differentiate between the two countries.[20]

Differing political cultures would be another possible explanatory factor. An argument could be made that while the Russian and Chinese Communists shared a common Marxist heritage, their attitudes toward the military were shaped by different cultural and political influences and concerns. The Bolsheviks, steeped in French revolutionary history and keenly aware of the destructive potential of the army (e.g., the Kornilov coup, treason during the civil war), were genuinely concerned about the possible emergence of Bonapartism in Russia. The fact that Trotsky, Tukhachevsky, and Zhukov were all suspected of Bonapartism and were subsequently removed from their posts could be cited to show the pervasive continuation of this attitude far beyond the civil war. By contrast, the political culture of the Chinese Communists was shaped under different circumstances.[21] The Chinese leaders, it could be argued, reacted against the instability, fragmentation, and weakness of the Chinese state in the 1911-49 period, especially in the 1911-27 period. They placed a high priority on the effective reintegration of the state.[22] The military, of necessity,would play a key role in accomplishing this task.

However, the utility of political culture as an explanatory variable is limited. The disintegration of Russia and the recurrent attempts by various foreign governmnets (for example, Poland and Japan) to annex parts of Russia during the civil war made the reassertion of strong central authority also a key Russian concern. Militarism was not a specifically Russian phenomenon but rather a general problem in all developing countries, including China. The Chinese Communists surely reacted negatively to the militarism rampant in China during the warlord period (1911-27). Militarism was even a problem within the party. In 1929 Mao attacked the "purely military viewpoint" that refused to recognize the supremacy of the party over the army.[23] From 1935 to 1937 Mao struggled against Chang Kuo-tao and his independent army. The image of irresponsible Bonapartism was always present in the form of the militaristic Chiang Kai-shek.[24] Thus, the problem of militarism and the need for strong authority to reintegrate the state existed in both Russia and China.

A final possible variable would be the level of economic development. One could argue that in an underdeveloped country with few major institutions, the army, as often the most modern, cohesive, and powerful institution with control of the instruments of violence, would tend to play a crucial role in the policymaking process.[25] As the society modernized, with the attendant creation of a number of strong institutions, the value and uniqueness of the army as a relatively modern and cohesive force would sharply decline, and its role in party and society affairs would correspondingly decline.

Although Russia in the 1920s and China from 1950 to 1971 were both underdeveloped countries, the role of the army differed sharply in the two countries. Furthermore, although Soviet society was underdeveloped in the 1920s, the army, far from playing a major role in the policymaking process, was actually weak and isolated from society. This variable might have some force in poorly integrated underdeveloped countries that lack an alternative mobilization force apart from the army; but, as Huntington has stressed, in Communist countries the party has provided an integrating organizational alternative to the army.[26] Thus, the variable of the level of development of society fails to differentiate significantly between the roles of the army in Russia and China.

These factors do provide some useful guidance and indicate the parameters within which army/party and army/society relations functioned. The level of military technology had a key impact on the relation between commanders and commissars within the army and on the question of a supportive military-industrial complex. The level of economic development helped define the number of key actors (besides the army) and the extent of available resources in the political system. The nature of the revolutionary political culture helped determine the degree of legitimacy which the party leadership would attribute to the political desires of the military leaders. Finally, and most importantly, the international political environment significantly determined the importance of the military factor (as opposed to the military sector) in the policymaking process. Indeed, the military factor may have been the most important factor in the massive campaigns of collectivization, industrialization, and modernization in the Soviet Union during the 1930s.[27]

We should also consider the possible role of pre-Communist traditional political culture. There are striking parallels between traditional army/state relations and Communist army/party relations in Russia and China. Many scholars have argued that the Soviet system has deep roots in the czarist period. Barghoorn has declared that "Soviet tendencies toward absolutist and autocratic preferences among alternative solutions for political problems were rendered highly probable by the preponderance of authoritarian over democratic behavior in the pre-revolutionary era."[28]

In czarist Russia, as in the Soviet Union from 1921 to 1940, the army tended to be subordinated effectively to civilian authority. For as Brzezinski has written,

> Traditions of military subordination to civil power are deeply ingrained in both Russian and American politics. . . . Unlike many autocracies, the czarist regime was not politically challanged by its military establishments, in spite of many defeats. . . . The Army officer corps . . . was one of the principal pillars of czarist rule. . . . The Soviet Union inherited a tradition of civilian control rooted in czarist concepts of absolute rule.[29]

Similarly Curtis has found that the military during the reign of Nicholas I "was completely dominated by the Tsar, a thorough autocrat."[30]

During the nineteenth century the czarist army demonstrated its loyalty by repeatedly crushing numerous internal revolts. [31] In 1849 it suppressed the Hungarian Revolution. Even during the popular 1905 Revolution, the army, despite some wavering, in Andolenko's words, "by remaining faithful to the throne ... broke the revolution."[32] Finally, in 1917, the army neither overthrew the czar nor took power in the period between the February and October Revolutions.[33]

Nevertheless, in a manner similar to that in the Soviet Union in the 1930s, the military factor and the needs of the army received great attention. Trotsky has argued that in czarist Russia,

> The history of Russia's state economy is an unbroken chain of efforts—heroic efforts in a certain sense—aimed at providing the military organization with the means necessary for its continuing existence. The entire government apparatus was built and constantly rebuilt in the interests of the treasury. Its function consisted in snatching every particle of the accumulated labor of the people and utilizing it for its own ends.[34]

During the eighteenth and much of the nineteenth century, at least 40 percent of the annual national budget was devoted to the military.[35] Furthermore, the military factor was so important that Pares could write about the reign of Peter the Great, "Reform, like every other activity of Peter the Great, grew out of the needs of the army."[36] Thus, while the czarist and Soviet armies were both rigidly subordinated to civilian, authoritarian regimes, both armies and their concerns were also the special object of attention of the regime.

Similarly, there exist some parallels between the pre-Communist period (1911-49) and the Communist era in China. The pre-Communist period demonstrated the great importance of armies in the policymaking process. From 1911 to 1927, the warlords primarily based their rule on military power.[37] Furthermore, the military and military thinking played an important role in the Kuomintang period (1927-49).[38] Pye has argued that

> From the days of the warlords to the succession crisis in Communist China, military power and the reality of armies have been consistent and dominant elements within Chinese politics. ... Military power has been the basic currency of modern Chinese politics ... the spirit of military organization finds its way into all manner of governmental and political organizations.[39]

However, traditional political culture generally refers not to the warlord and Kuomintang periods but rather to the pre-1911 period of Imperial China. Our analysis of this period is hampered, as Franke has noted, by the lack of first-rate studies of the military history of China.[40] Ping-ti Ho's view of the prevalence "of the civilian ideal in traditional Chinese governmental administration" seems to be a generally accepted view.[41] Fairbank and Needham would agree with Eisenstadt's analysis of the pre-1911 period, "In China, though in diffferent periods it enjoyed relatively great political significance, the army did not constitute a permanent semi-legitimate (or at least accepted) factor in the political process"[42] However, Franke has argued that the creation of regional armies to replace the ineffectual centrally controlled Banner armies during the Taiping Rebellion (1850-64) laid the base for future warlordism.[43] Mary Wright, noting the "powerful centripetal forces of the restored Confucian state" in the 1860s, has argued against this view.[44] She has stated

It is misleading to argue that because armies of this type later drifted away from a crumbling central authority, this was the aspect of greatest significance at the time they were first formed in the 1860s. This fallacy overlooks the aims that guided the actions of provincial leaders of the Restoration. They were interested not in securing satrapies for themselves but in assuring the survival of the Confucian order; only later when the Confucian order was clearly doomed did the disastrous *sauve qui peut* attitude become common.[45]

In summary, there appears to have been a disjunction between the pre-1911 period and the 1911-49 and 1950-71 periods.

We have seen the existence of some interesting parallels and a number of considerable differences between the traditional (or in the case of the 1911-49 period, the pre-Communist) and the Communist patterns of the role of the army in the policymaking process. However, even the parallels conceal sharp differences in the very nature of the armies. Unlike traditional armies, the Red Army and the People's Liberation Army were highly politicized forces with key functions of serving as "schools of Communism" and education. The officer corps of the two Communist armies were vastly more democratized than the elite-dominated officer corps of traditional armies. Furthermore, the traditional armies provide no significant clues as to the origins of the sharp differences between the two Communist armies in their roles in society. Thus, for example, while czarist armies, as in the military colonies in the first half of the nineteenth century, often engaged in economic production, the Red Army almost never performed such a function.[46] Nevertheless, some parallels do clearly exist. The crucial question is how these traditional cultural patterns were transmitted, if at all, between the pre-Communist and the Communist periods. This requires a study of the civil war periods, the key links between the pre-Communist and the Communist periods.

If we now turn to the literature on revolutions, we find some useful general, albeit little specific, guidance. Such authors as Huntington, Johnson, Tucker, and Wolf have pointed to the different natures of the Russian and Chinese revolutions.[47] Huntington has even elaborated these differences into "Western" and "Eastern" models of revolution.[48] Such authors as Wolf and Tucker have stressed that the Russian revolution represented the seizure of power by the small Bolshevik party at the head of worker uprisings in the cities.[49] At the same time parallel but uncontrolled peasant uprisings occured in the countryside. The small industrial proletariat was the "spearhead" of the Bolsheviks.[50] By contrast, the Chinese revolution, in Johnson's view, represented a "mass militarized insurrection" in the country-side.[51] Rather than seizing power in one quick blow, the Chinese Communists gradually built up and expanded their strength among the peasants in rural base areas. Eventually their alternative government became strong enough to take power. Thus, the method of coming to power and the base of support of the revolution differed sharply between the two movements.

The literature, however suggestive, does not explore the impact of these differences between the revolutionary movements on the future role of the army in society and party affairs in China and in Russia. In suggesting what might have been the impact of such differences, we should particularly keep in mind that both Russia and China were underdeveloped countries with peasant majorities at the time of the revolutions.[52]

The Russian Communists, seizing power on the base of the small industrial proletariat and lacking any army of their own, were in a vastly different position from the Chinese Communists. Lacking any experienced officers, they were forced to rely heavily on alien former czarist officers and inexperienced "red" commanders.[53] The army's high command had only tenuous links to the Stalinist faction that dominated the party in the 1920s. Alienated from the peasant majority by their Marxist ideology, radical social experimentation, and urban orientation, the Russian Communists were nevertheless forced to build a large army whose ranks were filled with peasants.[54] The lack of appeal to the peasant majority prevented the party from recruiting a large party stratum within the army. Under these conditions it was scarcely surprising that the Red Army, plagued by treason and desertion, was relatively ineffectual. Such an army would hardly seem likely to play a major role in party and society affairs after the end of the civil war.

By contrast, the Chinese Communists came to power only after an extremely prolonged civil war (1927-49).[55] The Maoist strategy, which entailed the creation of rural base areas and reliance on the peasantry, fostered the early creation of an army (1927) intimately fused with the party and involved in societal affairs. This army/party fusion and lengthy gestation period, coupled with the considerable appeal of the Communist movement to the peasants in the ranks, helped create an effective and revolutionary legitimated army by the end of the civil war.[56] Under these circumstances, the party could create its own officer corps and a large party stratum in the army. Such an army, with close ties to the party, could play a key role in party and societal affairs in the two decades after the end of the civil war.

In order to examine our hypothesis, we will make a detailed examination and comparison of the two civil wars. Although in the case of Russia the civil war period (1918-21) is easily definable, the same is not true for China. In a sense the entire 1927-49 period represented the civil war period in which crucial attitudes and relations were formed for the future role of the army in party and society affairs. However, the 1946-49 period—the "third civil war" in Chinese Communist terminology—proved preferable as a period of comparison to the Russian civil war period. This period reflected all the key elements of army/party and army/society relations as they developed over the entire 1927-49 period. Considerably more material was available on this period than on the preceding one. Indeed, a paucity of material available on the 1927-45 period would have made it difficult to cover adequately this period. Finally, the decisive nature of the 1946-49 civil war and its relatively short duration made it a good choice for comparison with the 1918-21 Russian civil war. Although often neglected by scholars, the civil wars had a profoundly formative impact in both countries.[57] In Russia and China the top political leaders in the two decades after the end of the civil war were prerevolutionary party members, significantly influenced by the experiences of the civil wars.[58] In Russia particularly, the middle-level party militants were largely men for whom the civil war was their first and dominant formative experience. The thinness of the party stratum in the army, the frequent treason and mass desertion of army officers and men, and the general ineffectiveness of the army alienated it from the party. The officer corps, dominated by ex-czarist officers, was largely alien to the Bolsheviks. By contrast, in China the large party stratum in the army, the army/party fusion, and the effectiveness of the PLA bound the army and party close together. The officer corps, especially at its top level, was intimately intertwined with the party leadership. Finally, within the army the civil wars played an important role in the formation of the Stalinist military faction in the Red Army and the field-army system in the People's Liberation Army.

The formative nature of the civil war period calls into question the considerable stress placed by such scholars as Daniels, Leites, and Fainsod on the importance of the pre-1917 period.[59] Fainsod has perhaps best expressed this commonly held view when he wrote,

> The period before 1917 was a proving ground in which doctrine was elaborated, organization tempered, tactics tested. In this crucible the strategy of 1917 was developed and Bolshevism as a system of governance took form. Still later the experiences of this period were to provide a set of precedents on the basis of which decisions would be defended and attacked, orthodoxies would harden and heresies be condemned. . . . Out of the totalitarian embryo would come totalitarianism full-blown.[60]

Yet, the army and the secret police were only created during the civil war and the very nature of the party was transformed in the course of the civil war.[61] The pre-1917 period tells us very little about the future role of the army in party and society affairs.

By placing such emphasis on the civil war periods in Russia and China, this book makes itself vulnerable to the charge that it represents a single-factor, monocausal analysis. There is undoubtedly a certain element of truth in such a description. However, two points are crucial in this respect. The Russian and Chinese civil wars are not simply another explanatory variable, such as level of military technology or international political environment. Rather they are political, social, and cultural phenomena, representing one of the crucial periods in the history of Russia and China. The civil war periods were of decisive importance in shaping the role of the army (and other institutions as well) in the two decades after the end of the civil wars. The emphasis on the civil wars is particularly necessary in view of the relative neglect of this period in Russia and China. There exist very few good analytic works on the civil war periods. Furthermore, other factors and variables are not neglected. Earlier we saw that such variables as international political environment and level of military technology played a role, albeit not a decisive role, in influencing the role of the army and especially the importance given the military factor. In Chapters 4 and 5 we will see the role that such factors as intra-army and intraparty struggles played in determining the role of the army in party and society affairs. Thus, while the civil war periods will be viewed as the single most important and heretofore neglected explanatory factor, many other possible variables will also be utilized.

Several major difficulties were encountered in writing this work. The principal difficulty involved the frequent lack of good data and material on the role of the army. In the case of Russia, the documentation of the civil war, with all its shortcomings, is adequate. However, while some good data and material is available on the 1920s, less is available on the 1930s. In the case of China, the problem has been even more acute. The problem of secrecy that generally surrounds the affairs of the military in any country, but especially in Communist countries, further complicates the matter. Furthermore, despite the numerous and important similarities between the two countries, there are, nevertheless, sharp differences in the nature of their political systems.

The potential significance of this work lies in its attempt to begin to fill two lacunae that exist in the literature concerning the role of the military in developing and Communist countries. One is the lack of an adequate explanation of the role of the military in developing countries, especially Communist countries, which have undergone a widespread, revolutionary transformation of society. The second is the seeming absence of any systematic explanation of a sharply divergent roles which the Chinese and Soviet armies have played in relation to party and society. By focusing on the nature and extent of the revolutionary transformation and the relation of the military to the transformation, I hope to fill some part of the first. By emphasizing the crucial experience of the decisive civil wars in forming army/party and army/society relations and influencing (as well as reflecting) the nature of the revolutionary transformation of society, I hope to fill part of the second. By emphasizing these two factors involving societal change in combination with other variables (such as level of military technology and international political environment), I hope to make a contribution to the literature of comparative Communist institutions.

NOTES

1. Paul Shoup, "Comparing Communist Nations: Prospects for an Empirical Approach," *American Political Science Review* 62, no. 3 (March 1968): 188. Ionescu has suggested that all Communist states share five common characteristics—largely born out of war, abolition of private ownership of means of production, telelogical, apparat-states, oppositionless. See Ghita Ionescu, *Comparative Communist Politics* (London: Macmillan, 1972), p. 43.

2. Donald Treadgold, ed. *Soviet and Chinese Communism: Similarities and Differences* (Seattle: University of Washington Press, 1967), pp. xvii-xviii. Especially in the last fifteen years there has emerged a burgeoning literature in the area of comparative communism. The growth of the field is epitomized by the appearance of the journal, *Studies in Comparative Communism*. For a sample of some of the work done in the field, see Zbigniew Brzezinski and Samuel Huntington, *Political Power: USA/USSR* (New York: Viking Press, 1964), Frederick Fleron, ed., *Communist Studies and the Social Sciences* (Chicago: Rand-McNally, 1969), Chalmers Johnson, ed., *Change in Communist Systems* (Stanford: Stanford University Press, 1970), and Robert Tucker, "On the Comparative Study of Communism," *World Politics* (January 1967). It is interesting to note that while in the

literature on developing countries there exists a substantial number of works on the role of the military, the same cannot be said about the literature in comparative communism. The relative neglect of Communist armies as a subject of study is illustrated by the fact that not one of the fifteen articles in the Treadgold volume is concerned directly with the role of the armies.

3. This is not to ignore the fact that four of the five members of the Standing Committee of the Chinese Politburo during the Cultural Revolution were civilians; but the army exercised considerable, and at times decisive, power during the latter part of the Cultural Revolution, especially at the regional level.

4. With the brief exception of Marshal Zhukov in 1957, no professional military man had ever been elevated to the Politburo in Soviet history until Defense Minister Grechko was chosen in 1973.

5. Furthermore, while the Chinese army, after a period of Soviet emulation in the 1950s, moved toward elements of a "red" model in the 1960s, the Russian army generally evolved in the 1921-40 period toward an "expert" model.

6. Indeed, Huntington has argued that the existence of the party has been critically important to Communist successes. As he has stated, "In the modernizing countries of Asia and Africa, the stress on organization has been the crucial characteristic differentiating communist from other nationalist movements." See Samuel Huntington, *Political Order in Changing Societies* (New Haven: Yale University Press, 1968), p. 339.

7. S.E. Finer, *The Man on Horseback* (New York: Praeger 1962), pp. 93-109.

8. Morris Janowitz, *The Military in the Political Development of New Nations* (Chicago: University of Chicago Press), pp. 3-4; Hans Speier, *War and the Social Order: Papers in Political Sociology* (New York: G.W. Stewart, 1952), p. 4; Samuel Huntington, "Political Development and Political Decay," in *The Military and Modernization*, ed. Henry Bienen (Chicago: Aldine-Atherton, 1971), p. 204.

9. Edward Shils, "The Military in the Political Development of New States," in *The Role of the Military in Underdeveloped Countries*, ed John Johnson (Princeton: Princeton University Press, 1962), pp. 44-52; Janowitz, *The Military in the Political Development of New Nations*, pp. 3-8; Huntington, *Political Order in Changing Societies*, pp. 193-263; Finer, *The Man on Horseback*, pp. 88-109.

10. Although the American military-industrial complex has been discussed and studied, very little work has been done on the equivalent military-industrial complexes in the Soviet Union and China.

11. Gordon Craig, *The Politics of the Prussian Army, 1640-1945* (New York: Oxford University Press, 1955), pp. xvi-xvii.

12. The "expert" model implies an orientation toward a high degree of military professionalism and a high level of military technology. By contrast, the "red" model, with its emphasis on the political nature of the army, would imply a substantial army involvement in party and society affairs. See Franz Schurmann, *Ideology and Organization in Communist China* (Berkeley: University of California Press, 1968), pp. 51-53, for a discussion of the red/expert dichotomy.

13. Harold Lasswell, "The Garrison-State Hypothesis Today," in *Changing Patterns of Military Politics*, ed. Samuel Huntington (New York: Free Press, 1962), pp. 51-69.

14. N.I. Shatagin and I.P. Prusanov, *Sovetskaya armiya—armiya novogo tipa* (Moscow: Voenizdat, 1957), p. 103. In 1921 Frunze stated that "Between our proletarian state and the entire remaining bourgeois world there can be only one condition—long, unyielding desperate war . . . ." See *Voennaya nauka i revoliutsiya* v. 1 (1921), p. 39. The Twelfth Party Congress in 1923 "charge [d] the Central Committee not to let escape from view the danger of possible new intervention attempts on the side of the more irreconcilable elements of the imperialist camp" See *KPSS o vooruzhennykh silakh sovetskogo soyuza, dokumenti 1917-1968* (Moscow: Voenizdat, 1969) p. 204. In 1927, after a series of anti-Soviet incidents in such cities as London, Warsaw, and Peking, a war scare developed in the Soviet Union.

15. *50 Let vooruzhennykh sil SSSR* (Moscow: Voenizdat, 1968), p. 194. The considerable expansion in the size of the armies of all of Russia's potential enemies in the 1930s further sharpened the feeling of encirclement. The massive industrialization and technological transformation of the Red Army in the 1930s was directly tied to the international environment. The sense of isolation was expressed by Stalin in 1937 when he told the Central Committee, "Capitalist encirclement is no empty phrase. It is a very real and unpleasant fact . . . there are many countries . . . waiting for an opportunity to attack . . . " See J.V. Stalin, *History of CPSU(B)* (New York: International Publications, 1939), p. 274. The formation of the Anti-Bolshevik Pact and the Japanese attacks in 1938 and 1939 even further reinforced the feeling of isolation.

16. H.S. Dinerstein, *War and the Soviet Union* (New York: Praeger, 1962), p. 2. He further stated, "In the years following the civil war the Soviet leaders were not unreasonable in suspecting that the 'capitalist' nations might well try at some favorable juncture and dislodge the Soviet regime even by violent means."

17. Tang Tsou has observed that the Chinese leaders, by stationing many divisions in Fukien Province opposite Taiwan, have taken the Nationalist threat with "complete seriousness." See Arthur Huck, *The Security of China* (New York: Columbia University Press, 1970), p. 39.

18. *Survey of China Mainland Press*, No. 750, February 18, 1954, p. 14.

19. The major program of building bomb shelters in China during the late 1960s demonstrated the seriousness with which the Chinese took the perceived Russian threat. It is important to stress that we are only dealing here with Chinese perceptions of the situation, not with the actual reality of who was threatening whom.

20. Furthermore, changes in the international political environment evidently did not manifest themselves in changes in army/party or army/society relations. During the 1920s, although the Soviet Union faced a hostile external environment, the power and influence of the army remained weak. Although the international political environment deteriorated sharply from the Soviet view in the 1930s, the power of the army—especially during the Great Purges—actually declined.

21. The more than two decades spent by the bulk of the Chinese Communist leadership in the countryside before the taking of power contrasted sharply with the experiences of prison, underground work, and exile in Siberia and Western Europe of most of the Russian Communist leadership before 1917.

22. As Samuel Huntington has written, "Surely one of the most outstanding achievements of the mid-twentieth century was the establishment in China in 1949 for the first time in a hundred years of a government really able to govern China." See *Political Order in Changing Societies*, p. 342.

23. Mao Tse-tung, *Selected Works* (Peking: Foreign Languages Press, 1967), v. 1, pp. 105-108.

24. Barrington Moore has stressed the militaristic nature of the Kuomintang and Chiang Kai-shek and has drawn some striking parallels between policies of the Kuomintang and the European fascists. See Barrington Moore, Jr., *Social Origins of Dictatorship and Democracy* (Boston: Beacon Press, 1967), pp. 187-201.

25. In a modified form Huntington has made this argument. See *Political Order in Changing Societies*, pp. 192-263.

26. Huntington has stressed that "organization has been the distinctive source of communist strength." Ibid., p. 340.

27. It is one of the fascinating paradoxes which this book examines that the military factor could be so important while the military sector was basically excluded from the policymaking process in the Soviet Union.

28. Frederick Barghoorn, "Analytic Framework: Soviet Politics in Comparative and Historical Contexts," *Studies in Comparative Communism* 4, No. 3-4 (July/October 1971): 53. For similar views see Merle Fainsod, *How Russia Is Ruled* (Cambridge: Harvard University Press, 1965), ch. 1; Frederick Barghoorn, *Soviet Russian Nationalism*, reprint (Westport, Conn.:

Greenwood Press, 1976); and, by implication, Hugh Seton-Watson, *The Russian Empire* (New York: Oxford University Press, 1967).

29. Brzezinski and Huntington, *Political Power: USA/USSR*, pp. 332, 336. Brzezinski has elsewhere spoken of "a sense of political noninvolvement" that made it "difficult for any would-be Bonapartist leader to use the army as a cohesive unit for political purposes." See *Ideology and Power in Soviet Politics* (New York: Praeger, 1962), p. 49.

30. John Curtis, *The Russian Army Under Nicholas I, 1825-1855* (Durham: Duke University Press, 1965), p. 112. As he further stated, "Any doubt as to the ability of the authorities to keep the armed services under firm control must vanish before the evidence that the military leaders found it possible to use the army for a variety of repressive measures against the people of Russia..." (p. 273).

31. This is not to ignore the serious Decembrist Revolt in 1825 and the sporadic revolts in the military colonies, as in 1831. However, the army was generally loyal. For the Decembrist Revolt, see Anatole Mazour, *The First Russian Revolution, 1825* (Stanford: Stanford University Press, 1964).

32. C.R. Andolenko, *Histoire de L' Armée Russe* (Paris: Flammarion, 1967), p. 301. Trotsky has similarly written, "The Russian proletariat in December foundered not on its own mistakes but on a more real force: the bayonets of the peasant army." See Leon Trotsky, *1905*, trans. Anya Bostock (New York: Random House, 1971), p. 296.

33. The relative inactivity of the Russian army (except for the abortive Kornilov coup) was particularly notable given the power vacuum which developed during this period. As Richard Pipes has observed, "... Bonapartism proved to have been largely an imaginary threat. The Russian generals turned out to be remarkably apolitical." See "Communism and Russian History," in *Soviet and Chinese Communism: Similarities and Differences*, ed. Treadgold, p. 22.

34. Trotsky, *1905*, p. 5.

35. See Curtis, *The Russian Army Under Nicholas I*, p. 99; Mazour, *The First Russian Revolution, 1825*, p. 38; and George Vernadsky, *A History of Russia* (New York: Alfred A. Knopf, 1967), p. 174.

36. Bernard Pares, *A History of Russia* (New York: Alfred A. Knopf, 1947), p. 201.

37. See Hsi-hsiang Chi, *The Chinese Warlord System, 1916 to 1928* (Washington: American University Press, 1969); Donald Gillin, *Warlord— Yen Hsi-Shan in Shansi Province, 1911-1949* (Princeton: Princeton University Press, 1967); and Lucian Pye, *Warlord Politics* (New York: Praeger, 1971).

38. Barrington Moore has emphasized that Chiang Kai-shek was preeminently a military leader. See *Social Origins of Dictatorship and Democracy*, pp. 187-201.

39. Lucian Pye, *The Spirit of Chinese Politics* (Cambridge: MIT Press, 1968), p. 194.

40. "Comments by Herbert Franke," in *China's Heritage and the Communist Political System*, ed. Ping-ti ho and Tang Tsou (Chicago: University of Chicago Press, 1968), 1, p. 46.

41. Ping-ti Ho, "Salient Aspects of China's Heritage," in *China's Heritage and the Communist Political System*, ed. Ho and Tsou 1, p. 15.

42. John K. Fairbank, *The United States and China* (New York: Viking Press, 1962), pp. 50-51; Joseph Needham, "The Past in China's Present," *The Centennial Review* 4 (1960): 154; S.N. Eisenstadt, *The Political System of Empires* (New York: Free Press, 1969), p. 172.

43. Wolfgang Franke, *A Century of Chinese Revolution*, trans. Stanley Rudman (Columbia; University of South Carolina Press, 1970), pp. 37-38. Franke has called Tseng Kuo-fan, the key organizer of the new Imperial armies used to defeat the Taiping Rebellion "the ancestor of the later 'warlords' " and has added, "After his time the troops were no longer under the direct control of the Emperor and the central government but of individual leaders. . . . After the fall of the dynasty political power devolved entirely on the warlords."

44. Mary Wright, *The Last Stand of Chinese Conservatism—The T'ung-Chi Restoration, 1862-1874* (Stanford: Stanford University Press, 1962), p. 198.

45. Ibid., p. 221.

46. Mazour, *The First Russian Revolution, 1825*, pp. 38-43.

47. Huntington, *Political Order in Changing Societies*, pp. 264-277; Chalmers Johnson, *Revolutionary Change* (Boston: Little, Brown & Company, 1966); Robert Tucker, *The Marxian Revolutionary Idea* (New York: W.W. Norton, 1969), pp. 137-160; Eric Wolf, *Peasant Wars of the Twentieth Century* (New York: Harper & Row, 1969), pp. 91, 298-300.

48. Huntington, *Political Order in Changing Societies*, pp. 264-277 Huntington's models suffer from a number of problems. His analysis never goes to the fundamental question of why there should even be "Western" and "Eastern" models. His models are based on extremely few cases 3.5 cases for the Western pattern, 2+ cases for Eastern pattern). He cannot explain why the first half of the Chinese revolution (collapse of the Imperial regime) followed the Western model rather than the expected Eastern model. Huntington argues that "dual power" was a distinguishing characteristic of the Eastern model (p. 271). Was not the situation in Russia between the two

revolutions in 1917 precisely one of "dual power" shared between the Soviets and the provisional government? He asserts that "In the Western revolution the principal struggles are between revolutionary groups; in the Eastern revolution they are between one revolutionary group and the established order" (p. 271). Yet, is the Kuomintang, which in the 1920s had been a revolutionary party reformed on Soviet lines, to be merely considered the "established order" (as the Manchu dynasty had been)? Or is it not more profitable to consider the Kuomintang, as Barrington Moore has done, as a movement seeking "to push China along the reactionary road to the modern state?" See Moore, *Social Origins of Dictatorship and Democracy*, p. 201. His discussion emphasizes that in the Western model the revolutionaries "fight out from the capital to the countryside" and seek to expand the political participation of the people; but this ignores the dual nature of the October Revolution. For while the Bolsheviks seized power at the head of workers' insurrection in the cities, "the peasantry," in Eric Wolf's words, "in the meantime staged its own uprising in the countryside, parallel with the industrial insurrection in the cities but in essential independence of them. . . ." See Wolf, *Peasant Wars in the Twentieth Century*, p. 298. The peasantry also played a key role in the 1905 Revolution. Thus, Huntington's analysis, while interesting, generalizes too broadly from too few cases.

49. Wolf, *Peasant Wars of the Twentieth Century*, p. 91; Tucker, *The Marxian Revolutionary Idea*, p. 147; The literature has tended to treat the October Revolution as a Bolshevik coup d'état. Robert Tucker has called it a "revolutionary coup," and Chalmers Johnson has called it a "conspiratorial coup." See Tucker, *The Marxian Revolutionary Idea*, p. 147, and Johnson, *Revolution and the Social System*, (Stanford, Calif.: Hoover Institution, 1964), p. 50. However, given the mass popular base of the Bolsheviks (as reflected in absolute majorities in the Petrograd and Moscow Soviets) and the Blanquist overtones of the word "coup", it would be preferable to say that the Bolsheviks seized power at the head of worker uprisings in the cities.

50. Tucker, *The Marxian Revolutionary Idea*, p. 147.

51. Chalmers Johnson, *Revolution and the Social System*, p. 57.

52. The attitude of the peasant majority toward the Communists played a crucial role in determining the nature of the revolution and the nature of the army. For an analysis of the importance of the peasantry in revolutionary movements, see Moore, *Social Origins of Dictatorship and Democracy*.

53. The vast majority of Bolsheviks before 1917 had spent their time in jail, underground work, or exile. Very few had served in the czarist army, even as a private.

54. The Bolsheviks had almost no roots in the countryside. In 1916 they had precisely four rural party cells in all of rural Russia. In 1917 only 7.8

percent of the party members came from peasant orgins. *See* G. Sharapov, *Razreshenie agrarnogo voprosa v rossii posle pobedy oktyabr'skoi revoliutsii* (Moscow: Gosizdat, 1961), p. 114. Furthermore, most of those members of peasant origin were undoubtedly soldiers, rather than peasants living in the countryside. For an excellent analysis of the "remarkable weakness" of the Bolsheviks in the countryside, see Teodor Shanin, *The Awkward Class* (London: Oxford University Press, 1972). The Bolsheviks were quite candid about the alienation of the peasantry to their cause (especially after the threat of the Whites taking power had passed). In March 1919, Stalin asserted, "I must say that those non-working class elements—the peasants—who constitute the majority in our army will not voluntarily fight for socialism." *See* J.V. Stalin, *Works* (Moscow: Foreign Language Publishing House, 1953-1955), v. 4, p. 250 and Yuri Petrov, *KPSS-rukovoditel' i vospitatel' krasnoi armii (1918-1920)* (Moscow: Voenizdat, 1961), p. 204.

55. The Chinese Communists themselves consider that they fought three civil wars in the 1927-49 period.

56. Donald Klein considers it a "truism" that "up to 1949 the Party, the Bureaucracy and the Army were virtually one and the same. Almost all of the full Central Committee members once held a high rank in the Red Army." *See* Donald Klein, "The 'Next Generation' of Chinese Leaders," *China Quarterly*, No. 26 (April/June 1966): 82. For the nationalist and agrarian reform appeals of the Communists, see Chalmers Johnson, *Peasant Nationalism and Communist Power* (Stanford: Stanford University Press, 1962) and Jack Belden, *China Shakes the World* (New York: Harper & Brothers, 1949).

57. In view of the importance of the civil war periods, it is striking that there exists such a paucity of good studies on the subject, especially in the case of the Russian civil war.

58. Although the pre-civil war periods were undoubtedly important in shaping the views of the top party leaders, the civil war periods were probably at least as important. The roots of many aspects of Stalinist policies in the 1930s—including the "war against the kulaks" and the Great Purges—are at least more explicable in terms of the civil war period (e.g., frequent treason, Allied intervention, feeling of Bolshevik isolation, numerous peasant uprisings). The roots of the Great Leap Forward and the Cultural Revolution in China reside in the "Yenan syndrome" of the Chinese Communist leadership.

59. Daniels has argued that "Given the fact of the party's forcible seizure of power [in 1917], civil violence and a militarized dictatorship of revolutionary extremism followed with remorseless logic." *See* Robert Daniels, *Red October* (New York: Scribners, 1967), p. 218; Nathan Leites, *A Study of Bolshevism* (Glencoe: Free Press, 1953), p. 18.

60. Fainsod, *How Russia Is Ruled*, p. 59. Such analyses generally stress the "conspiratorial" and authoritarian tendencies of the Bolsheviks and Lenin in the pre-1917 period.

61. The secret police was founded only in December 1917.

PART I

The Civil Wars

chapter 1

THE NATURE OF THE RED ARMY AND THE PEOPLE'S LIBERATION ARMY

In this and the next two chapters we will analyze the origins of the sharp differences in character between the two armies during their civil wars (1918-21 in Russia, 1946-49 in China).[1] As Philip Selznick has written, "The study of institutions... requires a genetic and developmental approach, an emphasis on historical origins and growth stages."[2] This is particularly important given the highly formative nature of the two civil wars.

Both armies functioned in strikingly similar environments. This is hardly surprising for as Robert Tucker has observed,

> With but two exceptions (Czechoslovakia and East Germany) the typical habitat of communist revolution has been a country of pre-capitalist or at most semicapitalist economic formation, and one that has shown a tendency to stagnate in its further economic development and modernization. It has been a country heavily populated by peasants and dependent upon agriculture, although usually with at least a small industrial working class and some development of modern industrial economy; a socially and politically as well as economically backward country, with very sharp class divisions and political institutions of traditional authoritarian complexion.[3]

As Table 1 shows, both armies reached a roughly similar size of 3 to 5 million men by the end of their civil wars. Both armies, given the large size of their countries, were forced to operate over vast land masses. While the Red Army during the civil war operated with a perimeter of as much as 5,000 miles, the PLA engaged in marches of thousands of miles.

Table 1   Size of Red Army and People's Liberation Army During Civil Wars

(Millions of soldiers)			
Date	Size of Red Army	Size of PLA	Date
3-18	.1	1.3	6-46
12-18	1.0	2.0	6-47
6-19	1.8	2.8	6-48
1-20	3.0	4.0	6-49
10-20	5.5	5.0	6-50

Sources: Politicheskoe Upravlenie RKKA, 1918-1928 let krasnoi armii—albom diagram, p. 6; Direktivi glavnogo kommandovaniya krasnoi armii (1917-1920), p. 139; A. S. Bubnov et al., Grazhdanskaya voina (1918-1921), v. 2, p. 87; A. S. Bubnov, O krasnoi armii, p. 224; John Gittings, The Role of the Chinese Army, p. 304.

The underdeveloped nature of both countries was reflected in the ranks of the armies. While 75 percent to 80 percent of the Russian soldiers were peasants, so were the "vast majority" of Chinese soldiers.[4] Illiteracy plagued both armies. In Russia in January 1918, 50 percent of the army was illiterate; even by January 1920, after considerable educational effort, 14 percent of the army was illiterate. Similarly, as late as 1950 the Chinese People's Liberation Army contained a "great percentage" of illiterates.[5]

Both armies shared a number of revolutionary features. Both the Red Army and the People's Liberation Army abolished the traditional system of ranks and titles, important symbols of a regular, stratified army. As class conscious organizations, both armies excluded men of undesirable class origin. In the words of the Eighth Party Congress in 1919, "The Red Army, as the arm of the proletarian dictatorship, must of necessity have an openly class character, i.e.,be recruited exclusively from the proletariat and semi-proletariat state of the peasantry which stand close to it."[6] Both armies were highly egalitarian in terms of pay and living conditions. In Russia even the officers "were restricted to an extremely spartan mode of life."[7] In China, even when a formal pay scale was introduced at the end of the civil war in 1950, a divisional commander received little more than three times as much as a private.[8] The party stratum played a crucial role in the functioning of both armies. In the Red Army not only did the Communists form the "overwhelming majority of the 14,000 winners of the Order of the Red Banner in the civil war, but they justified Trotsky's accolade as a "Communist order of samurai."[9] Both armies made major use of commissars and prohibited the election of officers.

LEVEL OF MILITARY TECHNOLOGY

Perhaps the most striking similarity shared by the two armies in their civil wars and by Communist armies in more recent civil wars was the low level of military technology, reflecting the underdevelopment of these various countries. Modern weaponry, such as airplanes, tanks, submarines, and self-propelled heavy artillery, first emerged in quantity in the armies of the major Western countries by the end of World War I. By 1918 the French air force, with 3,300 airplanes, deployed 260 squadrons on the western front. The British air force numbered 300,000 men.[10] After the use of 378 tanks at Cambrai in 1917 had achieved "stupendous success," the Allies, utilizing hundreds of tanks in such battles as those at Soissons and Amiens in 1918, transformed the war into a "tank war."[11] The cult of quick firing, massed modern artillery was so strong that at the Battle of the Somme in 1916 British and French guns fired 1.7 million shells in a mere eight days.[12] The extensive use of the newly developed German submarines (U-Boats) to sink shipping was an important element in the war. All major Western armies relied heavily on mechanized transportation.[13]

Against this standard, it is instructive to measure the Russian army in 1920 and the Chinese army in 1950. By examining seven key areas within the armies—infantry weapons, artillery, tanks, airplanes, ships, transportation, and supplies—which reflect the level of military technology, it can be demonstrated that both armies operated at a relatively similar primitive level of military technology, one far lower than the technology used by the Western armies at the end of World War I.

Despite the capture of large quantities of weapons from the enemy, "inheritance" of some weapons from other armies, and substantial local arms production, both armies suffered acute shortages of modern infantry weapons. Although the Red Army inherited the supplies of the czarist army, this advantage was offset in part by the fact that many soldiers deserted with their weapons. Hampered by a severe shortage of material, workers, and arms plants, industry produced the meager total of 15,400 machine guns and 1.28 million rifles during the civil war for the ultimately 5 million man army.[14] In 1919, the 134 active brigades of the Red Amy, as determined by the 1918 table of organization, lacked 87 percent of the needed carbines (837,000), 65 percent of the needed machine guns (14,500) and 35 percent of the needed infantry rifles (239,000).[15] In May 1919, Vatsetis could report, "When the operation on the fronts may take a decisive turn, we will not have the necessary number of bayonets."[16] At its nadir, in the summer of 1919, ammunition production was so low that the stock of bullets on the southern front would have been inadequate for a single regiment in one day of heavy fighting in World War I.[17] A similarly bleak situation prevailed in the Chinese army, despite the capture of huge quantities of arms during the civil war.[18] Even by the end of 1948 the PLA's arms arsenals could produce only 50 percent of the army's needs.[19] Soldiers were often allowed to fire only fifty rounds before going into combat.[20]

Similar problems plagued the artillery in both armies. Neither army possessed an adequate production base or enough skilled commanders to direct the use of the existing limited artillery, and both relied heavily on captured and inherited artillery. In Russia the active army in 1919 lacked 60 percent (2,700) of the needed field guns and often possessed less than one artillery piece per mile of front.[21] As Bubnov has observed, "The role of artillery . . . was considerably less than at the time of the imperialist war."[22] The Chinese army possessed almost no experience with massed artillery before 1948. Only in that year did the People's Liberation Army create an artillery and engineering corps. Some major army units, such as the First Field Army, made little use of artillery even at the end of the war. Hanson Baldwin commented about the PLA in 1951, "It has artillery, but relatively little of it, and the ammunition supply is limited."[23]

Tanks played a minimal role in both armies during the civil war. The Red Army and the People's Liberation Army, lacking indigenous production capacity, skilled repairmen, and qualified tank commanders, both relied exclusively on captured obsolete tanks.[24] Possessing only about 100 such tanks by 1920, the Red Army, even in the major campaign against Wrangel in October 1920, deployed not a single tank. By contrast, Wrangel had forty-five tanks and armed cars.[25] Gusev later declared that "The participation of tanks" in the civil war was "insignificant."[26] Similarly, so minimal was the tank force in the Chinese army that Mao Tse-tung in 1948 asserted that the PLA had "mastered the tactics of storming heavily fortified points" although "the People's Liberation Army had neither aircraft nor tanks."[27] Possessing no tanks before 1946 and only 622 old, obsolete captured tanks by June 1950, the PLA made minimal use of tanks. The First Field Army never used any at all in the civil war.[28]

Similarly, the air forces, like the tank forces, were quite small and in their infancy. Both the Red Army and People's Liberation Army air forces suffered from an acute shortage of trained pilots and adequate fuel. The two air forces possessed only a minimal or nonexistent production base; and neither air force contested enemy control of the skies.[29] Furthermore, inheriting only an "inconsiderable quantity" of obsolete, diverse, and poorly powered airplanes from the czarist army, the Red Army air force possessed only 300 to 350 active airplanes in the civil war.[30] So infrequently was the air force used that Commander in chief Kamenev later observed that the capture of a single airplane in the 1920 Polish campaign increased Soviet air capabilities by 50 percent.[31] In 1920, a Soviet publication noted, "There was almost no air force."[32] Even more pitiful was the People's Liberation Army Air Force. Formally organized only late in 1948, it consisted of only eighty-six old, serviceable airplanes by January 1950.[33] So hampered was this small air force by numerous crashes and low combat capability that "the Nationalists regarded the PLA as having no air force at all."[34]

The state of naval power was as primitive and insignificant as that of air power. Both navies were crippled by the lack of any production capacity and by the marked preference of experienced naval commanders and personnel to fight in the armies opposing the Communists. As a result, neither navy could prevent the domination of the sea by enemy fleets.[35] Possessing only a small inheritance from the czarist navy, the Soviet fleet in the civil war, in Yuri Petrov's words, "did not play an active role in the rout of the interventionists and their white guard allies."[36] By 1921 the position of the navy was "extremely difficult" for the fleet had been "almost annihilated in the world war and civil war."[37] Frunze later concluded that by 1921 "In sum all this signified that we had no fleet."[38] The Chinese navy was even more pathetic. Created only in April 1949, the PLA navy consisted mainly of 200 to 300 small gunboats and wooden sailing junks, interspersed with a few cruisers, destroyers, and submarines.[39] Consequently, Hanson Baldwin has termed the Chinese navy in 1950 a "negligible" factor while Lin Tsun has concurred by calling it "nothing," "dilapidated," and consisting of "only a few warships."[40]

Both armies possessed relatively primitive transportation systems. Operating in underdeveloped countries, they were hindered by the lack of a good system of roads and the absence of an automobile or tractor industry. In Russia the disintegration of the rail system badly hampered the deployment of Red Army troops. In April 1919, in a secret telegram to Lenin and Sklyansky, War Commissar Trotsky complained that "Meanwhile there is extremely little wheeled transport on the eastern front and a total insufficiency of horses."[41] Not until the end of the 1919 did any large number of Red Army men move eastward by train; even in 1920 and 1921 transportation by horse and cart was quite common. In China, the PLA heavily relied on an even more primitive yet more effective mode of transportation—walking. During the civil war the Chinese army demonstrated a capacity to march an average of fifty miles during the day and twenty to thirty miles during the night. Not until 1948 did the PLA make any extensive use of trucks, from among the 22,000 vehicles captured from the Kuomintang.[42] The primitive state and paucity of Chinese roads and highways, the mobile, guerrilla tactics of the army, and the lack of mechanized transport all contributed to the pre-modern nature of military transportation.

Finally, neither army possessed a modernized supply system. The Russian system was antiquated and often hopelessly inadequate. In November 1918, War Commissar Trotsky confided to Lenin, Sverdlov, and Nevsky that military freight moved an average of thirty-three miles a day![43] In January 1919, while the central supply depots were reported empty, Stalin and Dzerzhinsky wrote to Lenin about an army division whose "units were in action for five days literally without bread or other food."[44] In May 1919, in a message to Trotsky, Lenin excoriated the "scandalous arrangement and slovenliness of the supply system which is leading the army towards total collapse."[45] By February 1920, Lenin still called the situation on the railroads "quite catastrophic" while the armies on the western and northern fronts had only three to five day supply of grain on hand.[46] Even by October 1920, the problem of supplies remained so critical that Trotsky could note in a secret telegram that "Even the better-off armies are in effect wholly unprepared for the winter."[47]

Although more technologically primitive, the Chinese supply system was somewhat more effective. The simple system relied on massive manpower, horses, and carts. During the Liaoning, Huai-Hai, and Ping-chin campaigns in 1948 and 1949 the army utilized 5.4 million civilian service workers and 1 million head of animals.[48] These millions of peasants pushed wheelbarrows full of food, gas, and ammunition to the battle areas. Logistics were limited to short forays close to base. As the system was highly decentralized, no uniform system of supply and equipment was established during the civil war. The lack of technology, however, sufficiently limited the supply effort that Whitson has characterized of the PLA in 1949 as a "poorly equipped and supplied force" with meager rations.[49]

While the Chinese army functioned at a somewhat lower level of technology than the Russian army, both armies functioned at a relatively primitive level. Both also demonstrated a number of revolutionary features. In these aspects the Russian and Chinese armies were quite similar to other successful Communist armies in their civil wars.

However, these important similarities obscured major differences between the armies that was significant for their future development. These differences involved the nature and size of the proletarian and party strata in the army, the mechanisms of social control within the army, the degree and success of decentralization of command, and the effectiveness and degree of institutionalization of the armies.

These differences generally reflected differences in the existence of a lengthy gestation period for the army and in the manner in which the party came to power.

PARTY STRATUM

Lacking any gestation period before the civil war or popular appeal to the peasant masses, the Red Army possessed only a small party stratum of roughly 5 percent of the total Red Army during the civil war.[50] So important were the Communists that the Red Army considered units that were less than 5 percent Communist to be ineffective, 6 percent to 8 percent to be satisfactory, and 12 percent to 15 percent to be shock troops.[51] By these standards, the Red Army contained many ineffective units, some satisfactory units, and few shock troops. By these same standards, the Chinese army, which was 24 percent Communist in 1950, consisted almost entirely of shock troops.[52]

A key difference lay in the fact that the Russian Communists relied heavily on the small urban proletariat while the Chinese Communists relied on the peasant masses. Trotsky has estimated that 15 percent to 18 percent of the Red Army soldiers in 1920 were of proletarian origin.[53] Their value was considered sufficiently great that units with a low (4 percent to 10 percent) working-class component were considered unstable while those with a high (20 percent to 27 percent) working-class component allegedly distinguished themselves.[54] The peasant majority in the army was so remote from the Bolsheviks that Trotsky admitted in 1920, "It seemed as if all the mass of peasantry was unanimous in its enmity to the proletariat and Communist Party."[55] By contrast, the peasants formed the bulk of the active support for the Chinese Communists. The working class played a role of minimal importance in the People's Liberation Army.

CONTROL MECHANISMS

Differences between the two armies in their civil wars were also evident in mechanisms of control exercised largely over peasant masses in the ranks. The very high rates of desertion and treason and low level of combat effectiveness in the Red Army forced it to rely heavily on threats of coercion. Capital punishment and collective liability for units were introduced in 1918. As Trotsky admonished the party's Central Committe in a May 1919 secret telegram, "... there must be no stopping short at the most savage measures— shooting, drafting to the units of the rear, levies, imprisonment in the concentration camps."[56] The threat of coercion played a far more important role than actual coercion. During the period from May to December 1919, of the 1.5 million deserters taken back into the army, 55,000 were sent to punishment units, 4,112 were sentenced to death, and 612 were actually executed.[57] As Lenin argued in a February 1920 speech, "We led the Red Army to victory by strict iron discipline as well as agitation."[58]

Although fear of severe punishment and even death may have partially motivated Red Army soldiers, utilitarian and normative motivations played an important role. Given the disintegration of the society and economy during the civil war, the army at least provided a minimal, if risky, living for the soldier and his family.[59] Despite intensive propaganda and agitation efforts by Bolsheviks, normative commitment among the Red Army soldiers, especially the peasant soldiers, remained quite low. The thinness of the Communist stratum in the army prevented the effective penetration of the key primary units. The forcible confiscation of surplus grain by requisition squads, the persecution of the church, the organization of communes and poor peasants' committees, and the prominence of Jews in the Bolshevik leadership (for example, Trotsky, Kamenev, Zinoviev, Radek, Sverdlov) deeply alienated the peasantry from the Bolsheviks. Only among workers and Communists did normative motivation play a key role. Fear of the return of the landlord and the czar provided the major motivation for most peasant soldiers.

By contrast, the Chinese army relied far more heavily on normative commitment and psychological coercion and de-emphasized physical coercion. Agrarian reform and nationalism, reinforced by extensive propaganda in the villages and relief during times of scarcity, provided a powerful basis for normative commitment among the peasant soldiers. The large Communist stratum in the army created a far broader base for normative motivation in the Chinese army than in the Russian army and allowed the party to penetrate the crucial primary units.[60] These Communist soldiers could lead the primary units in action. They conducted intensive political indoctrination, self-criticism, mutual criticism, and surveillance within a well-structured primary group. Even the most illiterate, apathetic peasant soldiers became capable of reciting revolutionary slogans and acting in an acceptable manner. This intricate mixture of psychological coercion and normative belief functioned so well that a study of Chinese POWs in the Korean War labelled it "a remarkably effective and largely self-operating system of human control" and declared that "failure of personnel to identify with Communist goals, even widespread opposition to the goals and to the government, does not lessen the organizational strength of Communist armies.... They tended to perform the tasks expected of them with perseverance and competence regardless of their subjective feelings...."[61] Furthermore, the soldiers perceived utilitarian motivation in a number of material and educational benefits for themselves and their families if they performed well in the army.[62] In this context, the threat of physical coercion could be de-emphasized, to be used only in extreme situations.

COMMAND STRUCTURES

Sharp differences also existed in the stratification and centralization of the command structures of the two armies. These differences are particularly interesting in view of the similarities that existed between the two armies in the civil wars. Janowitz has observed that in underdeveloped countries "military organization is rigidly stratified and authoritarian because of the necessities of command."[63] Certain factors promoted decentralized army command structures in both Russia and China. Both armies were revolutionary forces that frequently identified the more repressive and authoritarian aspects of traditional armies with the evils of the old society. In both countries a prolonged prior war combined with the devastation of the civil war created a disintegration of economy and society and an erosion of the power and legitimation of central rule. In underdeveloped Russia and China, the relatively primitive infrastructures of communication and transportation, the extension of the war over vast territories, and the involvement of millions of soldiers hampered effective centralized command. The low level of military technology in the two armies did not demand a high degree of centralization. Finally, the unleashing of revolutionary forces in Russia and China created local forces often difficult to control. Thus, army forces inhibited the development of highly centralized commands in the two armies.

Nevertheless, the effective command structures of the two armies differed sharply. The Red Army lacked any gestation period before the civil war to create and institutionalize a command structure. It possessed only a thin communist stratum in the ranks and was plagued by mass desertion in the ranks and treason in the officer corps. Most of the army was ineffectual. While the Red Army in 1920 numbered more than 5 million men, only 700,000 to 800,000 were considered effective fighting men.[64] Numerous local forces—partisans, local Communists, commissars, soviets, and republics—fought vigorously to evade central control.

Indeed, Trotsky has aptly characterized the civil war as a struggle "for the creation of a centralized, disciplined army, supplied and administered from a single center."[65] The strong centralist push of War Commissar Trotsky and the army and party leadership from above met strong resistance from below, especially in 1918 and 1919. Central control barely existed in much of the army in this period. Most troops in 1918 were provided not by the central authority but by local soviets and republics, atamans, and partisans. The bulk of the fighting was done on a very decentralized and uncoordinated basis.[66] Future Marshal Yegorov, in an August 1918 note to Lenin, caustically observed that "A survey of all the operations in progress on the various fronts indicates that they contain no definite uniform conception or purpose" and that there existed an "evident failure to work out any plan of compaign against the existing enemy."[67]

Central control was extended, although slowly, in the Red Army. The irregular partisan groups, that fiercely fought the imposition of central authority, played, especially in the Ukraine and Siberia, in Marshal Sokolovskii's words, "an important role in the victorious outcome of the civil war."[68] By the end of 1919 some effective central control had been extended over the partisans. Similarly, by the end of 1918 local army Communists were so powerful that many cells, electing even army bureaus from below, sought to direct the army administration and elect the commissars. Only in 1919, with the creation of the Red Army Political Administration, was central control established over the local army party cells.[69] This same organization also extended control over the commissars who in 1918 had possessed a fairly autonomous body of their own. Finally, in 1919 the army extended central control over the military activities of the local soviets and republics.

Given the ineffectiveness of most troops, the key levels of command in the Red Army in the civil war were the central leadership and a corps of victorious officers and units. The central leadership exercised broad control over operations. Regional fronts had no continuity as regionally based units were generally those of the lowest quality and saw little action. Talented commanders, such as Tukhachevsky and Frunze, were moved from front to front. Reliable units often appeared on three or even four fronts. Budenny's First Cavalry Army fought Denikin, Wrangel, Makhno, and the Poles. The Latvian Rifles Division not only guarded the Kremlin but helped defeat Denikin and Wrangel. As Marshal Budenny described the Latvian Rifles, "in harsh battles of the civil war I saw you always at leading outposts, at most responsible sectors where was decided the fate of proletarian revolution. With courage unprecedented in history, with iron, indestructible pride you defended the approaches to conquests of the October Revolution."[70] In certain areas, notably the Ukraine, independent atamans and partisans played a major role throughout the civil war. The symbol of the Russian civil war was War Commissar Trotsky in his armored train, replete with miniature field headquarters and detachments of soldiers, frantically traveling 105,000 kilometers in thirty-six train trips as he sought to rally lagging troops everywhere.

By contrast, given the lengthy gestation period (1927-45) and large party stratum, the Chinese army created a far more decentralized command during its civil war. So simple was the role of the Chinese high command that Gittings has observed that the PLA "had no effective structure of centralized command."[71] The sketchiness of the broad plans of the high command reflected the experience of almost twenty years of guerrilla warfare and the lack of almost any large-scale campaigns until 1947. Instead, the five regional field armies, with their core of experienced party officers and geographic base in the ten to twenty years preceding the civil war, formed the effective higher level of the command structure.[72] Even this level exercised only broad but not tight or detailed control over operations. Indeed, the field headquarters of the Second Field Army (consisting of 360,000 men) was so small that it could be packed up on carts or a few horses and moved within one hour![73] The emphasis on small unit infantry fire and maneuver, the lack of modern military technology, and the absence of a modern system of transportation and communication were reflected in the very sketchy plans communicated to the field commanders. So highly decentralized were operations that few commanders ever led more than 40,000 men in combat. Staff work, quite primitive in nature, was confined to the divisional level and above. The highly decentralized command structure, with its roots in the pre-1946 era when scattered soviets were controlled by quasi-autonomous army commanders, owed much of its effectiveness to the existence of a large, experienced, and dedicated group of Communist commanders at all levels of the army.[74]

LEVEL OF INSTITUTIONALIZATION

Finally, and quite importantly, there existed sharp differences in the levels of effectiveness and institutionalization of the two armies. While effectiveness can be measured on the battlefield, institutionalization is a less tangible but also quite important element in an army. As Philip Selznick has written,

Institutionalization is a process. It is something that happens to an organization over time, reflecting the organization's distinctive history, the people who have been in it, the groups it embodies and the vested interests they have created and the way it has adapted to its environment. In what is perhaps its most significant meaning "to institutionalize" is to infuse with value beyond the technical requirements of the task at home.[75]

The multimillion man Red Army, founded only in 1918 at the beginning of the civil war, was literally formed on the battlefield in the course of the civil war. The lack of any prior gestation period and the absence of an experienced group of Communist commanders severely hampered the institutionalization of the army.

By contrast, the People's Liberation Army, formed in 1927, possessed almost a twenty-year gestation period before the beginning of the civil war in 1946. During this lengthy period the army evolved the "socially integrating myths" so important for the institutionalization of an army. Many key events, such as the Nanchang Uprising (1927) and Long March (1934-35), although technically military defeats, became powerful integrating symbols of a glorious revolutionary past. The great victories of the Chinese army, especially in the 1948-49 period, reinforced the potency of the integrating myths. The lengthy gestation period, by permitting the creation of a large and experienced corps of Communist officers and establishment of effective mechanisms of control within the army, greatly aided the institutionalization of the PLA.

What lessons can we draw from the experiences of the Russian and Chinese armies during their civil wars? Probably the major one concerns the importance of the level of military technology. A low level of military technology in victorious revolutionary armies is compatible with either a high or low level of effectiveness and institutionalization. It is compatible with either a highly politicized unified army (PLA) or an internally divided army with a low level of political consciousness (Red Army). It is compatible with a future rapid modernization of the army (PLA in the 1950s) or a decade of stagnation in the level of military technology (Red Army in the 1920s). In contrast, while level of technology does not appear to be of decisive importance, the effectiveness of the army and the relation of the army to the party are of critical importance to its future development. An effective army, closely tied to the party (as the PLA), would play an important role in the policymaking process. An ineffective army, isolated from the party (as the Red Army), would not play a key role in the policymaking process. More a threat than an opportunity, the army would need to be thoroughly reconstructed before it could play a major role. Thus, the effectiveness and degree of institutionalization of the army in the civil war would have an important impact on the future development of the army.

NOTES

1. It is important to note that the 1946-49 Chinese civil war did not occur in a vacuum but as part of the 1927-49 period of often intense fighting. The

four-year decisive civil war in many ways represented the culmination of trends which developed during the earlier period. However, due to the inability of the author to read Chinese and the fact that to focus on this period would distort and alter the primary focus of the later period, it was decided to omit any direct analysis of the 1927-45 period, except in a brief summary at the end of chapter 2.

2. Philip Selznick, *Leadership in Administration*, (Evanston, Ill.: Row, Peterson, 1957), p. 141. He distinguished between technically instrumental but expendable "organizations" and value infused "institutions." see pp. 21, 40.

3. Robert Tucker, *The Marxian Revolutionary Idea*, (New York: W.W. Norton, 1969), p. 137.

4. Jack Belden, *China Shakes the World* (New York: Harper & Brothers, 1949), p. 330; *Sbornik statisticheskikh svedenii po soyuzy SSR 1918-1923*, p. 94.

5. *Russian Review* 1, no. 13 (April 1924): 296; Robert Rigg, *Red China's Fighting Hordes* (Harrisburg, Pa.: Military Service Publishing Company, 1952), p. 145. A survey of Chinese POWs in the Korean War showed that 81 percent possessed less than three years of education while only 7 percent had more than six years of education. See William Bradbury et al., eds., *Mass Behavior in Battle and Captivity—The Communist Soldier in the Korean War* (Chicago: University of Chicago Press, 1968), p. 342.

6. *VKP (B) v rezolyutsiyakh* (Moscow: Gosizdat, 1941), v. 1, p. 287.

7. Erich Wollenberg, trans., *The Red Army* (London: Secker and Warburg, 1959), pp. 182-183.

8. Rigg, *Red China's Fighting Hordes*, p. 123.

9. Yuri Petrov, *KPSS—rukovoditel' i vospitatel' krasnoi armii* (Moscow: Voenizdat, 1961), p. 255; Lev Trotsky, *Kak vooruzhalas' revoliutsiya* (Moscow: Vyshii Voenni Redaktsionni Soviet, 1924), v. 2, b. 2, p. 7.

10. Robin Higham, *Air Power: A Concise History*, (New York: St. Martin's, 1972), p. 39; Charles Sims, *The Royal Air Force* (London: Adam and Charles Black, 1968).

11. J.F.C. Fuller, *Tanks in the Great War, 1914-1918* (London: John Murray, 1920), pp.192-198. See also G. LeQ. Martel, *Our Armored Forces* (London: Faber and Faber, 1943), p. 38; Douglas Orgill, *The Tank* (London: Morrison and Gibb, 1970), pp. 20-73.

12. Raymond Aron, *The Century of Total War* (Boston: Beacon Press, 1954), p. 21.

13. Theodor Ropp, *War in the Modern World* (Durham: Duke University Press, 1959), p. 231.

14. V.D. Sokolovskii, *Soviet Military Strategy*, translation (Englewood, N.J.: Prentice-Hall, Inc., 1963), p. 227. The Russian army inherited nearly

3,000 cannon, more than 10,000 machine guns, 1.3 million rifles, and nearly 800 million bullets from czarist reserves. See *Istoriya grazhdanskoi voina v SSSR* (Moscow: Gosizdat, 1961), v. 3, p. 306.

15. *Voennye-istoricheskii zhurnal* no. 11 (November 1960): 6.

16. *Direktivi glavnogo kommandovaniya krasnoi armii (1917-1920)* (Moscow: Voenizdat, 1969), pp. 319-321. Vatsetis also reported that the Red Army lacked 56.3 percent of needed machine guns and 20.4 percent of needed rifles.

17. N. Kakurin, *Kak srazhalas' revoliutsiya* (Moscow: Gosizdat, 1926), v. 1, p. 148.

18. The PLA has estimated that it captured 320,000 machine guns, 3.2 million rifles and pistols, and 508 million rounds of ammunition in the civil war. See *Chinese People's Liberation Army* (Peking: Foreign Languages Press, 1950), p. 10. As early as 1945 Chu Teh acknowledged that the "most difficult problem" for the PLA was "obtaining equipment and military supplies." See Chu Teh, *The Battle Front of the Liberated Areas* (Peking: Foreign Languages Press, 1962), p. 63.

19. William Whitson, ed., *The Military and Political Power in China in the 1970s* (New York: Praeger, 1972), p. 216.

20. Rigg, *Red China's Fighting Hordes*, pp. 153-154.

21. Sokolovskii, *Soviet Military Strategy*, pp. 215, 222. The army suffered from an "inadequately experienced command staff" which caused "big defects" in the use of artillery. See S.I. Gusev, *Grazhdanskaya voina i krasnaya armiya* (Moscow: Voenizdat, 1969), p. 94.

22. A.S. Bubnov, *O krasnoi armii* (Moscow: Voenizdat, 1958), p. 218.

23. Hanson Baldwin, "China As a Military Power," *Foreign Affairs* 30 (October 1951): 58.

24. Tank commanders, tending to come from the middle and upper classes, generally fought for the Whites or Kuomintang.

25. *Istoriya grazhdanskoi voiny v SSSR* (Moscow: Gosizdat, 1959), v. 5, p. 200. Vladimirtsev has noted that the majority of men in the Red Army had never seen tanks before the Wrangel campaign. See V.S. Vladimirtsev, *Partiya-organizator razgroma kontrrevoliutsii na yuge* (Moscow: Voenizdat, 1971), p. 263.

26. S.I. Gusev, *Grazhdanskaya voina i krasnaya armiya* (Moscow: Voenizdat, 1969), p. 95.

27. Mao Tse-tung, *Selected Works* (Peking: Foreign Languages Press, 1967), v. 4, p. 300.

28. William Whitson, *The Chinese High Command* (New York: Praeger, 1973), p. 462.

29. Most pilots either fought for the enemy or emigrated. Asher Lee, *The Soviet Air Force* (New York: John Day, 1962) p. 25; Rigg, *Red China's Fighting Hordes*, p. 321.

30. S.I. Aralov, *Lenin vel nas k pobede* (Moscow: Gosizdat, 1962), p. 75.

31. S.S. Kamenev, *Zapiski o grazhdanskoi voine i voennom stroitel'stvo* (Moscow: Voenizdat, 1963), p. 150.

32. Politicheskoe Upravlenie RKKA, *1918-1928 Let krasnoi armii-albom diagram* (Moscow: Voenni Vestnik, 1928), p. 11.

33. Richard Bueschel, *Communist Chinese Air Power* (New York: Praeger, 1968), pp. 17-18.

34. Ibid., p. 17.

35. Not only did the Whites dominate the Black and White Seas but even in the Baltic and Caspian Seas, Vatsetis, Gusev, and Kostayev could report in June 1919 that "The navel forces of the enemy have achieved absolute supremacy." See *Direktivi glavnogo kommandovaniya krasnoi armii (1917-1920)*, p. 328. The Chinese navy similarly played a minor role.

36. Yuri Petrov, *Stroitel'stvo politorganov, partiinikh i komsomolskikh organizatsii armii i flota (1918-1968)* (Moscow: Voenizdat, 1969), p. 281.

37. *KPSS i stroitel'stvo vooruzhennykh sily SSSR (1918-Juin, 1941)* (Moscow: Voenizdat, 1969), p. 281.

38. M.V. Frunze, *Izbrannye proizvedeniya* (Moscow: Voenizdat, 1967), v. 2, p. 87.

39. *Chinese People's Liberation Army*, p. 10; John Gittings, *The Role of the Chinese Army* (London: Oxford University Press, 1967), pp. 141-142.

40. Baldwin, "China As a Military Power."

41. *The Trotsky Papers*, ed. and trans. Jan Meyer (The Hague: Mouton, 1964), v. 1, p. 357.

42. *Chinese People's Liberation Army*, p. 10.

43. *The Trotsky Papers*, v. 1, p. 183.

44. J.V. Stalin, *Works* (Moscow: Gosizdat, 1947), v. 4, pp. 197-209.

45. *The Trotsky Papers*, v. 1, p. 487.

46. Ibid., v. 2, pp. 23, 323.

47. Ibid., v. 2, p. 323.

48. Gittings, *The Role of the Chinese Army*, p. 68.

49. Whitson, *The Military and Political Power in China in the 1970s*, pp. 189-191.

50. The Red Army was 5 percent Communist in December 1918, 5.1 percent Communist in January 1920, and 4.7 percent Communist in January 1921. See *Direktivi glavnogo kommandovaniya krasnoi armii (1917-1920)*, p. 139; A.S. Bubnov, et al., *Grazhdanskaya voina 1918-1921* (Moscow: Gosizdat, 1930), v. 2, pp. 87, 97.

51. Bubnov, et al., *Grazhdanskaya voina 1918-1921*, v. 2, pp. 67-68.

52. Gittings, *The Role of the Chinese Army*, p. 111.

53. Trotsky, *Kak vooruzhalas' revoliutsiya*, v. 2, bk. 2, p. 5. See also V.I. Lenin, *i sovetskie vooruzhennye sily* (Moscow: Voenizdat, 1967), pp. 83, 96, 105-238.

54. Voennyi vestnik, no. 6 (1928): 20.

55. Trotsky, *Kak vooruzhalas' revoliutsiya*, v. 2, bk. 2, p. 7.

56. *The Trotsky Papers*, v. 1, p. 393.

57. Bubnov, et al., *Grazhdanskaya voina 1918-1921*, v. 2, pp. 83, 87.

58. V.I. Lenin, *Collected Works* (Moscow: Foreign Language Press, 1960), v. 30, p. 321.

59. Soldiers at the front received an average of 2,184 calories per day while those in the rear received 1,504 calories per day. These rations were considerably greater than those received by civilians. However, disease and illness were rampant in the barracks, as in society. In 1919, 204.4 of every 1,000 soldiers and in 1920, 314.8 of every 1,000 soldiers suffered from typhus. See Politicheskoe Upravlenie RKKA, *1918-1928 Let krasnoi armii-albom diagram*, pp. 24, 26.

60. Shils and Janowitz have shown in their classic study of the Wehrmacht that the primary units were of critical importance in the army. See Edward Shils and Morris Janowitz, "Cohension and Disintegration in the Wehrmacht in World War II," *Public Opinion Quarterly* 12, no. 2 (Summer 1948): 12.

61. Bradbury, et al., *Mass Behavior in Battle and Captivity* p. 165.

62. These benefits included a plot of land, status, and security for his family if the soldier performed well in the army. See Lionel Chassin, *The Communist Conquest of China* (Cambridge: Harvard University Press, 1965), pp. 37, 161.

63. Morris Janowitz, "Military Elites and the Study of War," in his *Political Conflict* (Chicago: Quadrangle Books, 1970), p. 128.

64. Bubnov, et al., *Grazhdanskaya voina 1918-1921*, v. 2, p. 81.

65. Trotsky, *Kak vooruzhalas' revoliutsiya*, v. 1, bk. 1, p. 17.

66. For a good analysis of the state of the Red Army in 1918, see David Footman, *Civil War in Russia* (New York: Praeger, 1962).

67. *The Trotsky Papers*, v. 1, p. 95.

68. Sokolovskii, *Soviet Military Strategy*, pp. 222-223. Even as late as 1919, an estimated 80,000 partisans were active in Siberia and another 50,000 partisans were operating in the Ukraine.

69. D. Fedotoff White, *The Growth of the Red Army* (Princeton: Princeton University Press, 1944), p. 77.

70. S.M. Budenny, *Proidenny put'* (Moscow: Voenizdat, 1973), v. 1, p. 518.

71. Gittings, *The Role of the Chinese Army*, p. 24.

72. For the thesis of the centrality of the field army in Chinese Communist military history, see Whitson, *the Chinese High Command*.

73. Ithiel de Sola Pool et al., *Satellite Generals: A Study of Military Elites in the Soviet Sphere* (Stanford: Stanford University Press, 1955), p. 125; Rigg, *Red China's Fighting Hordes*, pp. 4-5.

74. However, Mao's denunciation of "mountaintopism" shows that at times the system became overly decentralized from the viewpoint of the top leadership.

75. Selznick, *Leadership in Administration,* pp. 16-17.

chapter 2

THE EFFECTIVENESS OF THE RUSSIAN AND CHINESE ARMIES

Four important indicators of battlefield capabilities—desertion, treason, mobilization of manpower, and the nature of the campaigns—show a consistent picture of a relatively strong and capable People's Liberation Army and a generally weak and ineffectual Red Army.

DESERTION

Desertion of soldiers and commanders is a particularly telling indicator of the state of any army. The Red Army suffered from mass desertion throughout the civil war. Indeed, its predecessor, the czarist army, had ultimately collapsed under the weight of desertion. Now, in the 1918-20 period, the largely peasant soldiers not only were weary of war but also were wary of the Bolsheviks and eager to occupy and farm their newly seized land.

In 1918 the Bolsheviks faced tremendous obstacles in the formation of the Red Army. During 1918 and the beginning of 1919 Soviet figures show that 917,250 men (out of nearly 4 million called up) refused even to appear for possible induction into the army. Furthermore, the Soviet historian Olikov has spoken of an "enormous percentage of evaders" in 1918 and declared that from July to December 1918, "The ranks of the army, in the usual meaning of the word, faded away."[1] In June 1918, for example, in the fighting against the Czech Legion, losses from enemy action were "slight" but losses from desertion and flight were "enormous."[2]

The situation remained grave in 1919. Severe measures, including confiscation of property, transfer to punishment units, and even exemplary executions, were introduced to curb desertion. Although some progress was made, Table 2, using Soviet data, shows that a remarkable 1,761,000 deserters were either apprehended in raids or appeared voluntarily under an amnesty. These huge numbers, almost equal to the number of men called up in 1919, did not include those who successfully avoided reentry into the Red Army. Table 2 also shows that even in the Petrograd Military District, a Bolshevik stronghold, no less than 88,500 deserters were arrested, and another 59,100 deserters appeared voluntarily during 1919.

Table 2   Red Army Desertion, 1919

| | Deserters | | |
Okrug	Arrested in Raids	Voluntary Appearance	Total
Moscow	151,631	214,722	366,353
Petrograd	88,548	59,095	148,133
Yaroslavl	71,899	108,215	180,114
Orlov	175,134	236,401	411,533
Western	75,047	140,086	238,470
Volga	93,393	60,804	162,202
Urals	87,324	76,264	163,589
Railroad	7,803	—	7,803
RSFSR	862,572	898,533	1,761,104

Source: S. Olikov, *Dezertir'stvo v krasnoi armii i bor'ba s nim*, pp. 30-31.

Whole armies, such as the Eleventh and Twelfth Red Armies on the southern front, simply disintegrated through mass desertion in the spring of 1919. In June 1919, Berzin, inspector of the Latvian army, reported that only 10,000 to 15,000 men remained of the 70,000 effectives mobilized less than a month earlier.[3] At the height of the Denikin offensive in October 1919, a remarkable 17.8 percent of all Red Army men on troop trains in the first half of the month and 21.8 percent in the second half simply deserted. At the same time, in the last half of October no less than 60 commanders and 9,239 men already on the front abandoned their positions and deserted.[4] Potyaev, a member of the Revolutionary Military Council of the western front, reported in a secret telegram to Lenin in December 1919, "Our units start to disintegrate before they have undergone formation and produce a colossal percentage (up to 70 percent) of deserters who carry their rifles away with them."[5]

Even the drawing to a close of the civil war in 1920 did not eliminate the problem entirely. In 1920, 1,100,000 deserters were either apprehended in raids or reappeared voluntarily.[6] In the Ukraine, Olikov refers to a figure of nearly 500,000 deserters in a five-month period and asserts that mass desertion there was stopped only at the end of 1920. Indeed, even in Russia no less than 118,273 men deserted the front during the first six months of 1920 alone.[7] Many troops in anti-Soviet rebellions, such as those of Makhno and Antonov, were Red Army deserters. Mashatov at the Tenth Party Congress in March 1921 went as far as to say that "from the army grew banditism."[8] Even in 1921 official Soviet statistics showed that 1,896 military administrators and 1,681 military commanders deserted while only 133 were killed in battle.[9]

By contrast, the People's Liberation Army, possessing a lengthy gestation period, large party stratum, and relatively favorable disposition of the peasants towards the revolution evidently possessed a low rate of desertion. While the testimony of Western observers, such as Derk Bodde, who deny the existence of any desertion at all in the army, strains credulity, available evidence has suggested a very low rate of desertion.[10] Official PLA statistics have no category for desertion. However, these same statistics also listed 17,700 prisoners of war taken by the Kuomintang and 107,000 men missing in action in the civil war.[11] Even if desertion were concealed under these categories, they would suggest an order of magnitude vastly less than that of the Red Army which recorded 2.8 million deserters in only two years of the civil war.

American data on the Korean War supports these suppositions. Under much less favorable circumstances than the civil war, the Chinese army, numbering 700,000 men at its height, suffered only 21,000 POWs.[12] The small number of Chinese POWs was remarkable in view of the vastly superior enemy firepower, the great casualties suffered by the Chinese army, the lack of any decisive victory, and the inevitable disillusionment with the general lack of success of the "people's war" in the Korean countryside. Thus, desertion seemed to have been a far lesser problem in the Chinese army than in the Russian army.

TREASON

Treason is another telling indicator of the cohesion and effectiveness of an army. As with desertion, treason was a far greater problem in the Red Army than in the PLA. Treason in the Red Army occurred against a backdrop of numerous foreign interventions, foreign plots, and anti-Soviet actions. Treasonous activity was especially endemic among three unlikely, but important, allies of the Bolsheviks—the *voenspets*, atamans ("Cossack Leaders"), and non-Bolshevik radicals.[13]

Although the majority of *voenspets* ("ex-czarist officers") were passively loyal, a minority were traitors. Lenin declared in March 1920, "Thousands of former officers, generals, and colonels, of the czarist army betrayed us and sold us, and thousands of the finest Red Army men perished as a result, that you know."[14] Indeed, given their upper-class backgrounds and close ties with czarism, it was hardly surprising that a considerable majority of *voenspets* served in the White, rather than the Red, Army.[15] In July 1918 the majority of teachers at the General Staff Academy, led by Commandant Andogsky, left for the Urals to join Kolchak while only a minority remained to found the Red Army General Staff Academy.[16]

Treason was especially prevalent among those *voenspets* who fought in the Red Army during 1918. In May 1918, former Admiral Shchastny, commander of the Baltic fleet, was shot for not rescuing the fleet and allowing it to be used against the Bolsheviks.[17] In June, former Admiral Sablin and a majority of naval officers refused a direct order to sink the Black Sea fleet in view of the imminent German threat.[18] In July 1918, former General Boguslovsky, commander of the North Urals-Siberian sector, went over to the Whites.[19] That same month the fall of Ufa was greatly eased by the treason of former colonel Makhin, chief of staff of the Ufa Red Army.[20] In August 1918, former General Nosovich, deputy commander of the southern front, fled to the Whites after he and his fellow *voenspet* Kovalevsky, chief of staff of the North Caucasus Military District, were arrested for systematically sending information to Krasnov.[21]

August 1918, a critical month for the existence of the government, was also a banner month for treason and accusations of treason. The loss of Archangel to foreign interventionists was aided by the treason of former Admiral Vikorst, commander of the local flotilla, and the *voenspet* Potapov, commander of the armies of the White Sea Military District.[22] The retreat of the Red Army from the Far East was hastened by the "vile traitorous role" played by the command of local military gunboats and the ship committee of the Amur River flotilla.[23] In an August 1918, in a secret telegram to Lenin, War Commissar Trotsky claimed that around Commander in chief Vatsetis (himself a *voenspet*) were *voenspets* "many of whom commit acts of treachery," while in the navy "the percentage of traitors among them" was "higher."[24]

In October 1918, the former Cossack officer Sorokin, commander in chief of the North Caucasus Red Army, emulating his predecessor Avtonomov, revolted and shot a number of key party and government leaders. Although the revolt was soon suppressed, by January his army had disintegrated, easing Denikin's advance.[25] Similarly, the treasonous activity of a number of *voenspets* in the Third Army paved the way for the fall of Perm in December. Stalin reported there occurred "an incredible, almost wholesale desertion of responsible officers to the enemy."[26]

In March 1919, an uprising in Gomel led by the *voenspet* Strekopytov gained the support of the majority of local army units and led to the shooting of the entire Military Revolutionary Staff.[27] In May, former Colonel Vsevolodov, having served as commander and chief of staff of the Ninth Army, went over to Denikin.[28] That same month the defection of the commander of an Estonian division, Ritt helped the Whites to capture Pskov.[29] In June *voenspets* led by Neklyudov spearheaded an uprising and seized the key forts of Krasnaya Gorka and Seraya Loshad on the approaches to Petrograd.[30] Lundquist, the *voenspet* chief of staff of the Seventh Army, not only reported regularly to Yudenich but even worked out plans for his October offensive on Petrograd![31]

Treason by *voenspets* did diminish considerably as victory neared, and the enemy became an old national antagonist (Poland) in

1920. Enough acts continued to occur that Lenin in March 1920 bemoaned the "treachery" of the *voenspets* which "cost us tens of thousands of lives."[32]

The weakness of the revolution, especially in the Ukraine and the south of Russia, forced the army to rely heavily on local atamans and would-be atamans, who were notoriously undependable. The revolts of Golubov, Grigoriev, and Mironov were typical instances of this group. In May 1919 Grigoriev, former ataman and Petlyurist officer, served as chief Soviet commander in the southwest. He revolted and seized the cites of Kherson, Nikolayev, and Ekaterinoslav. The entire front against Denikin collapsed as many soldiers joined him, attracted by slogans emphasizing free trade, "Soviets without communists," and Ukrainian nationalism. Other units remained neutral. The revolt was finally suppressed with "extraordinarily grave consequences for the southern front" as Makhno had him shot.[33] In August 1919 Mironov, former Cossack colonel and would-be ataman, led his Red Cossack Corps in revolt at Saransk, thereby undermining the front at a critical time and causing "great harm" to the Soviet effort. After Budenny's First Cavalry Army suppressed the revolt, Mironov was condemned to death but was reprieved.[34]

Finally, the radical allies of the Bolsheviks often posed considerable problems for the Red Army. The abortive revolt of the Left Socialist Revolutionaries in Moscow in July 1918 touched off several army revolts. Abandoning Kazan, the Left SR commander of the eastern front, Muraviev, raised a revolt and called for renewed war against Germany. Although Muraviev was soon shot, Lenin later asserted that "the treachey of Muraviev" had "cost the lives of tens of thousands of workers and peasants" for "he had opened up almost the entire front to the enemy and caused us a number of reverses."[35] In Yaroslavl, a protracted Left SR revolt was supported by the chief of the military district and entire command staff of an armored division. In January 1919, the Left SR War Commissar of Turkestan Osipov led a bloody revolt which, with the active support of the entire command staff of the local garrison, led to the shooting of top party leaders before it was suppressed.[36]

In July 1920, Left SR Sapozhkov, the commander of a cavalry division, staged an uprising which seized Buzuluk. Several Red Army units, attracted by his slogans against forced requisitions, joined him before he was shot.[37] The three revolts of Makhno, the politically conscious anarchist and frequent Soviet ally, repeatedly troubled the Red Army. His last revolt, which began in November 1920, was finally suppressed only nine months later after a long and arduous campaign.[38] Revolts by radical allies frequently disrupted the Red Army during the civil war, especially as such allies could not easily be dismissed as White Guards.

The end of the main fighting of the civil war in November 1920, with the destruction of Wrangel's forces, did not bring the expected end to such dangerous army revolts. Rather it fostered a new and even more dangerous wave, based on discontent with the regime. In December 1920, Vakulin, an army battalion commander, led a revolt in the Don. Although Vakulin was killed in February 1921, by March, his original band of 500 men had grown to almost 6,000 bayonets and sabers under his successor, Popov. Twice whole Red Army battalions were seized by his units. Only four months after the beginning of the revolt did his band disintegrate.[39]

Vakulin's band was not alone. The remnants of Sapozhkov's revolt had rallied under a new leader, Serov. Their numbers reached 3,000 men during 1921 in actions along the Volga.[40] Elsewhere, on the left bank of the Ukraine, in January 1921, Maslakov, a brigade commander in Budenny's First Cavalry Army, revolted and joined Makhno. This greatly strengthened Makhno, and Maslakov's revolt was not crushed until March 1921.[41] The Makhno revolt continued to trouble the Red Army during the first eight months of the year. And, in March 1921, the Kronstadt sailors, once the "pride of the revolution," staged a revolt. The suppression of the sailors was a difficult and protracted affair. It is little wonder that Lenin in March 1921 could assert that "We are barely holding on," especially in view of unrest in the factories and mass discontent in the countryside.[42]

Treason, and the fear of treason, was so pervasive in the Red Army that in 1919 the commander in chief of the Red Army, the *voenspet* Vatsetis, was even briefly arrested on suspicion of treason.[43] By contrast, treason was virtually unknown in the Chinese army during the civil war. The thought that Chu Teh, the commander in chief of the PLA, could have been a traitor would have been inconceivable in China. The only known major case of treason in the 1946-50 period occured in January 1946, six months before the beginning of the civil war, when Ho P'eng-chu's 40,000 troops defected back to the Kuomintang.[44] Although numerous cases of treason occurred in the Kuomintang armies, not one major case of treason occurred in the PLA during the civil war.[45] Indeed, treason had not been a major problem in the Chinese army since the early years of formation, in the 1927-37 period.[46] Thus, treason and desertion showed the same pattern in each of the two armies.

MOBILIZATION

The mobilization capacity for key campaigns is another indicator of the effectiveness of the two armies, especially given their roughly similar size and low level of technology. Tables 3 and 4 show a considerably higher mobilization capacity for the Chinese army than the Russian army. During the time of the three major campaigns detailed in the tables (Denikin, Polish, and Wrangel for the Red Army; Liaohsi-Shenyang, Huai-Hai, and Peking-Tientsin for the PLA), the armies were roughly the same overall size.[47] During these three campaigns, the Red Army mobilized 89,000 to 140,000 troops while the PLA mobilized 600,000 to 900,000 troops. Of course, the disparity was lessened by the smaller size of White forces. However, unlike the PLA, the Red Army evidently was at a numerical disadvantage in two of its three major campaigns.

Table 3   Size of Red Army Mobilization for Key Campaigns

Campaign	Dates	Red Army Troops	Enemy Troops
Kolchak	4/19	101,400	136,000
Denikin	4/19-9/19	140,800	153,000
Polish	7-8/20	89,000	130,000
Wrangel	10-11/20	133,000	34,000

Sources: L.M. Spirin, *Razgroma armii kolchaka*, pp. 89-91; N. Kakurin, *Kak srazhalas' revoliutsii*, v. 2, pp. 306-307; V.D. Sokolovskii, *Soviet Military Strategy*, p. 218; *Istoriya grazhdanskoi voiny v SSSR*, v. 5, p. 200.

The Red Army repeatedly suffered from poor mobilization capabilities. When the landing of an Allied force of more than 100,000 men in Archangel in the summer of 1918 posed a potential threat to Petrograd and Moscow, the Red Army initially could muster less than 15,000 troops to oppose it.[48] In March 1919, the 1.5 million man Red Army mobilized only 100,000 troops to oppose Kolchak's 136,000 bayonets and sabers.[49] In May 1919, Commander in chief Vatsetis reported to the General Staff that "In general for the current decisive operations we not only are not stronger than our opponents but numerically are considerably weaker."[50] In the crucial Polish campaign of 1920 future Marshal Tukhachevsky later argued that "numerical weakness" hindered the Red Army as the "enemy went on the attack twice as powerful as us."[51] Thus, the Red Army was repeatedly hindered by its very poor mobilization capabilities.

Table 4   Size of PLA Mobilization for Key Campaigns

Campaign	Dates	PLA Troops	Kuomintang Troops
Seizure of Kaifeng	6/48	200,000	250,000
Seizure of Tsinan	9/48	240,000	100,000
Liaohsi-Shenyang	9-11/48	700,000	472,000
Huai-Hai	11/48-1/49	600,000	555,000
Peking-Tientsin	1/49	900,000	521,000

Sources: O. Edmund Clubb, *Twentieth Century China*, p. 288; V.I. Glunin, *Tret'ya grazhdanskaya revoliutsionnaya voina v kitai* (1946-1949), p. 140; William Whitson, *The Chinese High Command*, p. 240; Mao Tse-tung, *Selected Works*, v. 4, pp. 264-266; *Tret'ya grazhdanskaya revoliutsionnaya voina v kitai*, p. 325; Jerome Ch'en, *Mao and the Chinese Revolution*, pp. 304, 306-307.

In general, the Red Army was unable to mobilize more than 5 percent of its total strength for key campaigns while the PLA could mobilize more than 25 percent of its total strength. While Soviet party leader Bubnov has estimated that only 11 percent of Red Army troops were even at the front in 1920 (and only one-fourth of them ever saw action), the United States Army Intelligence Division has estimated that 40 percent of the PLA troops were combat effective.[52] Thus, the Chinese army was also superior to the Russian army in mobilization capabilities.

CAMPAIGNS

Battle is the ultimate test for any army. An examination for each army of several campaigns during the civil war, a significant foreign campaign at the end of the civil war, and "bandit-suppression" campaigns after the end of the civil war highlights the relative strengths of the PLA and the weaknesses of the Red Army. The Red Army ultimately triumphed in each major campaign, but only with extreme difficulty. For as Lenin conceded in October 1921, "on each occasion—on the Kolchak front, on the Denikin front, on the Yudenich front, on the Polish front, and on the Wrangel front— ... we had been badly battered (and sometimes more than once)."[53] The Yudenich and Denikin campaigns in 1919 were particularly reflective of the problems of the Red Army on the battlefield during the civil war.

In September and October 1919, Yudenich's small northwest army, numbering 15,000 to 25,000 men, threatened Petrograd.[54] Although the Red Army numbered nearly 3 million men and the local Seventh and Fifteenth Armies counted 250,000 men, the Red Army could not contain Yudenich's forces which even Lenin called "weak, insignificant."[55] In a single week Yudenich advanced nearly 100 miles into the suburbs of Petrograd. The Politburo was forced to declare Russia a military camp, register all members of the Petrograd party, trade union, and government for military service and rush in troops from as far away as Moscow, Murmansk, and Tula.[56] Zinoviev even called for the evacuation of Petrograd. Some 4,500 Communists were rushed to the front while thousands more were inducted into the party at the front in order to increase willingness to fight for the revolution.[57] As a result, Yudenich was routed, and his army disintegrated, but the cost had been high. The extreme incompetence and inefficiency of the Red Army had escalated a minor attack by a small enemy force into a major crisis in which the very existence of the regime seemed to be at stake.

Similarly, the campaign against Denikin did not inspire confidence in the army. Although by the end of the summer, the Red Army considerably outnumbered Denikin's forces and possessed twice as many cannon and machine guns, it could not contain Denikin.[58] Indeed, during the summer and early fall of 1919, Denikin seized the

Crimea, Kherson, Odessa, Kiev, and Tsaritsyn. Footman has characterized the Red Army in the south as an "ineffectual and demoral-
ized" force which "seemed to be disintegrating."[59] From April to
October 1919, Denikin, with some exaggeration, claimed the taking
of 250,000 prisoners and the capture of 1,700 machine guns and 700
cannon.[60] Only after the mobilization of 10,000 Komsomolites,
30,000 Communists, and 36,000 trade unionists and the dispatch of
Budenny's First Cavalry Army and the Latvian Rifles Division to the
ranks of the Red Army on the southern front did the Red Army
proceed to rout Denikin in the fall of 1919.[61]

The performance of the Red Army in the Polish campaign of 1920
was even more inglorious. Indeed, the independence of such small
countries as Poland, Finland, Latvia, Lithuania, and Estonia was due
in large measure to the weakness of the Red Army in a series of
campaigns against them in the 1919-20 period. The Red Army performance in the Polish campaign was markedly inferior to that of the
PLA in the Korean War. Yet, the Red Army possessed a number of
advantages in its Polish campaign. In Marshal Tukhachevsky's
words, "The Party concentrated here its best forces." The Red Army
sent four of its five future marshals (Tukhachevsky, Yegorov, Budenny, and Voroshilov) and many other key officers to direct the
campaign.[62] The Polish campaign inspired such nationalist fervor
that many *voenspets*, such as General Brusilov, rushed to join the
army. Although the Red Army suffered from poor mobilization capability, it did not lack adequate firepower or air and sea supremacy, as
the PLA did in Korea. Furthermore, the Polish army, unlike the
American army in Korea, was a distinctly second-rate fighting
force.[63] Given these advantages, the Red Army, in an initially successful counterattack after a disastrous Polish advance which had
taken Kiev in May 1920, did reach the gates of Warsaw in August
1920.

However, the counterattack by a weak Polish army led to the
disintegration of Tukhachevsky's command and a "wild rout" of the
Red Army.[64] In the aftermath, the Poles took 66,000 POWs while
another 30,000 Red Army men were disarmed in East Prussia. A
renewed Polish campaign in September (the battles at Niemen and
Szczara) resulted in 50,000 more Russian POWs, the loss of Rovno,
Tarnopol, Pinsk, and Grodno, and an overall "disaster" for the Red

Army.[65] The rout was finally halted only outside Minsk in October 1920 when the Polish army overran its supply lines and the Polish government obtained an armistice.

The campaigns against small revolts at the end of the civil war did little to improve the dismal picture. The Kronstadt, Makhno, and Tambov revolts of 1921 were hardly very threatening from a military viewpoint. Even the Kronstadt sailors, who occupied strong defensive positions, numbered only 15,000 men. Antonov's 20,000 to 50,000 men in the Tambov revolt consisted of "simple peasants, armed with axes, cudgels, pitchforks, and a scattering of rifles and pistols."[66] Makhno's forces, equally ill-equipped, often numbered as few as 2,500 to 3,000 men.[67] In the Ukraine in 1921, the Red Army seized from numerous rebel bands all of 30 cannon, 333 machine guns, 2,667 rifles, 227 revolvers, and 2,375 sabers, not much more than it confiscated from the local civilian population.[68] Thus, these small rebel forces should have posed no great threat to the 5 million man Red Army.

And yet, the Red Army, despite great numerical superiority and considerable firepower, not only found it impossible to crush the revolts alone but in the process tended itself to become a threat to the regime. The Soviet historian Trifonov drily noted that a "significant part of the armaments and military supplies of the bands were acquired in fighting" with the Red Army. He further observed that Red Army units "demonstrated unpreparedness for conducting so-called little wars" and that "Pursuing bandits tired military units, evoked a morbid mood among the population and Red Army men."[69] The weakness of the army angered Lenin who, in a February 1921 note to Sklyansky on the Makhno campaign, complained that "Our military command has ignominiously failed, letting Makhno go (despite a gigantic preponderance of force and strict orders to trap him)."[70]

A clear pattern of army impotence and even rebelliousness emerged in the suppression of the Kronstadt, Tambov, and Makhno revolts in 1921. In the Kronstadt revolt, the Seventh Army in Petrograd, the logical instrument for suppressing the revolt, was so unreliable that units were disarmed and confined to the barracks, for it was felt that "They might well refuse to fire on the rebels or even go over to their side." Even buttressed by reliable units, kursanti ("officer cadets"), Communists, and Chekists, the first army assault across the admittedly dangerous open ice against Kronstadt was a miserable failure. Despite the presence of Cheka machine gunners in the rear of the troops, some soldiers defected to the rebels, others refused to advance and at least one group even sent a delegation to the rebels to find out their demands. As Avrich has concluded, "Troops chosen for their reliability had faltered at the crucial moment."[71]

The army similarly failed, and even became a threat to the regime, in the Tambov and Makhno revolts. It is no accident that the official five-volume Soviet history of the civil war chose to ignore these campaigns.[72] When regular army units were first sent to Tambov, many soldiers and commanders deserted to Antonov.[73] Similarly, in late November 1920, a Red Army division surrounded Makhno's small force of perhaps 2,500 men but was routed. Makhno claimed the capture of 6,000 Red Army prisoners, 2,000 of whom allegedly promised to fight for Makhno. Three days later, two more Red Army divisions were routed by the small Makhno forces, and Makhno this time claimed the capture of 8,000 to 10,000 men.[74]

In lieu of regular military action by the Red Army, the Bolsheviks relied primarily on a mixture of political concessions, Chekist repression and massive military force.[75] Political concessions played a major role in undermining the political base of revolts. The New Economic Policy (NEP), introduced in March 1921, pacified the peasantry by replacing the hated forced requisitions with a tax in kind and by creating private markets to trade peasant surpluses. It was no accident that it was only after the introduction of NEP that Makhno was forced to leave Russia for Rumania (August 1921) and Antonov was killed by a special Cheka unit (June 1922). It was further no accident that NEP, together with increased rations for Petrograd workers, was introduced on the day before the launching of the second assault against the Kronstadt rebels. In referring to the Antonov and Makhno peasant revolts, Soviet historians Gusev and Eritsyan have noted, "The transition to the NEP created the decisive precondition for the full extirpation of SR-kulak banditry."[76]

Chekist repression was particularly important in the suppression of the Makhno and Tambov revolts. Antonov-Ovseenko, in a special report to Lenin in August 1921, described the important role of the Cheka in the Tambov area. In pro-bandit villages, the entire male population was put on trial. All families of bandits were sent to concentration camps as hostages. If the bandit did not surrender within two weeks, his family was deported and its property confiscated. The senior working member of the family was liable to be shot if weapons were found during Cheka searches. Antonov-Ovseenko reported that 5,000 hostages were currently in concentration camps, 663 bandits and hostages had been shot, and several hundred homes had been burned.[77] Similarly, in the Makhno revolt, the Cheka played a major role by hanging all active pro-Makhno activists found in each village searched by them.[78] Singleton has asserted, "Against a backdrop of mass executions and burning villages, the Red Army finally crushed the partisans."[79]

Finally, many elements were used to reinforce and at times replace regular army units. In all three campaigns the Red Army ultimately mobilized a crushing numerically superior force (90,000 men against Makhno, 50,000 men against the Kronstadt rebels, and 35,000 men against the Tambov rebels).[80] Outstanding military commanders, such as Tukhachevsky (Kronstadt and Tambov) and Frunze (Makhno), directed the Red Army forces, backed by significant quantities of military equipment. The party carried out mobilizations of Communists, including the sending of 300 delegates to the Tenth Party Congress to Kronstadt.

The party also repeatedly relied on an admixture of non-army units to supplement, and even replace, the army. The party mobilized ChON units (Communist units of special assignment) which, in Trifonov's words, were "a reliable military support of party and Soviet government . . . (who) distinguished themselves in fighting with the bands." By December 1921, ChON units, with a 41,000 man cadre force and a temporary additional force of 329,000 men, were fighting in such diverse areas as Tambov, Volga, Western Siberia, Belorussia, and Karelia.[81] In addition, Cheka army units, originally organized in 1919, played a key role as they "annihilated in fierce fighting dozens of big and small bands."[82] Repeatedly the party utilized whole battalions of kursanti as a reliable fighting force. In the Ukraine the regime relied heavily on KNC units (committees of poor villages), which numbered 730 detachments with 56,000 men by June 1921. These units, according to Trifonov, played an "outstanding role in liquidating kulak banditism in the Ukraine."[83] Using all these diverse elements, the army was eventually able to defeat the enemy.

The comparison with the People's Liberation Army, with its "high morale and a remarkable zest for the offensive" and "pervasive aura of invincibility" is absolute and compelling.[84] The last two years of the Chinese civil war witnessed a "triumphal march" across the huge land mass of China.[85] From the fall of Mukden in November 1948 to the capture of Canton in October 1949, the PLA advanced approximately 2,000 miles, a phenomenal average of six miles every day. One military analyst has extravagantly called this feat "unique in the military history of the world."[86] The PLA offensive from September 1948 to January 1949 alone resulted in the capture of Peking and Tsinan and the loss of 1 million men and 400,000 rifles by the Kuomintang.[87] Thus, the PLA, in contrast to the Red Army, by its swift advances at the end of the civil war manifested a strongly offensive spirit and a high level of effectiveness on the battlefield.

These qualities were also much in evidence during the Chinese intervention in the Korean War. While the Red Army had disintegrated quickly under the blows of a second-rate military power in the Polish campaign, the PLA successfully resisted the attacks of the army of the world's leading superpower, the United States. The forces of the United Nations (largely American and Korean) possessed almost total air and sea supremacy as well as a vast superiority in firepower. The long Chinese supply lines were vulnerable to enemy air and sea power. Furthermore, the narrow width of the Korean peninsula greatly hindered Chinese mobility while the alien population did not respond to Chinese propaganda. Despite these adverse factors largely not faced by the Red Army (except for the enemy population), the PLA (in the guise of the Chinese People's Volunteers), in a large-scale offensive starting from the Yalu in November 1950 drove the United Nations forces completely out of North Korea in three weeks. By January 1951, the Chinese army had taken Seoul. General Ridgeway, the American commander in Korea, conceded "severe" defeats and "tragic" losses for the American army. He asserted that the Americans faced a "near disaster" on the Yalu during the Chinese offensive.[88] By June 1951, after a moderately successful Western offensive and the failure of several Chinese offensives, a stalemate went into effect around the 38th parallel. Thereafter, despite massive American firepower, the Chinese army was neither routed nor dislodged from its positions. Indeed, despite an estimated 600,000 casualties, the PLA lost only 21,000 men taken as prisoners by the enemy.[89]

The Chinese army's performance in Korea elicited respect from various military experts. General Chassin concluded that the Chinese campaign in Korea "demonstrated that its defensive capabilities are as remarkable as its capabilities for offensive action."[90] Alexander George cited an American Marine Corps history that characterized the Chinese army as "a first-rate army when judged by its own tactical and strategic standards" and as a "formidable" army.[91]

Finally, in sharp contrast again to the Red Army, the PLA evidently successfully conducted large-scale "bandit suppression" campaigns in 1950. In Hunan Province alone the PLA deployed 200,000 troops for this campaign. In 1950 in the Southwest Military Region nearly 500,000 bandits were reportedly eliminated.[92] During the period from May 1949 to May 1951, over 1 million bandits were reportedly inactivated in the Central South Military Region.[93] No secret police units, party levies, mobilizations of officer cadets, political concessions, or extensive coercion seemed to have been necessary. Thus, the PLA demonstrated itself to be an effective force in great contrast to the ineffectiveness of the Red Army.

The PLA emerged far stronger than the Red Army from the civil wars. Indeed, the Bolsheviks won the civil war *virtually in spite of* the largely weak an ineffectual Red Army. It was little wonder that Lenin in December 1920 bluntly asserted that "We do not possess one-hundredth of the forces of the combined imperialist states"[94] and in October 1921 speculated that "Perhaps they [the Whites] would have crushed us had any of the capitalist states that were fighting us mobilized a few army corps in time."[95] In sharp contrast, the Chinese Communists won their civil war to a large degree *precisely because of* the People's Liberation Army. Despite certain deficiencies in modern technology, the PLA at the end of the civil war was a powerful, effective fighting force.

THE EARLY DEVELOPMENT OF THE CHINESE ARMY (1927-45)

In order to better understand the origins of the differences between the two armies, it is necessary to examine the gestation period of the Chinese army, the period from 1927-45. During this time the Chinese Communists faced many of the same problems as did the Bolsheviks in their civil war. The creation of a revolutionarily legitimate and militarily effective army was a protracted process. This gestation period, is divided into two natural parts—the first period, from 1927-36, began with the Nanchang Uprising and ended with the consolidation of a decimated army in Yenan after the Long March, and the second period witnessed a steady rise in the power of the Chinese army during the Anti-Japanese War.

In the 1927-36 period the Chinese Red Army grew from a ragtag force of several thousand men to a disciplined army of tens of thousands of men after the Long March. Its officer corps, almost completely Communist and highly talented young men, gained invaluable experience by 1936. Nearly a decade after its founding, the army represented far more in potential than in achievements. It had actually shrunk from roughly 300,000 men in 1934 to only 40,000 men in 1937. Its most famous exploits in this period—such as the Nanchang Uprising (which founded the army in August 1927) and the Long March (October 1934 to October 1935)—were actually serious military defeats in which a large part of the Communist forces disintegrated. The glory of these events lay largely in their symbolism and in the preservation of a nucleus for the army.

A number of serious problems hampered the development of the Chinese Red Army (renamed the People's Liberation Army in 1946) in its early years. These problems can be seen in comparison to the early years of the Russian Red Army. Most importantly, the Chinese army did not represent a central government or even a significant part of the country. The army and party lacked legitimacy and the resultant capacity to mobilize large numbers of men and significant material resources. There was no large inherited stockpile of weapons and existing governmental bureaucracy, such as the Bolsheviks found in place after the October Revolution. Furthermore, given the strength of the central government and the remaining warlords, the army was largely confined to remote, inhospitable areas of the country (such as the Chingkan Mountains and Yenan) or condemned to flight from the enemy (the Long March of 368 days). These structures severly hampered the development of an army, especially as these base areas tended to have small populations and food problems. The lack of a stable base also limited work with the local population.

The army faced a number of significant internal military problems as well, including great difficulties in establishing any form of constant, centralized control over numerous partisan groups and base areas, widely separated by large distances and hostile enemy forces. Until 1931 there was no regular system of partisan forces. Only in that year did the army succeed in ending an anarchical deployment of scattered and largely autonomous guerrilla forces. Until 1933 in the Kiangsi Soviet there were great differences in the strength and often level of independence of various army units. In that year a military reform simplified and standardized the size and table of command for units under central control. Only at that time did the Chinese Red Army cease to be a congery of loosely organized units and come instead under effective central control.[96]

Furthermore, unlike the Russian army's successful move to gain control over Ukrainian and Siberian partisans in its civil war, the Chinese army center had very little to offer these groups in terms of weapons, resources, and manpower. The problem of "mountain-topism" (excessive localism), which occurred in both large and small units, was one Mao repeatedly denounced. While in 1928 there were at least eight major and semi-independent "Red armies," there were at least three separate armies that made the Long March in the 1934-36 period.

Furthermore, the Chinese Communists faced specifically Chinese problems in the creation of a viable revolutionary force. After the overthrow of the Imperial dynasty in 1911, China fell under the sway of innumerable warlords for the next sixteen years. These petty warlords, linked to a particular region, used their military power solely for the satisfaction of personal and even criminal needs. Their armies were devoid of any national or political character. Their unbridled militarism highlighted the dangers inherent in the creation of armies lacking political direction. Although the Kuomintang in the 1920s had higher national and political goals than the warlords, its armies too were of the more traditional type. The Kuomintang armies were congeries of many disparate units bound together by the personal loyalties of their leaders. Revolts were common against the at times nominal central leadership. There was no sense of unity.

The effectiveness of the Kuomintang units, while greater than that of the warlord armies, was not very high. Neither the warlords nor the Kuomintang had succeeded in elevating the traditionally lowly place of the soldier in Chinese society.

These problems were accentuated by the weakened state of the party in the latter half of 1927 when it was called upon to create an army. Numbering only 58,000 members at its height in April 1927, the party had most of its support in the cities. However, the leader of the Kuomintang, General Chiang Kai-shek, was sufficiently strong to expel them from their urban bases. In April 1927, Chiang's forces massacred the Communists in Shanghai by the thousands. The bulk of the party members, who had joined only in the previous two years, were killed, driven underground, or forced to leave the party. From an important national political force in China in the early months of 1927, the Chinese Communist party had been reduced to a small band of isolated revolutionaries by the end of 1927. At least one-third of its top leaders were executed by Chiang's secret police. By November 1927, there were less than 20,000 Communists left in the country, perhaps 4,000 of whom could be considered active.[97]

Beginning in the summer of 1927, the remaining Communist forces fled in small groups to the countryside. Here the prognosis was not much better. Having successfully completed the Northern Expedition to unite China, Chiang Kai-shek was at the height of his power. Communist influence within the Kuomintang, despite a key Communist role in the running of the Whampoa Military Academy, remained rather small. There was no massive peasant revolt waiting to be led by the Communists. Mao's Autumn Harvest Uprising ended in a disastrous failure. Attempts at revolts in the cities met no better fate. Later, in December 1927, the Canton Commune was easily crushed by the anti-Communist forces.

It was against such a black backdrop that the Chinese Red Army was born out of a desperate revolt at Nanchang in August 1927. The revolt was engineered by Communist and pro-Communist officers in the Kuomintang army and police forces stationed at Nanchang and was led by Chu Teh, Yeh T'ing, and Ho Lung. The very weakness of the Nanchang Uprising underscored the grave difficulties faced by the Chinese Communists in the creation of an army of their own. Ho Lung was the commander of the Twentieth Kuomintang Army, Yeh

T'ing was the commander of the Twenty-fourth Kuomintang division, and Chu Teh was the chief of Public Security Forces. Within
three days after the beginning of the revolt on August 1, 1927, the
new Communist forces had to evacuate Nanchang. Far from being a
triumphant march southward, the army's journey from Nanchang
was marked by sharp defeats at Ch'ao-chou and Swatow. Only a
victory at Juichin preserved the force from total defeat. By the end of
August, the new army had dwindled from the original 21,000 combat
troops to only 8,000! The entire Tenth Army with 5,000 men had
defected to the Kuomintang, 1,000 men had been killed or wounded,
and a staggering 7,000 had been left behind sick or had simply
deserted.

There are two extant descriptions of the army on its march from
Nanchang that give a graphic idea of precisely how horrendous were
the difficulties faced by the Communists in the early days of the
creation of the army. Li Li-san, later the leader of the party from 1928
to 1930, vividly described the situation.

Propaganda work was extremely bad and none of the troops understood
the meaning of the revolt. Therefore the soldiers' morale was very shaky and
a great many of them deserted. During only three days' march we had lost
more than one-third of our actual strength, almost half the ammunition was
abandoned, the mortars were completely thrown away, and several of the
large cannon were also lost. The soliders who deserted or died of illness
approached four thousand (the 20th Army was worst, military discipline was
extremely bad, shooting and impressment of porters and such things hap-
pening all along) . . . .

Chang Kuo-t'ao, later one of Mao's rivals, has succinctly summa-
rized the challenge facing party leaders at this time, in words redolent
of those Trotsky might have used to describe the Russian Red Army
in its early days in 1918.

But, the 11th Army still could not be called a CP [Communist] Army or a
workers' and peasants' army and can only be called a disciplined Kuomintang army which included a large number of CP members. The 20th Army
can only be called an old-fashioned army which showed sympathy towards
us. The Revolutionary Committee was very confused, the Party's organizations were extremely negligent and the Party also did not perform its

functions. Both militarily and politically it was very juvenile and made abso-
lutely no preparations to seize political power. Thus, we were defeated and
dispersed, which certainly was pitiable.

As if these problems were not enough, the local peasant populations,
by all accounts, were passive or even hostile toward the new army.[98]

Having finally survived the march from Nanchang, the Chinese
Communists faced severe problems in the recruitment of soldiers
and officers in the early period. Now that its familiar urban base was
lost, the Communists had to recruit in the often uncongenial rural
areas. In 1927 and 1928, defection from the Kuomintang was the
greatest, single source of Red Army troops, and even by 1931 over
one-half of all Red Army soldiers were former Kuomintang soldiers.
Together with their military skills, they also brought with them all of
the negative features of the Kuomintang armies—opium smoking,
plundering and raping the local population, and even resorting at
times to open banditry.[99] Furthermore, most former Kuomintang
soldiers were more devoted to their commanders than to the Red
Army.

Two other significant sources of recruiting soldiers—bandits and
rural vagrants—also posed important problems for the fledgling
army. In December 1929, Mao declared that such elements déclassé
actually formed a majority among Red Army soldiers.[100] Often such
"bandit" soldiers were unreliable and returned to their past practices
soon after they joined the army. Another key source of recruitment
lay in the local peasant population. However, as Mao reported in
November 1928 to the Central Committee, "Few peasants in border
areas are willing to serve as soldiers. Since land has been divided up,
they have all gone to till."[101] Those peasants who were willing to serve
in the army were often both culturally and politically illiterate or
semiliterate. Thus, recruitment of soldiers was an extremely difficult
problem for the Red Army in the early years.

Officer recruitment posed similar challenges. There shortly emerged
a talented nucleus of Communist officers in the army, such as Chu
Teh, Liu Po-cheng, and Ho Lung. As in the early days of the Russian
Red Army, however, the bulk of the officers were former enemy
(here Kuomintang) officers with little affinity for communism. Often
of aristocratic and landlord origins, they were at best apolitical and at

times even hostile to the revolution. Needed for their skills, these officers were mainly interested in promotion and status. They brought a militarist caste to the army. Often they tried to maintain the loyalty of their men to themselves rather than to the Red Army. Yet, such men were indispensable in the early years.

The Red Army also faced difficulties with the same "partizansh-china" (partisanship) that plagued the Soviet army. Those partisan leaders who led their units in guerrilla actions proved difficult to integrate into a regular army. Furthermore, another problem common to both armies in the early days was the demand for ultraleftist democracy in the army. This spontaneous radicalism from below fought the imposition of the discipline and centralization necessary for the creation of an effective army.

Given all these difficulties in the creation of the capable and legitimate army, it was little wonder that the Chinese Communists faced problems of desertion and treason of at least as great a magnitude as the Russian Communists in the early days. As we have already seen, mass desertion plagued the Chinese army at its inception in the Nanchang Uprising. During the revolt, at least one-third of all troops had defected during the first month. The situation was hardly better with officers. When Chu Teh late in 1927 permitted officers and men to leave his small force without fear of reprisal, more than 300 officers and men left, including his chief of staff.[102] Mao fared little better. In the last few months of 1927 in the Chingkan Mountains, Mao's first two army commanders, Yu Sha-t'ou and Chang Hao, both defected to the Kuomintang.[103] Only the arrival of Chu Teh, an experienced officer, rescued the situation early in 1928.

The problems of desertion and treason were particularly acute in 1928, the first full year of the new army's existence. In the summer of 1928 the small Red Army suffered a setback when a battalion commander, Yuan Chung-chuan, deserted to the enemy along with two companies (which later were brought back).[104] During 1928 at least thirty-three leading army officers defected to the Kuomintang![105] This high turnover of officers had a deleterious effect on the functioning of the army. By November 1928, Mao could report to the Central Committee that only one-third of the troops of Ho Lung and Yeh T'ing, a Guards' Regiment, and units of peasant militiamen which had been in the Chingkan Mountains a year before remained in the

Red Army. And, ominously, he noted that a few troops deserted after each battle.[106]

As the fortunes of the Red Army improved, the rate of desertion and treason declined sharply, but the intensity of intraparty conflict soon led to bloody conflict within the army and dire accusations of treason leveled against top army and party leaders.

The Futien Mutiny marked a high point in bloody internal military conflict. In November 1930 the Red Army captured documents at Kian indicating that an anti-bolshevik corps of Kuomintang secret agents had penetrated even the top levels of the Red Army and the Communist party. Several key leaders were implicated. Based on these documents, Mao's General Front Committee in Kiangsi ordered the arrest of 4,400 Red Army officers and soldiers, the political commissar of the Twentieth Red Army, Hsieh Han-ch'ang, and all but two of the twenty-three members of the Southwest Kiangsi Provincial Action Committee. Mao charged that the committee leaders, who were supporters of the Maoist rival Li Li-san, were under the influence of the anti-bolshevik corps. In December 1930, a battalion political commissar, Liu Ti, led a mutiny which freed the imprisoned leaders in Fukien, arrested the chairman of the Kiangsi Soviet, and allegedly shot over 100 Maoist supporters in Futien. The freed rebel leaders now proceeded to call for Mao's overthrow and the establishment of a rival soviet. Looking for support from the Central Committee, the rebels accused Mao of seeking to become a "Party Emperor" and charged that his gradualism in agrarian reform represented a rightist deviation. The convergence of Kuomintang troops on Southeast Kiangsi at this time in the beginning of the First Encirclement Campaign forced an uneasy truce between the Maoists and the rebels.

The three major army commanders in the area, P'eng Teh-huai, Chu Teh, and Huang Kung-hueh, then proceeded to throw their unreserved support behind Mao. Praising his agrarian and military policies, they argued that Mao was a true Bolshevik. Not wishing to offend the Central Committee and now possessing considerable numerical superiority over the rebels, the Maoists waited for an opportune moment to strike. In January 1931, the Central Committee in Shanghai abolished both the Maoist General Front Committee and the Southeast Kiangsi Provincial Action Committee. Instead, it named a new Central Bureau for Soviet Areas with the three members from Kiangsi being Mao, Chu Teh, and a third Maoist, Tseng Shan. Assured now of party support, Mao moved quickly to expel all the rebels from the party. Using the tensions created by the unsuccessful First Encirclement Campaign, he turned public wrath against the accused traitors.

In the period from May to July 1931, the Red Army invaded and occupied the rebel areas. Over 4,000 rebels were captured. Mao chaired the Revolutionary Tribunal which officially charged the rebels with being members of the anti-bolshevik corps. Mass public trials were held and three of the five leaders were executed. By various estimates, as many as 2,000 to 3,000 rebel officers and men were liquidated in the affair.[107]

In September 1931, the Red Army discovered the alleged Huangpo plot in the Oyuwan Soviet which bordered on three provinces. The commander of the First Army, General Hsu Chi-shen, a Whampoa cadre, had previously deserted the party but had returned. Now he was accused of planning an uprising against the party. He was executed along with 170 members of the Political Department of the First Army. Two divisional commanders, one divisional commissar, eight regimental commanders, and 700 party members of the Oyuwan Soviet were purged.[108]

Treason continued to be a serious problem in 1932. Hou Chung-yung, commander of the 1st division, and Kuo P'ing-shang, commander of the 2nd division, led a revolt against the army. Kuo eventually surrendered to the Kuomintang along with his regimental commander.[109] Later that year Chi Chen-tung, commander of the Fifth Army, was accused of being an active counterrevolutionary and was imprisoned. In May 1932, the commander of the Fifteenth Army, Hsung Chung-yueh, and his chief of staff, Hsiao Hsi-chen, allegedly conspired against the leadership. In a proclamation issued that month, future Defense Minister Lin Piao (himself, ironically, later purged as a traitor in 1971) proclaimed that "For the defense of the revolution and the Red Army we must liquidate these counterrevolutionary elements from the Red Army."[110]

Gradually, the problems of treason and desertion diminished; they were still major concerns in times of acute crisis. In 1934, facing the final Fifth Encirclement Campaign, the Communists massively stepped up army recruitment. The new recruits, however, lacking military training or political indoctrination, all too often decamped.[111] During the Long March the large forces under Chang Kuo-t'ao ignored Maoist advice and set off on their own Long March. Indeed, the Long March truly solidified the officer corps and weeded out all dissidents. With the ouster of Chang Kuo-t'ao and the reduction in political significance of the members of the Returned Students' Clique in 1937 and 1938, the problems of desertion and treason sharply dropped in significance.

Desertion and treason in the 1927-36 period also reflected a critical problem in Chinese military development—the lack of a centralized, unified party leadership for much of the period. Mao himself did not formally ascend to the leadership of the party until the Tsunyi conference held during the Long March in January 1935. In the 1927-34 period leadership of the party had at least nominally been in the hands of Moscow-oriented Communists who generally favored urban proletarian revolution—Li Tao-chao and Ch'en Tu-hsiu (1927), Li Li-san (1928-30), and Wang Ming and the Returned Student Clique (1931-34). Mao and his comrades were frequently at variance with the official leadership. Indeed, there is a general belief that in the aftermath of the failure of the Autumn Harvest Uprising in the fall of 1927 Mao himself was purged from the Central Committee.[112] Although his general influence increased again in the next few years, in the 1932-34 period he seemed to play almost no role in the army. Indeed, in 1932 Chou En-lai displaced Mao as the chief political commissar of the army. Only with the Long March did Mao finally rise to the preeminent position which he retained for the rest of his life. Furthermore, as we have seen, rival leaders, such as Chang Kuo-t'ao, commanded their own independent armies until the end of this period. These problems of political leadership hampered the smooth development of the Chinese Red Army.

However, despite these problems, the Chinese Communists began to create a new type of army in the first decade of its existence. They stressed egalitarian pay and a breakdown of traditionally elite status for officers. The officers and men received the same food and clothing. Soldiers were given some freedom of speech and a role in rooting out corruption which had been endemic in all Chinese armies. All battles were discussed before and afterwards at general meetings of the soldiers. The army performed a major educational function in teaching literacy to the frequently illiterate peasants. The commissars taught classes and gave political instruction to the officers and men. Through the Communist Youth and Communist party organizations, the party sought to strengthen its hold over the army.

The army also participated extensively in various functions outside the barracks. For both political and economic reasons, the army helped in the destruction of land deeds and in the sowing, plowing, and reaping of crops. It played a powerful role in agrarian reform. The army helped investigate class stratification in the villages, organized local peasants' associations, and helped redistribute the land. Through the formation of village party branches and the spreading of party propaganda in the countryside, the army significantly aided the development of a strong rural base. These roles also aided the army in improving the political consciousness of the soldiers in its ranks and its relations with the local population which could aid it in times of crises.

In short, the initial 1927-36 period had profound consequences for the development of the Chinese army. Although the army had lost upwards of 90 percent of its strength in the Long March and numbered only 40,000 to 50,000 men in 1937, it had laid a strong base for future growth. A system of political commissars and political control had been institutionalized. Effective Communist control now existed over the army. A talented and dedicated Communist officer corps, strengthened by innumerable battles, had been created. The political leadership was now unified under the general direction of Mao. Dissident and incompetent officers had been weeded out in the hardships of the first decade. The basic problems of treason and desertion had been brought under control.

The 1937-45 period of the Anti-Japanese War marked a consolidation of all of these trends and witnessed the perfection of the structure and functioning of the army. By the end of 1945, the Chinese Red Army had completed a nineteen-year gestation period resulting in a legitimate and highly effective army. This new army in only three short years would sweep the highly trained and well-equipped multi-million man force of Chiang Kai-shek from the mainland. From a force of only 40,000 men in 1937, the army grew to 1 million men by

1945. While the party ruled only five small base areas with perhaps 2 million people in 1937, by 1945 it would rule 19 large base areas with 100 million people.

By 1937 the Red Army had created a capable, elite officer corps virtually fused with the party elite; but it needed to train a new, much larger officer corps which could cope with future, much grander tasks. The army, after its own unfortunate experiences with former Kuomintang officers, wished to avoid mass dependency on such unreliable officers. It wanted to hold down the number of its *voenspets* to a minimum. The creation of the Red Army Academy at Juichin in 1933 and its reemergence at Yenan in 1937 was an integral element in the formation of such an officer corps. During this 1937-45 period the academy trained over 100,000 officers and political workers, many of whom played an important role in the army. The creation of a large, competent, and Communist officer corps was to be a major factor in future Communist successes.

Furthermore, the party succeeded in creating a large party stratum within the army in this period. Leadership at the primary unit level is critical to success in battle. The ability of the army to place a Communist or several Communists in charge of each small basic unit greatly enhanced the fighting capability of the army. These Communists could lead by example, direct the elaborate system of psychological control, explain the war, and deflect any criticism of the party. Chalmers Johnson, in his excellent study, *Peasant Nationalism and Communist Power*, has shown the powerful appeal of nationalism which the war against Japan afforded the Chinese Communists.[113] The twin appeals of agrarian reform and nationalism were extremely effective in recruiting such diverse elements as peasants and middle-class students into the party. The party expanded from perhaps 40,000 members in 1937 to over 1 million members by 1945. In other words, at least 20 percent to 25 percent of all soldiers belonged to the party by the end of the gestation period. This figure contrasted sharply with the Russian Red Army where no more than 4 percent of all soldiers and officers were Communists during the civil war.

An effective, partly decentralized command system emerged in this period. The regional field army system, which Whitson has ably described in his work, began to function in the 1937-45 period, giving the army maximum flexibility and providing it with extensive knowledge of local terrain and people.[114] Only an elite Communist officer corps closely tied to the party enabled the party to overcome the obvious latent danger of warlordism. The Hundred Regiments Campaign in 1941 demonstrated the enhanced military capability of the army. However, the severe Japanese response to this campaign and the blockade against the Communists by both the Japanese and the Kuomintang forced the Communists on the defensive for the remainder of the war. By this period, however, the army had successfully institutionalized its basic patterns of behavior.

Finally, we should look briefly at the role of the army in party affairs. In the Soviet case we have seen that a non-Communist and relatively ineffective officer corps, dominated by upper-class voenspets and non-party commanders, played only a minor role in political decision-making. By contrast, in China the very nature of protracted rural insurrection led to such an interpenetration of army and party that one could speak of an army/party fusion. The Seventh Party Congress held in 1945 demonstrated the powerful role of the military in party affairs. Indeed, many of the key events in party history, such as the Long March, were primarily military in nature.

The Chinese army in a sharply different context thus faced many of the same problems in creating an effective and legitimate army as did the Soviet army. The problems of institutionalization of approved behavioral patterns, of party control over an army possessing the instruments of violence, were considerable in both armies in the early years of existence. Major problems of desertion and treason plagued both armies. The imposition of effective centralized control over masses of partisans and over a peasant-dominated army was a common problem. The overall level of military technology was relatively primitive in both armies by the standards that existed at the end of World War I. The role of a dedicated but thin party stratum was critical. Neither the Russian army nor the Chinese army received any significant external military assistance, either in the form of equipment or advisors.

Furthermore, as we have seen, the Chinese faced significantly greater obstacles than the Russians. The Russian Red Army, representing the central government in Moscow, could mobilize 48,400 *voenspets* and 215,000 ex-czarist noncommissioned officers into the army. It could conscript millions of peasants, rely on central lines of supply and communication, and use large stocks of czarist war supplies. The Chinese had none of these advantages and had to scrounge for captured weapons and recruits.

Yet, the state of the Chinese army was far superior to that of the Russian army at the end of their respective civil wars. Only the existence of the protracted gestation period and the agrarian nature of the Chinese revolution can account for these differences, for it was these factors which gave potency to the Chinese Army.

These differences had major implications for army/party and army/society relations in the two decades after the end of the civil wars. By that time, the 5 million man armies, possessing the major instruments of violence and functioning as the only major integrated organization besides the party and government, posed both a threat and an opportunity to the Communist parties. Given the great tasks of reconstruction and socialist development which faced the parties in both underdeveloped countries at the end of the civil wars, a strong effective army with revolutionary legitimation, such as the People's Liberation Army, could be a major asset. By contrast, a large, weak, and ineffectual army, such as the Red Army, which was incapable of suppressing even minor revolts without posing a threat to the regime, would primarily represent a potential threat to the party. Only through massive demobilization and extensive renewal could this threatening, hostile, and alien institution become an effective, positive force. During the interim period, which would be elongated by economic weakness and the press of other, more urgent needs of economic reconstruction, the army could hardly play a major role in society or within the party. Such weakness further eroded the claims of the army for a key role within the party, as the party, through the use of coercive power, sought to mainly control the army.

Thus, the great weakness and ineffectualness of the Red Army severely limited the future role of the Soviet army in party and societal affairs as much as the considerable strength of the People's Liberation Army greatly enhanced its future role in party and societal affairs.

NOTES

1. S. Olikov, *Dezertir'stvo v krasnoi armii i bor'ba s nim* (Moscow: Voennoi Tipografii Upravleniya, 1926), pp. 13, 32.

2. David Footman, *Civil War in Russia* (New York: Praeger, 1962), p. 141.

3. N. Kakurin, *Kak srazhalas' revolyutsiya* (Moscow: Gosizdet, 1926), (1919-1920), v. 2, p. 208.

4. Olikov, *Dezertirstro* pp. 30-31. The vast bulk of the deserters were not politically motivated. In eight months in 1919 the army labeled 779,800 deserters as "weak willed" while only 116,200 deserters were labeled as "malicious deserters" and 30,500 were put on trial (p. 33).

5. *The Trotsky Papers*, ed. and trans. Jan Meyer, 2 vols. (the Hague: Mouton, 1964, 1971), v. 1, p. 797.

6. A. S. Bubnov et al., *Grazhdanskaya voina 1918-1921* (Moscow: Gosizdet, 1930), v. 2, p. 83.

7. Olikov, *Dezertirstro*, pp. 34-35.

8. Desyatyi s'ezd RKP (b), Mart 1921 goda, *Stenograficheskii otchet* (Moscow: Partizdat, 1933), p. 303.

9. Bubov et al., *Grazhdenskaya*, v. 2, p. 98.

10. Derk Bodde has cited a Chinese account that claimed that in some units of Lin Piao's army, which marched all the way from Mukden and Harbin to near Peking, there existed not a single deserter. See Derk Bodde, *Peking Diary—A Year of Revolution* (New York: Schuman, 1950), p. 103.

11. The official PLA statistics for the civil war, which are not broken down for the July 1948 to July 1949 period, show 11,100 POWs for the war excluding that one-year period. If we prorate the captured/casualty rate for the other years of the war, we reach the overall figure of 17,700 POWs cited on p. 51. We followed a similar procedure for men missing in action. See *Tret'ya grazhdanskaya revoliutsionnaya voina v kitai*, pp. 105, 113, 118.

12. William Bradbury, et al., *Mass Behavior in Battle and Captivity—The Communist Soldier in the Korean War* (Chicago: University of Chicago Press, 1968), p. vii. Furthermore, many of those taken prisoner were not deserters but soldiers encircled by superior enemy forces.

13. Each group possessed loyalties at times greater than those it owed to the Red Army. The primary loyalty of the atamans was to their region and local power while that of the radicals was to their leftist political views. The *voenspets*, with the majority of their fellow officers in the White armies, owed primary allegiance to their class and conservative political views. All were temporary allies on whom the Bolsheviks, lacking any reliable experienced Communist stratum in the officer corps, were forced to rely during the civil war.

14. V.I. Lenin, *Collected Works* (Moscow: Politizdat, 1969), v. 30, p. 430.

15. In the summer of 1919, 65 percent of all czarist generals, lieutenant colonels, and colonels were serving the White armies, mainly that of Denikin. See A.M. Spirin, *Klassy i partii v grazhdanskoi voine v Rossii (1917-1920)* (Moscow: Mysl, 1968), p. 290.

16. S.A. Fedyukin, *Sovetskaya vlast' i burzhuuznye spetsialisty* (Moscow: Mysl', 1965), p. 72.

17. *Arkhiv russkoi revolyutsii* (Berlin: 1922), v. VII, p. 251.

18. *Ocherkii istorii Krasnodarskoi organizatsii KPSS* (Krasnodar: Krasnodarskoe Knizhdat, 1966), pp. 218-220.

19. *Istoriya grazhdanskoi voiny v SSSR* (Moscow: Gosizdat, 1957), v. 3, p. 228.

20. P.G. Sofinov, *Ocherki istorii vserossiiskoi chrezvychainoi komissi (1917-1920)* (Moscow: Gosizdat, 1960), p. 78.

21. Ibid., pp. 67, 82, 94.

22. *Arkhiv russkoi revolyutsii*, v. III, p. 19.

23. *Grazhdanskaya voina na Dal'nem Vostoke (1918-1922)* (Moscow: Nauka, 1973), p. 104.

24. Leon Trotsky, *My Life*, (New York: Charles Scribner's Sons, 1930), p. 399.

25. *Ocherkii istorii Krasnodarskoi organizatsii KPSS*, p. 231; *Istoriya grazhdanskoi voiny v SSSR*, v. 3, p. 259.

26. J.V. Stalin, *Works* (Moscow: Gosizdat, 1951), v. 4, p. 208.

27. *Istoriya grazhdanskoi voiny v SSSR*, v. 4, p. 170.

28. *The Trotsky Papers*, v. I, pp. 542-543.

29. *Ocherki istorii Pskovskoi organizatsii KPSS* (Leningrad: Lenizdat, 1971), p. 126.

30. *Pravda*, July 12, 1919; S.F. Naida and A.P. Aleksashenko, *Kommunisticheskaya partiya v period inostrannoi voennoi interventsii i grazhdanskoi voiny* (Moscow: Gosizdat, 1959), v. 2, p. 24.

31. Sofinov, *Ocherki istorii*, p. 182; *Iz istorii vserossiskoi chrezvychanoi komissii 1917-1921 gg: sbornik dokumentov* (Moscow: Gosizdat, 1958), p. 335.

32. Lenin, *Polnoe sobraniye sochineniya*, v. 30, p. 395.

33. *Istoriya grazhdanskoi voiny v SSSR*, v. 4, pp. 176-178.

34. The Mironov saga did not end here. Joining the party in 1920, he was awarded the Order of the Red Banner for his role as commander of the Second Cavalry Army in the campaign against Wrangel in the fall of 1920. In 1920 he was arrested by the Cheka and shot. Several years after his death he was rehabilitated. See *Istoriya grazhdanskoi voiny v SSSR*, v. 4, pp. 218, 225.

35. Lenin, *Collected Works*, v. 29, p. 80.

36. Spirin, *Klassy i partii v grazhdanskoi voine v Rossii (1917-1920)*, p. 207; and Sofinov, *Ocherki istorii*, p. 66.

37. *Inostrannaya voennaya interventsiya i grazhdanskaya voina v Srednei Azii i Kazakhstane* (Alma Ata: Nauka, 1964), v. 1, p. 106; *Istoriya grazhdanskoi voiny v SSSR*, v. 3, p. 360.

38. For three accounts of the Makhno movement and its final suppression, by a Makhno follower, a Soviet author, and a Western leftist respectively, see P. Arshinov, *Istoriya Makhnovskogo dvizheniya (1918-1921)* (Berlin: Group of Russian Anarchists in Germany, 1923), pp. 167-203; V.V. Rudnev, *Makhnovshchina* (Kharkov: Knigospilka, 1928); Max Nomad, "The Epic of Nestor Makhno," *Modern Monthly* 9, no. 8 (March 1936): 490.

39. Ilya Trifonov, *Klassy i klassovaya bor'ba v SSSR v nachale NEPa* (Leningrad: Leningrad University Press, 1964), p. 260. Also, see Oliver Radkey, *The Unknown Civil War in South Russia* (Stanford: Hoover Institution, 1976), p. 405.

40. Radkey, *The Unknown Civil War*, p. 392.

41. Trifonov, *Klassy i klassovaya*, pp. 273-275; *The Trotsky Papers*, v. II, p. 404.

42. Lenin, *Polnoe sobraniye sochineniya*, v. 43, p. 82.

43. Vatsetis was soon exonerated of the charges but was eventually replaced by another *voenspet*, Kamenev. See *The Trotsky Papers*, v. 1, p. 595.

44. Lionel Chassin, *The Communist Conquest of China*, trans. Timothy Osato and Louis Gelas (Cambridge: Harvard University Press, 1965), p. 122.

45. According to official PLA statistics, more Kuomintang generals (105) defected to the PLA than were killed in battle (67) during the civil war. Ibid., p. 208.

46. Treason, defined in the broadest sense as actions taken against the Maoist faction in a military manner (and therefore often little more than vicious factional rivalry at times) was quite common in the early 1927-37 period. In the summer of 1928, the small, fledgling Red Army suffered a setback when a battalion commander, Yuan Chung-chuan, defected to the enemy with two companies (which were later brought back). See Mao Tse-tung, *Selected Works* 4 vols. (Peking: Foreign Languages Press, 1967), v. 1, p. 98. In December 1930, in the Futien Mutiny, the Twentieth Red Army, in open revolt, arrested the chairman of the Kiangsi Soviet and many officials and officers, including the army commander. Labeling the rebels the "antibolshevik group," Mao and Chu Teh used loyal forces to crush the revolt. Some 2,000 to 3,000 officers and men were liquidated in the suppression of the revolt. See Donald Klein and Anne Clark, *Biographic Dictionary of*

Chinese Communism, 1921-1965 (Cambridge: Harvard University Press, 1971), v. 1, p. 729; Jacques Guillermaz. *A History of the Chinese Communist Party, 1921-1949* (New York: Random House, 1972), pp. 186, 216-217. In September 1931, the army discovered the alleged Huangpo plot and executed the commander, Hsu Chi-sen, and 170 members of the Political Department of the First Army. Two divisional commanders, one divisional commissar, eight regimental commanders, and 700 party members of the Oyuwan Soviet were purged. See Jerome Ch'en, *Mao and the Chinese Revolution* (New York: Oxford University Press, 1967), p. 164; Guillermax, *A History of the Chinese Communist Party*, pp. 217-218. Two months later two key Communist commanders, Kuo Ping-sheng and Lung P'u-lin, defected to the Kuomintang. See Ch'en, *Mao*, p. 174. In 1932 the commander and chief of staff of the Fifteenth Army, Hsung Chung-yueh and Hsaio Hsi-chen, allegedly conspired against the leadership. In a proclamation issued in May 1932, future Defense Minister Lin Piao proclaimed that "For the defense of the revolution and the Red Army we must liquidate these counterrevolutionary elements from the Red Army." See Thomas Robinson, *A Politico-Military Biography of Lin Piao* (Santa Monica, Calif.: Rand Corporation, 1971), v. 1, pp. 79-80. By 1938, the defection of Chang Kuo-t'ao, a major rival of Mao, accelerated the process of unification of the army. Furthermore, the Long March had weeded out all but the most dedicated men. At Tsunyi in 1935, Mao had formally ascended to the leadership of the party.

47. Both armies numbered roughly 3 million men in this period.

48. William Chamberlin, *The Russian Revolution 1917-1921* (New York: Grosset & Dunlap, 1963), v. 2, p. 402.

49. *KPSS i stroitel'stvo vooruzhennykh sily SSSR (1918-June 1941)* (Moscow: Voenizdat, 1959), p. 141.

50. *Direktivi glavnogo kommandovaniya krasnoi armii (1919-1920)* (Moscow: Voenizdat, 1969), pp. 326-327.

51. M.N. Tukhachevsky, *Izbranny proizvedeniya*, v. 1 *(1919-1927)* (Moscow: Voenizdat, 1964), pp. 151, 155. Of course, he may have somewhat exaggerated the numerical weakness of the Red Army in order to exonerate his role in the defeat.

52. A.S. Bubnov, *O krasnoi armii* (Moscow: Voenizdat, 1958), p. 244; United States Department of State, *United States Relations With China* (Washington, D.C.: Government Printing Office, 1949), p. 322.

53. Lenin, *Polnoe sobraniye sochineniya*, v. 33, p. 63.

54. Potyaev estimated Yudenich's forces at 15,000 men, Kakurin and the official Soviet history of the civil war have estimated his forces at 18,500 men, while Trotsky estimated them at 25,000 men. See *The Trotsky Papers*, v. 1,

p. 793; Kakurin, *Kak srazhalas' revoliutsiya*, v. 2, p. 330; *Istoriya grazhdans-koi voiny v SSSR*, v. 4, p. 329; Trotsky, *Moya zhizn'*, p. 424.

55. Lenin, *Collected Works*, v. 30, p. 68.

56. *Istoriya grazhdanksoi voiny v SSSR*, v. 4, pp. 336, 339.

57. Indeed, the "party week" in the entire Red Army brought some 60,000 new members into the party in October 1919. See V.S. Vladimirtsev, *Partiya—organizator razgroma kontrrevolyutsii na yuge* (Moscow, Voenizdat, 1971), p. 143.

58. While Denikin's forces outnumbered those of the Red Army at the beginning of the campaign (see Table 3), by July 1919 the Red Army outnumbered Denikin's armies (171,600 to 151,500). See Kakurin, *Kak srazhalas' revolyutsiya*, v. 2, p. 249.

59. Footman, *Civil War in Russia*, pp. 247-275. Denikin reached Orel, within 250 miles of Moscow, before being finally repulsed.

60. Winston Churchill, *The World Crisis* (New York: Scribners, 1929), v. 5, p. 260. Given the generally small size of Red Army forces, Denikin is undoubtedly exaggerating the number of POWs. However, their numbers were probably considerable.

61. A.A. Grechko, *Vooruzhennye sily sovetkogo gosudarstvo* (Moscow: Voenizdat, 1974), p. 27.

62. These officers included future War Commissar Frunze, Kork, Sollogub, Sergeyez, Kamenev, and Kakurin. See *Istoriya grazhdanskoi voiny v SSSR*, v. 5, p. 96.

63. Major General Fuller has described the "barefooted and tattered" Polish army as "improvised, chaotically equipped." See J.F.C. Fuller, *A Military History of the Western World* (New York: Funk and Wagnalls, 1956), v. 3, pp. 341, 349.

64. Georg von Rauch, *A History of Soviet Russia*, trans. Peter and Annette Jacobsohn (New York: Praeger, 1967); Tukhachevsky, *Izbrannye proizvedeniya*, v. 1 (1917-1927), pp. 151, 155.

65. Fuller, *A Military History*, v. 3, pp. 24, 360.

66. Paul Avrich, *Kronstadt 1921*(Princeton: Princeton University Press, 1970), p. 46.

67. Arshinov, *Istoriya Makhnovskogo*, pp. 189-197. Nomad has asserted that in the eight months of the campaign against Makhno, his forces rarely exceeded 3,000 men. See Max Nomad, "The Epic of Nestor Makhno III: The Last Fight," *Modern Monthly* 9, no. 8 (March 1936): 490. Indeed, when Makhno was initially attacked in November 1920, his immediate forces numbered only 150 to 200 cavalrymen. See Arshinov, p. 189.

68. Trifonov, *Klassy i klassovaya*, p. 241.

69. Ibid., pp. 5, 111, 113, 223.

70. Ibid., p. 168.

71. Avrich, *Kronstadt 1921*, p. 46

72. See *Istoriya grazhdanskoi voiny v SSSR*.

73. *The Trotsky Papers*, v. 2, p. 505. See also Radkey, *The Unknown Civil War in South Russia*.

74. Arshinov, *Istoriya Makhnovsbogo*, pp. 189-190. Some doubt could be cast on the accuracy of this work by a dedicated follower of Makhno. However, the details are generally plausible, given the great popularity of Makhno, his undoubted military skill, and his light treatment of prisoners (usually allowed to go home). Furthermore, the basic accuracy of the account is accepted by such Western authors as Footman. See Footman, *Civil War in Russia*, p. 292.

75. These measures were applied not only in the Tambov, Makhno, and Kronstadt revolts but also in a number of less well-known revolts. Regular army units were also unreliable in suppressing the Sapozhkov, Maslakov, Grigoriev, and Mironov revolts. In the Sapozhkov revolt, Lenin wrote in August 1920 to the Saratov guberniya *ispolkom* that "Sapozhkov has succeeded in attracting to his side some Red Army units and part of the kulak population." See *Leninskii sbornik* XXXIV, p. 241. Red Army men, including a detachment of *kursanti*, deserted to Maslakov when sent to destroy his revolt. See *The Trotsky Papers*, v. II, p. 404. It is little wonder that it took Budenny's First Cavalry Army to suppress the Mironov revolt and Makhno's shooting of Girgoriev to end his revolt. A combination of ChON units, Tatar regiments, and Communist battalions were needed to suppress Sapozhkov's revolt. See *Istoriya grazhdanskoi voiny v SSSR*, v. 4, pp. 177, 225; Trifonov, *Klassy i klassovaya*, p. 259.

76. K. V. Gusev and Kh.A. Eritsyan, *Ot soglashatel'stvo k kontrrevoliutsii* (Moscow: Musl, 1968), p. 394.

77. *The Trotsky Papers*, v. II, pp. 533-535, 543-551.

78. Footman, *Civil War in Russia*, p. 292.

79. Seth Singleton, "The Tambov Revolt," *Slavic Review* 25, no. 3 (September 1966): 510. It should be noted that Chekist "Red Terror" was matched by the "White Terror" on the other side.

80. Avrich, *Kronstadt, 1921*, pp. 193-203; Trifonov, *Klassy i klassovaya*, pp. 248, 250, 273.

81. Trifonov, *Klassy i klassovaya*, pp. 229, 243.

82. Ibid., p. 243.

83. Ibid., p. 149.

84. Chassin, *The Communist Conquest of China*, p. 258.

85. Trevor Dupuy, *The Military History of the Chinese Civil War* (New York: Franklin Watts, 1969), p. 100.

86. Chassin, *The Communist Conquest of China*, p. 258.

87. U.S. Department of State, *United States Relations With China*, p. 357.

88. Matthew Ridgway, *The Korean War* (Garden City, N.Y.: Doubleday, 1967), pp. 47, 73-74.

89. Allen Whiting, *China Crosses the Yalu* (New York: Macmillan, 1960), p. 122; John Gittings, *The Role of the Chinese Army* (London: Oxford University Press, 1967), p. 75.

90. Chassin, *The Communist Conquest of China*, p. 259.

91. Alexander George, *The Chinese Communist Army in Action* (New York: Columbia University Press, 1967), p. 3.

92. Whiting, *China Crosses the Yalu*, p. 164.

93. Gittings, *The Role of the Chinese Army*, p. 33.

94. Lenin, *Collected Works*, 4th ed. (Moscow: Gosizdat, 1941-65), v. 31, p. 441. In March 1920, decrying the "helpless" state of the army he similarly asserted of the Entente "And all they had to do was to employ a few hundred thousand soldiers of this army of millions in the war against us in the same way as they were employed in the war against Germany and the Entente would have crushed us. There cannot be the slightest doubt of this. . . ." Ibid., v. 30, pp. 383, 387.

95. Ibid., v. 33, p. 67. For an especially withering, if biased, view of the "feeble" nature of the Red Army, see Churchill, *The World Crisis*, v. 5 p. 241.

96. Peter Donovan, *The Red Army in Kiangsi, 1931-1934* (Ithaca, N.Y.: Cornell University East Asian Paper No. 10, 1976), p. 153.

97. C. Martin Wilbur, "The Influence of the Past: How the Early Years Helped to Shape the Future of the CCP," *China Quarterly*, no. 36 (October-December 1968); 23-31.

98. For the complete text of these two quotations, see C. Martin Wilbur, "The Ashes of Defeat," *China Quarterly*, no. 18 (April-June 1964): 3, 12, 34. See also Jacques Guillermaz, "The Nanchang Uprising," *China Quarterly* no. 11 (July-September 1963).

99. Donovan, *The Red Army*, pp. 32-35.

100. Stuart Schram, *The Political Thought of Mao Tse-tung* (New York: Praeger, 1963), p. 65.

101. Ibid., p. 195.

102. Agnes Smedley, *The Great Road* (New York: Monthly Review Press, 1956), p. 221.

103. John Rue, *Mao Tse-tung in Opposition, 1927-1935* (Stanford: Stanford University Press, 1966), p. 83.

104. Mao Tse-tung, *Selected Works*, v. 1, p. 98.

105. Donovan, *The Red Army*, p. 84.

106. Schram, *The Political Thought*, p. 195.

107. Ronald Suleski, "The Fu-t'ien Incident, December, 1930," in his *Early Communist China: Two Studies* (Ann Arbor: Michigan Papers in Chinese Studies no. 4, 1969). See also Klein and Clark, *Biographic Dictionary of Chinese Communism*, p. 729.

108. Guillermaz, *A History of the Chinese Communist Party 1921-1949*, p. 217.

109. Donovan, *The Red Army*, p. 85.

110. Robinson, *A Politico-Military History of Lin Piao*, v. 1.

111. Donovan, *The Red Army*, p. 133.

112. Rue, *Mao tse-tung*, p. 296.

113. Chalmers Johnson, *Peasant Nationalism and Communist Power* (Stanford: Stanford University Press, 1962).

114. William Whitson, *The Chinese High Command* (New York: Praeger, 1973).

chapter **3**

THE RUSSIAN AND CHINESE OFFICER CORPS

The officer corps is the essential "elite nucleus" that controls decision-making and provides leadership and continuity for the army. As Yuri Petrov has written:

The role of the command cadres in the construction of the army, in its fighting actions, is enormous. They are carriers of the class and military spirit of the army. The command staff serves as the skeleton of the army, its framework, unites separate parts into a unified organism.[1]

The low level of military technology of the two armies, which made the roles of the soldiers relatively simple and interchangeable, further enhanced the role of the officer corps.

RED ARMY OFFICER CORPS

The formation of the Red Army officer corps in the Russian civil war (1918-21) was "a big and extremely difficult task," for, in Marshal Tukhachevsky's words, there was "an almost complete absence in the first period of the existence of the Red Army of a politically mature and reliable command staff."[2] As War Commissar Voroshilov later recalled, "We were a strangely poor command group at the beginning of the building of the armed forces. The problem of commanders was the most difficult, the most painful, of all our work."[3] The problem was magnified by the fact that only 5 percent of the army in December 1918 belonged to the party.[4] Reliable proletarian and party elements could provide, in S.I. Gusev's words, "only a tiny number of experts in military matters."[5] Furthermore, during the first two years of the civil war, the Red Army, ultimately numbering more than 5 million men, prepared only 13,300 officers in inadequate command courses.[6]

As a consequence, the Red Army relied on a number of often antagonistic groups to fill out its officer corps during the civil war. At least seven groups, distinguished by military education, class origins, motivations, and political orientation, were represented in the Red Army officer corps during the civil war: senior *voenspets* (ex-czarist officers), junior *voenspets*, temporary junior officers, ex-NCOs, new revolutionaries, old revolutionaries, and partisans.[7]

Senior Voenspets

The senior *voenspets*, numbering at least 350 General Staff officers, more than 1,000 generals, and several thousand colonels from the czarist army, played a critical role in the civil war.[8] They held many top command posts and most key staff positions, including the post of commander in chief.[9] By the end of the civil war, senior *voenspets* Kamenev and Lebedev served as commander in chief and chief of staff of the Red Army; Kork, Petin, and Gittis commanded the Kharkov, Kiev, and Petrograd military districts; and Nemitts commanded the navy. Senior *voenspets* held the key instructional positions in military academies and schools. Their virtual monopoly of prior experience in senior command positions and their knowledge of military theory made them unique in the officer corps and invaluable in the civil war. At the same time, their lengthy service in the czarist army (generally more than twenty years), attendant close identification with czarism, frequent upper-class background, and strict adherence to traditional military philosophy isolated them from other groups within the officer corps. Their isolation from the party was demonstrated by an almost total lack of party membership.[10] Those serving in the Red Army frequently manifested their dislike for the revolution through desertion and treason.[11] Lenin himself declared that "Nine-tenths of the *voenspets* are capable of treason at any instant."[12] Extensive coercion, involving the use of commissars in the army and the sending of hostile officers and families of defecting officers to concentration camps, was often needed to make the senior *voenspets* contribute their skills to the Red Army.[13] While their numbers and influence declined sharply in the post-civil war period, the senior *voenspets* remained an important and visible element in staff and instructional positions throughout the 1920s. Such senior *voenspets* as Shaposhnikov even played a role in World War II.

Junior Voenspets

The junior *voenspets*, commissioned officers below the rank of colonel, formed the great bulk of the 48,400 ex-czarist officers in the Red Army during the civil war.[14] While far fewer junior than senior *voenspets* rose to important positions, the junior *voenspets* occupied a number of responsible positions. By 1921, junior *voenspets* Galler and Viktorov were serving as chief of staff and commander of the Baltic Fleet while Tukhachevsky had emerged as one of the leading army commanders. The junior *voenspets* were separated from the senior *voenspets* by their lower ranks, their much shorter service in the czarist army (typically four to ten years), their younger age, and often their more positive orientation toward the revolution. Some junior *voenspets*, such as Tukhachevsky, even joined the party. At the same time, their many years of training and service in the czarist army, often upper-class background, dedication to an army career, and marked preference of many of their compatriots for the Whites kept them from disappearing as an identifiable group within the army. So overwhelming was the preference of most *voenspets* for the Whites that there was one officer for every five to ten fighters in the armies of Kolchak, Denikin, and Wrangel compared to only one officer for every thirty to forty fighters in the Red Army during the civil war.[15] Although the overall influence of the junior *voenspets* declined as other groups obtained extensive training after 1921, a number of junior *voenspets*, especially party members, such as Kashirin, Levandovsky, and Tukhachevsky, played key roles in the 1921-37 period.

Temporary Junior Officers

The temporary junior officers, who attended abbreviated officer schools (less than one year in duration) created during World War I to replace the heavy war losses of the czarist army, formed 22 percent of the officer corps by 1921.[16] Possessing minimal theoretical military training and often limited experience, few temporary junior officers reached important positions during the civil war. They occupied a number of key secondary positions, however. Their relative youth (twenty-five to thirty-five years old), diverse class backgrounds, lack of identification with czarism, frequent sympathy with the revolution, and possession of some officer training and experience in an officer-starved army aided them in the civil war and augured well for the post-civil war era. Such temporary junior officers as Eideman, Fedko, Gaylit, Khripin, and Uborevich played important roles in the Red Army in the 1921-37 period.

Ex-noncommissioned Officers

The former czarist NCOs, who numbered 215,000 men in the Red Army, formed 13 percent of the officer corps by 1921.[17] Save for a few audacious cavalrymen, such as Budenny and Gorodovikov, who played key roles in the civil war, the ex-NCOs occupied second-echelon command positions and almost no staff positions. Overwhelmingly of peasant origin, the ex-NCOs were seriously handicapped by their very low level of education and lack of theoretical military training.[18] While most were probably apolitical, an elite element among them joined the party. Given the promotion of large numbers of ex-NCOs to officer status, career motivations undoubtedly played an exceptionally important role. Their modest contribution to the army was largely attributable to their badly needed practical skills.[19] These skills, combined with humble origins and a lack of identification with czarism, aided their progress in the post-civil war period. A number of ex-NCOs, such as Blyukher, Budenny, Bogdanov, Malinovsky, Rokossovsky, Timoshenko, and Zhukov, later became Red Army marshals in the 1930s and during World War II.

New revolutionaries

The new revolutionary commanders, primarily consisting of the 53,200 men who graduated from the short two-to-eight month command courses and the 25,000 men who were advanced from the ranks with minimal preparation at the front during the civil war, occupied largely secondary positions. A few new revolutionary commanders, such as Yakir, Khalepsky, and Zhloba, commanded important armies and divisions in the civil war. Most were severely limited by their lack of military education, minimal practical military training, and low level of education.[20] Yakir could later write: "I was never a military man and understood nothing previously in military matters. I began my military 'career' when I organized twenty to thirty brave men and pursued the Rumanians by truck."[21] Their extreme youth (96 percent of the graduates of command courses were less than twenty-five years old), revolutionary enthusiasm and courage, general party membership, and heavily proletarian and peasant origins distinguished them from other officers and favored their advancement after the civil war.[22] Many new revolutionaries gained the necessary military training in the 1920s. In 1921, the new revolutionary commanders, in Efimov's words, occupied a "very insignificant role" in the officer corps.[23] In the interwar period, however, such men as Yakir, Khalepsky, and Sedyakin played an important role. During World War II, a number of new revolutionary commanders, such as Chuikov, Grechko, Meretskov, Voronov, and Zakharov, became Red Army marshals.

Old Revolutionaries

The old revolutionary commanders, consisting primarily of several thousand Old Bolsheviks active in the revolutionary movement for many years before 1917, formed a small but crucial group in the officer corps during the civil war. By its end, Trotsky and Sklyansky were people's commissar and deputy commissar of military and naval affairs, respectively, while Muralov commanded the Moscow Military District, Sergeyev commanded the air force, and Raskolnikov commanded the Baltic Fleet. While Frunze, Voroshilov, and

Antonov-Ovseenko commanded fronts, Dybenko commanded the navy. Many other old revolutionary commanders directed army corps, armies, divisions, and brigades. They lacked military training or experience before the civil war.[24] Their many years of service to the party, unquestioned loyalty to the revolution, and close friendship with the old revolutionaries who ran the party and government made them unique and indispensable. Indeed, during the October Revolution in Petrograd, Trotsky had organized the insurrection, Antonov-Ovseenko had directed the storming of the Winter Palace, and Dybenko had commanded the sailors. Their often high level of education, frequent bourgeois origins, and the tendency of many to leave the army at the end of the civil war further differentiated them from the new revolutionaries and ex-NCOs. In the post-civil war period, their influence diminished so sharply that by 1935 only two of twenty men awarded the ranks of marshal and army commander (Voroshilov and Dybenko) were old revolutionaries, but, in the civil war, they formed an important, even crucial, element.

Partisans

The partisans, distinguished by their localist orientation, persistence in guerrilla warfare, rejection of traditional military philosophy, independence from central authority, and personal allegiance of their followers, formed a stratum operating quite independently from the rest of the Red Army. Despite frequent denunciations of *partizanshchina* by Lenin and Trotsky, Soviet historians have credited the partisans with being a "great help" as "they seized enormous territories in the rear of White Guards and interventionists."[25] Particularly important in Siberia and the Ukraine, the partisans raised and led substantial army units. As Rakovsky declared at the Eighth Party Conference in December 1919, "We liberated the Ukraine with the help of partisans. We did not have a regular army ... the Ukraine from Kharkov to Odessa and to Volochisk was liberated by partisans—by elements part revolutionary, part semi-bandit, which lived by self-supply; which plundered."[26]

Often they demonstrated considerable military ability. Mainly of Ukrainian origin, many partisans served in the czarist army where some, such as Mironov and Kazansky, achieved high ranks.[27] Although often fervent radicals, few partisans ever joined the party. Their allegiance to the army and the party was nearly always in doubt. Many partisans, such as Makhno, Mironov, and Grigoriev, raised serious and troublesome revolts against the Bolsheviks.[28] Given their exceptionally high death rate and general lack of discipline or allegiance to army or party during the civil war, it was scarcely surprising that few partisans played any role in the army after the end of the civil war.[29]

Officer Corps in 1921

Tables 5 and 6 graphically summarize the extremely heterogeneous nature of the Red Army officer corps at the end of the civil war. Janowitz has observed that in order to function effectively an army needs a basic congruence of norms, attitudes, and beliefs among its members, especially its leading ones. This congruence is usually provided by a prolonged period of professional socialization and isolation from society, often accompanied by a similarity of background characteristics (class, urban/rural origins, education).[30] Formed hastily on the battlefield in the course of the civil war and lacking any prior gestation period, the Red Army officer corps was plagued by sharp internal differences between the various groups in class, education, culture, and political orientation. Most ex-NCOs and many temporary junior officers came from the wavering peasant stratums, and most ex-NCOs, partisans, and new revolutionary commanders were poorly educated, even illiterate or semiliterate. By contrast, most senior and junior *voenspets* were relatively cultured, well-educated men from bourgeois and even noble origins. While many old revolutionary commanders also came from relatively privileged backgrounds, they were dedicated revolutionaries, while most *voenspets* were hostile to the revolution.

The mere use of *voenspets*, given their close association with czarism and upper-class origins, provoked sharp conflict within the officer corps and army. At a March 1918 meeting in the Kremlin, the "overwhelming majority" of military workers opposed the use of *voenspets* in the army. At the Eighth Party Congress in March 1919,

Table 5 A Partial List of Red Army Officer Corps, 1921-22
(Compiled from the 130 officers in seven categories)

War Commissar - Trotsky (old revolutionary)
Deputy War Commissar - Sklyansky (old revolutionary)

Staff

Chief of staff - Lebedev (senior *voenspet*)
Deputy Chief of staff - Shaposhnikov (senior *voenspet*)
Chief, All-Russian Main Staff - Samoylo (senior *voenspet*)
Head, Operations Board, Red Army Staff - Kolenkovskii (senior *voenspet*)
Chief of staff, Red Air Force - Novitsky (senior *voenspet*)
Chief of staff, Black Sea Fleet - Kondrat'yev (junior *voenspet*)
Chief of staff, Baltic Fleet - Galler (junior *voenspet*)
Chief of staff, separate Caucasian Army - Pugachyov (junior *voenspet*)
Chief of staff, Ukrainian and Crimean Red Army - Sollogub (senior *voenspet*)
Inspector, Soviet Air Force - Khripin (temporary junior officer)

Instruction

Head of Red Army Military Academy - Tukhachevsky 1921 (junior *voenspet*)
- *Lebedev 1922 (senior voenspet)*
Assistant Head of the Red Army Military Academy - Afanasyev (senior *voenspet*)
Head, Air Force Training Establishment - Zinovy'ev (temporary junior officer)
Professors, Red Army Military Academy - Nemitts, Neznamov, Kostayev, Samoylo, Snesarev, Svechin, Sytin, and Vatsetis (all senior *voenspets*)

Commanders

Commander in chief - Kamenev (senior *voenspet*)
Assistant Commander in chief, Cavalry - Budenny (ex-NCO)
Assistant Commander in chief, Siberia - Afanesyev (senior *voenspet*)
- Petrin (senior *voenspet*)
- Shorin (senior *voenspet*)
Navy - Nemitts (senior *voenspet*)
Air Force - Sergeyev 1921 (old revolutionary)
- Znamenski 1921+ (old revolutionary)

Commanders of military districts

Moscow - Muralov (old revolutionary)
Petrograd - Yegorov (senior *voenspet*)
North Caucasus - Voroshilov (old revolutionary)
Volga - Yefremov (new revolutionary)
Kiev - Petin 1921 (senior *voenspet*)
    - Yakir 1921+ (new revolutionary)
Kharkov - Kork (senior *voenspet*)
Western - Tukhachevsky (junior *voenspet*)
Siberia - Petin 1922 (senior *voenspet*)
East Siberia - Uborevich (temporary junior officer)
Altay - Gaylit (temporary junior officer)
Amur and TransBaikal - Lapin (new revolutionary)
Petrograd Fortified District - Sedyakin (new revolutionary)
Kronstadt Fortrees - Kuibyshev (temporary junior officer)

Baltic Naval Forces - Viktorov (junior *voenspet*)
Ukrainian and Crimean Armed Forces - Frunze (old revolutionary)
                                    - Eideman (temporary junior officer)
                                    - Uborevich (temporary junior officer)
Assistant Commander, Ukrainian and Crimean Armed Forces - Kork
                                            (senior *voenspet*)
Commander in chief, Armed Forces of the Far Eastern Republic
                                    - Eykhe (senior *voenspet)*
                                    -Blyukher (ex-NCO)
                                    -Avksentyevsky (temporary
                                        junior officer)

the "Military Opposition" was sufficiently powerful that by a considerable majority (37 to 20) the military section of the Congress
opposed the use of *voenspets* in command posts. Only after intense
lobbying by Lenin and Trotsky was this proposal defeated (174 to 95)
on the floor of the Congress.[31] Resentment of the *voenspets* was
especially strong among the ex-NCOs and new revolutionary commanders who felt that the *voenspets* had usurped positions rightfully
belonging to them by virtue of their humble origins and revolutionary
right. In return, the *voenspets* often scathingly deprecated these
groups for their lack of theoretical military training and often minimal
prior military experience. As one new revolutionary commander
reported, "We are treated with contempt" by the *voenspets* as "our

Table 6
Table 6 Key Groups Within the Officer Corps of the Red Army, 1921 (Typical member of group)

	Senior Voenspets	Junior Voenspets	Ex-NCO	Temporary Junior	New Revolutionaries	Old Revolutionaries	Partisans
Social Background							
1. Age	40-50	30-40	25-35	25-35	20-30	30-40	30-50
2. Urban/rural origins	Urban	Urban	Rural	Either	Either	Urban	Rural
3. Class	Noble/middle	All	Peasant	Peasant/middle	Worker/peasant	Middle	Peasant
4. Education	Higher	Higher	Lower	Higher/lower	Lower?	Higher/lower	Higher/lower
Military Characteristics (before 1918)							
5. Military training	Extensive formal theoretical	Moderate formal theoretical	Brief formal practical	Brief formal practical	None	None	Some
6. Czarist army posts	Colonel/general	Jr. Comm. posts	NCO	Junior posts	None	None	Junior
7. Military experience	20 years	10 years	4 years	1-3 years	0	0	4 years
8. Military philosophy	Traditional	Traditional	Revolut.	Revolut.	Revolut.	Revolut.	Anarchist

Beliefs and Motivations

9. RCP(B) membership	None	Few-civil war	Some-civil war	All-civil war	All-civil war	All-1905	Some-civil war
10. Dominant status	Theoretical expert	Less theoretical expert	Practical expert/new red	Practical expert/new red	New red	Old red	Unallied radical
11. Loyalty	Very suspect	Suspect	A little suspect	Proven	Proven	Proven	Very suspect
12. Primary motivation	Coercive	Coercive utilitarian	Utilitarian	Normative/utilitarian	Normative	Normative	Normative

Future

13. Future posts after end of civil war	Wholly military	Wholly military	Wholly military	Wholly military	Wholly military	Mainly military	Most dead/some military
Outstanding example	Kamenev	Tukhachevsky	Budenny	Fadko	Yakir	Frunze	Nestor

regimental commander never speaks to us Red Commanders. He regards us in general as small fry."[32] Nor was conflict limited to the officer corps. For according to Korablev, "consider(ing) all former officers counterrevolutionary 'golddiggers'," the soldiers "reacted sharply negatively to the attraction of former officers to the Red Army."[33]

Even at the end of the civil war, the officer corps was isolated from the party and even hostile to it. While in 1920 only 10.5 percent of all commanders were Communists, as late as 1921 less than 20 percent of all officers were Communists.[34] Neither Commander in chief Kamenev, Chief of staff Lebedev nor almost any of the leading staff officers were Communists. The level of political consciousness among the officers was low. Marshal Tukhachevsky called the political training of officers at that time "a great and exceedingly difficult" task, while Yuri Petrov has asserted that "a serious defect of the command cadre was its weak political preparedness."[35]

Although the Bolsheviks openly declared war on the bourgeoisie, nobility, and kulaks, the officer corps in 1921 was dominated by men from precisely those alien and hostile elements.[36] While it is no accident that no data are available on the social origins of top commanders in 1921, such data are available for 1924. Despite recurrent purges, even in 1924 a phenomenal 67.8 percent of all generals and 52.5 percent of all top commanders came from the "other" social background which generally denoted those of aristocratic, bourgeois, and landlord origins; nearly 50 percent of all top naval commanders were of noble origins as well.[37] This situation was undoubtedly worse in 1921. Table 5 shows that the junior and especially the senior *voenspets* dominated most important staff and instructional posts and many key command posts, including the top positions of commander in chief and chief of staff. No less than 35 percent of army officers and 71 percent of naval officers in 1921 were *voenspets*.[38] As Trotsky declared, "The chief command posts were occupied by military experts of the old school."[39] Thus, the Red Army relied heavily on men at best passive and at worst hostile to the party, for as Fedyukin has said, "Many of the former officers, although they were not directly traitors, were very unstable in political relations to the masses. Having fallen capture to the Whites they, without any special remorse, went to fight against Red Army men."[40]

In 1921, the officer corps was so weak that Gusev proclaimed it "the weakest of any army."[41] Tukhachevsky called its unreliability an "extremely, extraordinary evil for the Red Army."[42] In 1921, official Soviet statistics acknowledged that 1,681 commanders had deserted the army, while a mere 133 commanders had been killed in battle.[43] Furthermore, a phenomenal 43 percent of all officers possessed no military training at all in 1921.[44] The training of many other officers was so minimal that War Commissar Frunze later estimated that in 1921 "almost three-fourths of all our command structure" lacked any real theoretical military training. Even worse, over 14,000 officers had previously fought for the Whites in the civil war.[45]

The replacement of the weak, unreliable officer corps by a strong, reliable one was hindered by a number of factors. Even under the best of circumstances, the training of first-rate officers is a prolonged process. The devastated state of Soviet society in 1921 precluded the devotion of more than minimal resources to the army and its officer corps. Low pay (Red army commanders in 1925 received only 30 percent of the pay of czarist army commanders in 1913) and terrible housing conditions hindered recruitment.[46] Far from moving to strengthen the army in the early 1920s, the party carried out a demobilization of 90 percent of all army personnel and relegated military appropriations to a very low place in the budget in order to promote economic reconstruction.[47] Many of the most reliable officers (especially the old revolutionary commanders), who might have formed the nucleus of a new officer corps, were transferred to more immediate nonmilitary tasks. Many army Communists were uninterested in becoming officers and preferred to be demobilized.[48] Furthermore, the men of proletarian and peasant origins, on whom the party would rely in constructing a new officer corps, had great difficulty in mastering modern military science. Even in 1928, the average student admitted to military school possessed only three to four years of education.[49] Throughout the 1920s, those qualified men who aspired to become officers were overwhelmingly of undesirable class (nonproletarian, nonpeasant) background.[50] Finally, the development of a new officer corps was hampered by the weak state of military technology and low level of Soviet development in the 1920s.

Under these circumstances, the *voenspets* played an important role throughout the 1920s. I.B. Berkhin has written that in 1923,

In the central *apparat* there were a lot of backward and conservative elements from a number of old [czarist] *voenspets*, alien to the spirit of the Red Army, who in all ways were opposed to a leadership of the red commanders. . . . [51]

No less than 35 percent of all military men in the central *apparat* in 1923 were of noble origins.[52] In February 1923 *voenspets* constituted 82 percent of the commanders of rifle regiments, 83 percent of the commanders of corps and divisions, and 54 percent of the commanders of military districts.[53] Even in 1926, *voenspets* commanded six of eight military districts. As late as 1928, the teaching staff of the military academies was "composed primarily of officers of the czarist army, very advanced in age and often conservative in mood."[54]

This situation, in the words of a Soviet source, "aroused great anxiety in the party . . . it is very important to ensure a firm and stable proletarian nucleus in the Red Army."[55] Yet, in 1921, the proletarian nucleus numbered but 12 percent of the officer corps.[56] Until a new officer corps could be constructed, in the prolonged interim period a weak, unreliable *voenspet*-dominated officer corps, isolated from the party, would have grave consequences for the role of the army in party and societal affairs. This weakness prevented the army from serving as a model for society or from performing societal activities. Lacking legitimacy or ties to the party, the officer corps had little influence in party affairs. Instead, the party was motivated to strengthen its hold over such an alien and potentially threatening army through the use of a number of coercive measures. The party created separate and powerful secret police units, reinforced the secret police network in the army, and periodically strengthened the power of commissars within the army. Only when the officer corps had been thoroughly reconstructed properly to perform its military function, would the role of the army in party and societal affairs be reexamined. By the early 1930s, however, the reconstructed officer corps still remained apart from the Stalinist faction which dominated the party and other institutions.

PEOPLE'S LIBERATION ARMY OFFICER CORPS

In contrast, during the decisive Chinese civil war (1946-49), the state of the People's Liberation Army officer corps was far superior.

In the first decade of its existence (1927-37), the Chinese Communist army had been racked by problems similar to those of the Soviet army in its early days. Desertion was frequent and widespread in the early years; treason, (from the Maoist perspective) represented a major and recurring problem. In both the Futien Mutiny in 1930 and the Huangpo plot in 1931, the Maoists in the army used force to suppress opposition. They executed a large number of dissidents and allegedly treasonous rivals.[57] In 1932, the disclosure of a plot by two leading army officers led future Defense Minister Lin Piao to proclaim, "For the defense of the revolution and the Red Army we must liquidate these counterrevolutionary elements from the Red Army."[58] The Long March weeded out all but the most dedicated and devoted men, while at Tsunyi in 1935 Mao ascended formally to the leadership of the party. By 1938, with the final defection of Chang Kuo-t'ao, a key Maoist rival, the Chinese army was well on its way to becoming a reliable and effective force.

By 1946, the PLA had forged a large, cohesive, homogeneous, experienced, and effective officer corps, especially at the elite level.[59] Unlike the Soviet army, the Chinese army had a prolonged gestation period (1927-45), the experience of almost innumerable campaigns, popular nationalist and agrarian reform appeals, and a large party stratum before the beginning of the civil war 1946. The lengthy gestation period enabled the Chinese army to fill its officer corps with graduates of its own military schools and to eliminate dissidents. In contrast to the severe paucity of party-trained officers in the Red Army, in China perhaps 100,000 cadres graduated from the party-run military academies at Juichin and Yenan in the 1933-46 period.[60] In addition, while the Soviet army exhibited a sharp diversity of class backgrounds, the PLA reflected the agrarian nature of the Chinese revolution and produced a relatively homogeneous officer corps in terms of a low level of education and overwhelmingly rural origins. While their technical qualifications were as unimpressive as those of the Soviet officers, the elite Chinese officers had at least received their training under revolutionary and quasi-revolutionary auspices.[61] The extensive political and military training and military experience of Chinese Communist troops before the beginning of the civil war in 1946 shaped an officer corps radically different from that of the Red Army in 1918.

In contrast to the changing composition and nature of the Soviet officer corps during the civil war, the Chinese officer corps demonstrated amazing continuity over a period of several decades.[62] Five of the ten marshals named in 1955—Ho Lung, Chu Teh, Yeh Chien-ying, Liu Po-ch'eng, and Hsu Hsiang-chen—planned and led the small forces of 20,000 to 30,000 men in the abortive Nanchang Uprising which founded the Chinese army in August 1927.[63] The nine leaders of the Eighth Route Army in 1937 were still the key officers during the decisive civil war (1946-49). Indeed, eight of the nine officers became marshals in 1955. This impressive continuity at the elite level substantially aided the creation of a smoothly functioning officer corps, especially given the highly decentralized nature of operations. The People's Liberation Army field armies were far more stable than the Soviet armies since they contained both an experienced core of officers and a geographic base in the ten to twenty years preceding 1946. In William Whitson's words, "Until the end of 1948 ... each field army fought independent campaigns in essentially the same area in which it had operated during the Sino-Japanese War."[64]

The bulk of the Chinese officer corps possessed extensive military experience by 1946. Having typically joined the Chinese army in its infancy in the late 1920s, an elite commander had often seen sixteen to nineteen years of arduous military service by 1946.[65] He had usually fought in such key campaigns as the five encirclement campaigns (1931-35), the Long March (1934-34), and the Hundred Regiments' Campaign (1940). Furthermore, a small but important group which included no less then five future marshals—Ho Lung, Liu Po-ch'eng, P'eng Teh-huai, Chu Teh, and Yeh Chien-ying—had seen seven to fifteen years of service in warlord and Kuomingtang armies before 1927. Such prolonged service in the PLA and prior military experience helped create effective officers with an esprit de corps.

The relation of the Chinese officer corps to the party differed markedly from that of the Soviet officer corps to its party during the civil war. While the vast majority of Soviet officers were not party members, nearly all Chinese officers were.[66] The same general situation prevailed at the elite level of the two officer corps. While eleven of twelve key Chinese officers (91.7 percent) belonged to the party's

Central Committee in 1950, only one of the twelve key Soviet officers (8.3 percent) belonged to its party's Central Committee in 1921. Furthermore, four of the twelve key Soviet officers—Commander in chief Kamenev, Chief of staff Lebedev, Navy Commander Nemitts, and future Marshal Shaposhnikov—did not even belong to the party in 1921. Also, six of the eight Soviet officers who belonged to the party had joined only recently, in the 1917-20 period. By contrast, all key Chinese officers were party members. Their median date for joining was 1927, or almost twenty years before the beginning of the civil war. Indeed, a significant stratum among key Chinese officers had even joined in the party's infancy (1922-24) when membership was very small.[67]

Similarly, there was a marked pattern of isolation of the Soviet officer corps from the party and a near fusion of a Chinese officer corps and the CCP. While 50.6 percent of the members of the Chinese Communist party Central Committee were military men in 1950, only 10 percent of the members of the Russian Communist party Central Committee consisted of army representatives in 1921.[68] Furthermore, while nearly all the Chinese military men were full-time career officers (and future marshals) holding key command positions in the army, all the Soviet military men (Trotsky, Frunze, Bubnov, and Voroshilov) were essentially party representatives in the army. Their primary loyalty was owed to the party, not the army. They were not career officers in any sense of the word.

In this context, it is scarcely surprising that Andrew Nathan considers it a well-known fact that "the Chinese Communist Party and its Army have formed throughout their history a single institutional system with a single elite performing simultaneously the functions of political and military leadership."[69] Associated with the most important revolutionary events, such as the Long March, the Chinese officers were both a key political force and a highly legitimated revolutionary element. Unlike the Soviet officer corps, the Chinese officer corps emerged from the civil war as a strong, relatively cohesive, legitimate and effective revolutionary group. Possessing a large and important party stratum, it stood ready and able to serve as a suitable partner for the party, with which it had been intertwined in the 1927-49 period, in important post-civil war tasks.

SOURCES OF DISPARITY IN ROLES OF CHINESE AND RUSSIAN MILITARY

The sharp differences in the roles of the Soviet and Chinese armies in the two decades after the end of their civil wars reflected at least in part differences in the nature of the two officer corps at the end of the civil wars. The lengthy gestation period of the Chinese army, the highly military nature of any protracted agrarian revolution, and the development of popular nationalist and agrarian reform appeals to the peasant masses helped create an army/party fusion. These factors produced a highly effective and revolutionary legitimated officer corps by the end of the civil war. The Chinese officer corps could draw on a large army party stratum (24 percent of the army) by the end of the civil war. The effectiveness of the officer corps was reflected in the outstanding performance of the PLA, which made a triumphant 6,000 mile march across the face of China in the last two years of the civil war. The effectiveness and legitimacy of the officer corps and army was particularly important in an underdeveloped country, such as China. Such countries generally lack large-scale, effective, and legitimate organizations. These traits enabled the army to play a key role in the policymaking process in the two decades after the end of the civil war. This was particularly true during difficult campaigns for the revolutionary transformation of society, such as the Cultural Revolution.

In contrast, the Red Army officer corps, lacking a gestation period, a large party stratum, and broad appeal to the peasant masses, was formed hastily on the battlefield during the civil war. It was composed of very heterogeneous and often antagonistic elements. Neither red nor expert, the Red Army officer corps, like the army in general, was exceptionally weak and ineffectual, even by the end of the civil war.[70] The Red Army was unable to suppress even small-scale revolts, such as Makhno and Tambov, without resorting to extensive reinforcement, Chekist coercion, and political concessions. In 1920 and 1921, the army was repeatedly racked by treasonous and serious revolts by such Red Army officers as Sapozhkov, Maslakov, and Makhno and by the heretofore exemplary Kronstadt sailors. The weak Red Army was routed in the disastrous Polish campaign of 1920.

The problems of the Red Army officer corps stemmed in large measure from the narrow base of the revolution and the method of coming to power, which precluded the creation of an experienced party-dominated officer corps before the beginning of the civil war. The key role of the *voenspets* in the civil war further eroded the legitimation of the officer corps. Neither highly legitimate nor especially effective, needing to be thoroughly reconstructed, the officer corps could scarcely play a key role in party affairs for many years after the end of the civil war. Given its partial control of the instruments of violence, it represented as much a threat as an asset to the party.

In short, greater attention should be paid to the remarkably formative influence of the civil war periods. The sharply different roles of the secret police in the Soviet Union and China, for example, can be traced in part to differences in the nature of the civil wars. As shown by the Great Purges in the late 1930s, the role of the secret police in the Soviet Union has been greater and more visible than in China. The presence of a legitimate and highly effective army in China, in combination with mass peasant support, precluded the rise of a rival secret police force or the extensive use of physical coercion. (Indeed, during most of the two decades after the end of the civil war, the secret police troops in China were directly subordinated to the army.) The lack of these two factors in the Soviet Union during the civil war forced the creation of secret police troops both to substitute for the army (as at Tambov) and to carry out extensive coercive activities within the army. These secret police troops also served as a counterweight to an unreliable and ineffective army. Because of the lack of mass support in Russia, the Cheka used physical coercion extensively during the civil war.

This analysis could be extended to other Communist countries. Eastern European Communist parties, generally lacking a mass base and armed forces, needed the help of the Soviet army to seize power. Given the smallness of the parties, the limited resources, and other more immediate priorities, the reconstruction of inherited unreliable and ineffective armies, generally dominated by non-party reactionary officers from the previous regime, was a lengthy and arduous process. In the interim, the parties relied on extensive secret police forces to carry out the domestic repression necessitated by the lack of mass support. Furthermore, the secret police troops, combined with the presence of Soviet troops in the countries and Soviet officers in the officer corps, counterbalanced the power of the armies and directed secret police networks within the armies.[71]

By contrast, in such Communist countries as Yugoslavia and Cuba, an army was created in a popular rural insurrection before the seizure of power. Although the new regimes did establish secret police forces, they were on a smaller scale than those of the Soviet Union. The effectiveness and legitimacy of the army and its officer corps gave the army a considerable amount of political influence, which allowed it to overshadow and submerge rival security forces.[72]

Comparative analysis of the civil war periods has been relatively ignored in the study of Communist countries, even though, as shown, these formative periods are important in their consequences. The differing natures of the Russian and Chinese civil wars affected the characteristics of their officer corps and considerably influenced the role of the army in their decision-making process for the following two decades. Careful study of the civil war periods may further clarify their influence upon the future development of institutions and the evolution of policies in Communist countries.

NOTES

1. Yuri Petrov, *KPSS-rukovoditel' i vospitatel' krasnoi armii (1918-1920)* (Moscow: Voenizdat, 1961), p. 18.

2. D. A. Voropaev and A. M. Iovlev, *Bor'ba KPSS za sozdanie voennykh kadrov* (Moscow: Voenizdat, 1960), p. 12; M. N. Tukhachevsky, *Izbrannye proizvedeniya*, v. 1, *1919-1927* (Moscow: Voenizdat, 1964), p. 93.

3. K. E. Voroshilov, *Stat'i i rechi* (Moscow: Partizdat, 1937), p. 575.

4. *Direktivi glavnogo kommandovaniya krasnoi armii (1917-1920): sbornik dokumentov* (Moscow: Voenizdat, 1969), p. 139.

5. S. I. Gusev, *Grazhdanskaya voina i krasnaya armiya* (Moscow: Voenizdat, 1958), p. 97.

6. A. S. Bubnov et al., eds., *Grazhdanskaya voina 1918-1921* (Moscow: Gosizdat, 1930), v. 2, pp. 94-96.

7. This sevenfold division of the officer corps is more comprehensive and detailed than the threefold division of Lerner, the fourfold division of Erickson, the fivefold division of White and the sixfold division of Trotsky. See respectively, Ithiel de Sola Pool et al., *Satellite Generals: A Study of Military Elites in the Soviet Sphere* (Stanford: Stanford University Press, 1955), pp. 3-4; John Erickson, *The Soviet High Command* (London: Macmillan, 1962), p. 80; D. Fedotoff White, *The Growth of the Red Army* (Princeton: Princeton University Press, 1944), p. 64; Lev Trotsky, *Kak vooruzhalas' revoliutsiya* (Moscow: Vyshii Voenni Redaktsionni Soviet, 1924), v. 3, P. 2, p. 227.

8. Peter Kurzhin, "Lenin and the Soviet Armed Forces," *Studies on the Soviet Union* 9, no. 1 (1970): 33.

9. Vatsetis and Kamenev served as the two commanders in chief during the civil war. On the eastern front, no less than four senior *voenspets* (Kamenev, Olderogge, Samoilo, and Vatsetis) served as front commanders while five senior *voenspets* (Bonch-Bruyevich, Kolenkovsky, Lebedev, Olderogge, and Sollogub) served as front chiefs of staff. Four senior *voenspets* (Gittis, Sytin, Yegorov, and Yegoryev) were commanders of the southern front during the civil war.

10. Only one (Yegorov) of the thirty-two senior *voenspets* in the group belonged to the party during the civil war. Even the senior *voenspet* Bonch-Bruyevich, brother of the leading Bolshevik, wrote, "Yet I never did join the Party and do not belong to it even now, while in those days before the October Revolution, the Party and its aims were actually quite alien to me." See M. Bonch-Bruyevich, *From Tsarist General to Red Army Commander* (Moscow: Progress Publishers, 1971), p. 125.

11. During 1918 alone, such senior *voenspets* as Vikorst, Bogoslavsky, Nosovich, and Makhin defected to the Whites. So too did the majority of *voenspets* in the air force. See Yu. Korablev, *V. I. Lenin i sozdanie krasnoi armii* (Moscow: Nauka, 1970), p. 325. The problem of treason by *voenspets* plagued the Red Army throughout the civil war. As Lenin declared in March 1920, "Thousands of former officers, generals and colonels of the Tsarist army betrayed us and sold us, and thousands of Red Army men perished as a result . . . ." See V. I. Lenin, *Collected Works*, (Moscow: Gosizdat, 1941-1965), v. 30. p. 403.

12. V. I. Lenin *Polnoe Sobranie sochinenii* (Moscow: Politizdat, 1967-1970), v. 43, p. 242.

13. Numerically, the 5,200 commissars in the army in December 1919 could hardly scrutinize all 48,000 *voenspets*. However commissars had the right to remove and even arrest commanders. As Sverdlov said, "If nevertheless under these eyes they try to do something, then we directly declare

to them that they will be immediately executed." See S. A. Fedyukin, *Sovetskaya vlast' i burzhuuznye spetsialisty* (Moscow: Mysl; 1965), pp. 55, 85.

14. Bubnov et al., *Grazhdanskaya voina 1918-1921*, v. 2, p. 91.

15. I. Gusev, *Grazhdanskaya voina i krasnaya armiya*, p. 79; A. S. Bubnov, *O krasnoi armii* (Moscow: Voenizdat, 1958), p. 224.

16. Trotsky, *Kak vooruzhalas' revoliutsiya*, v. 3, P. 2, p. 227. Over 250,000 such officer positions were created during World War I. See Fedyukin, *Sovetskaya vlast' i burzhuuznye spetsialisty*, p. 52.

17. Bubnov, et al., *Grazhdanskaya voina 1918-1921*, v. 2, p. 95; Trotsky, *Kak vooruzhalas' revoliutsiya*, v. 3, P. 2, p. 277.

18. The bulk of the ex-NCOs probably possessed no more than a primary education. Gorodovikov, for example, dropped out of school at the age of eight to become a shepherd. As ex-NCO Marshal Budenny later wrote with particular reference to ex-NCOs, "For us, commanders and political workers of the young Red Army, things were incomparably harder than for the former ex-czarist officers and generals. Very few of us had the necesary military education." See. S. M. Budenny, *Proidenny put'* (Moscow: Voenizdat, 1973), v. 3, p. 397.

19. Marshal Zhukov, an ex-NCO, has written, "The backbone of the old army were the NCOs who instructed and knit together the mass of soldiers. Candidates for NCO training were virtually handpicked and sent to special courses which as a rule gave exemplary training." See G. K. Zhukov, *Vospominaniya i razmyshleniya* (Moscow: Novosti, 1969), p. 36. During the civil war, 22,000 ex-NCOs were appointed platoon commanders. See Fedyukin, *Sovetskaya vlast' i burzhuuznnye spetsialisty*, p. 50.

20. Petrovsky has acknowledged that the graduates of the command courses were essentially well-trained privates with a good sense of duty. See D. A. Petrovsky, *Voennaya shkola v gody revoliutsii* (Moscow: Voenizdat, 1924), p. 58. These courses were brief, extremely inadequate, and conducted under "exceedingly difficult" conditions. The barracks often lacked fuel and as many as one-third of the *kursanti* (officer cadets) lacked shoes. See D. A. Voropaev and A. M. Iovlev, *Bor'ba KPSS za sozdanie voennykh kadrov* (Moscow: Voenizdat, 1960), p. 21. Furthermore, only 12.1 percent of the *kursanti* had completed middle school, and 62.7 percent had less than four years of education. See N. F. Kuz'min, *V. I. Lenin vo glave oborony sovetskoi strany 1918-1920* (Moscow: Voenizdat, 1958), p. 77. Only a smaller number of new revolutionaries, such as Yakir, were well educated.

21. N. D. Roitman and V. L. Tsetlin, *Polkvodets-kommunist* (Kishiniev: Kartya Moldovenyaske, 1967), p. 6.

22. During the civil war 54 percent to 70 percent of the graduates of the command courses joined or already belonged to the party. See Voropaev and Iovlev, *Bor'ba KPSS za sozdanie voennykh kadrov*, p. 21. Among the graduates of the command courses, 67 percent to 81 percent were allegedly of proletarian and peasant origins. See A. F. Danilevsky, *V. I. Lenin i voprosy voennogo stroitel'stva na VIII s'ezde RKP (B)* (Moscow: Voenizdat, 1964), p. 24.

23. Bubnov et al., *Grazhdanskaya voina 1918-1921*, v. 2, p. 104.

24. In Trotsky's words, applicable to most old revolutionary commanders, "Was I prepared to do military work? Of course not. I had not even had the benefit of service in the Tsarist army. My army-service years I had spent in prison, exile and abroad." See Leon Trotsky, *My Life* (New York: Scribners, 1930), p. 349.

25. Lenin stated in August 1919, "Fear like the plague the unruly guerrilla spirit, the arbitrary actions of isolated detachments and disobedience to the central authority for it spells doom as the Urals, Siberia and the Ukraine have demonstrated." See Lenin, *Collected Works*, v. 29, p. 512. See also *50 let vooruzhennykh sil SSSR* (Moscow: Voenizdat, 1968), p. 160.

26. Vos'maya konferentsiya RKP (B), Dekabr' 1919, *Protokoly* (Moscow: Gosizdat, 1961), p. 98.

27. This is particularly noteworthy in view of the small role played by Ukrainians in the regular Red Army. During the civil war, Russians formed a disproportionate 77 percent of Red Army soldiers and officers. See G. V. Kuz'min, *Grazhdanskaya voina i voennaya interventsiya v SSSR* (Moscow: Voenizdat, 1958), p. 349.

28. The charismatic quality of many partisans, the personal allegiance of their men, frequent local support, undeniable anti-White orientation, and the often considerable military talent of their leaders made partisan revolts very troublesome to the Red Army. For the Makhno revolt, see P. Arshinov, *Istoriya Makhnovskogo dvizheniya (1918-1921)* (Berlin: Group of Russian Anarchists in Germany, 1923) and V. V. Rudnev, *Makhnovshchina* (Kharkov: Knigospilka, 1928).

29. In one group of partisans, nine of the fifteen were dead by 1923 and one other (Makhno) was in exile. Only three partisans (Apanasenko, Kazansky, and Shchetinkin) pursued military careers in the 1920s.

30. Some heterogeneity in backgrounds, career patterns, and beliefs is to be expected in any officer corps. The creativity of men of unusual backgrounds (such as the Jews Yakir and Feldman in the Red Army and Rickover in the American navy) or of men with an adaptive career pattern (such as Dr. Leonard Wood in the American army) has often helped to prepare the

110   THE CIVIL WARS

armed forces for needed change. Furthermore, as Coser has shown, some conflict may even be functional for an organization. See Lewis Coser, *The Functions of Social Conflict* (Glencoe, Ill.: Free Press, 1956). Beyond a certain point, however, sharp differences in backgrounds and beliefs will harm the functioning of the officer corps.

31. Danilevsky, *V. I. Lenin i voprosy voennogo stroitel'stvo na VIII s'ezde RKP (B)*, pp. 28, 70; Yuri Petrov, *Partiinoe stroitel'stvo v sovetskoi armii i flote (1918-1961)* (Moscow: Voenizdat, 1964), pp. 71-74.

32. Petrovsky, *Voennaya shkola v gody revoliutsii*, p. 237.

33. Korablev, *V. I. Lenin i sozdanie krasnoi armii*, p. 257.

34. Petrov, *Partiinoe stroitel'stvo v sovetskoi armii i flote*, p. 179; Trotsky, *Kak vooruzhalas' revoliutsiya*, v. 3, P. 2, p. 277.

35. Tukhachevsky, *Izbrannye proizvedeniya*, v. 1, p. 93; Petrov, *Partiinoe stroitel'stvo v sovetskoi armii i flote*, p. 127.

36. As Lev Kritsman has written, "The entire social order of this epoch was penetrated with the spirit of ruthless class exclusiveness .... The bourgeois was transformed into a scorned and outcast existence—into a pariah. ... The stigma of belonging to the exploiting class could open only the road to concentration camp, to jail and, in the best case, to hovels which remained after the proletarians were resettled in the best homes." See Lev Kritsman, *Geroicheskii period velikoi russkoi revolyutsii* (Moscow: Gosizdat, 1925), p. 79.

37. Bubnov et al., *Grazhdanskaya voina 1918-1921*, v. 2, pp. 105, 109. A commission headed by Gusev found that a phenomenal 45 percent of the commanders in the 1923-1924 period were of undesirable social origins. See I. B. Berkhin, *Voennaya reforma v SSSR (1924-1925)* (Moscow: Voenizdat, 1958), p. 58; *Voenno-istoricheskii zhurnal*, no. 5 (1963): 16.

38. *KPSS i stroitel'stvo vooruzhennykh sily SSSR (1918-June 1941)* (Moscow: Voenizdat, 1959), p. 221; Voropaev and Iovlev, *Bob'ba KPSS za sozdanie voennykh kadrov*, p. 41.

39. Trotsky, *My Life*, p. 451.

40. Fedyukin, *Sovetskaya vlast' i burzhuuznye spetsialisti*, p. 43.

41. Gusev, *Grazhdanskaya voina i krasnaya armiya*, p. 121.

42. Tukhachevsky, *Izbrannye proizvedeniya* v. 15, p. 93. Indeed Denikin has estimated that 70 percent of the *voenspets* seized by the Whites fought well and only 10 percent tried to return to the Red Army. See C. A. Alekseev, *Denikin, Yudenich, Wrangel* (Moscow—Leningrad: Gosizdat, 1931), p. 69.

43. Bobnov et al., *Grazhdanskaya voina 1918-1921*, v. 2, p. 98.

44. M. V. Frunze, *Izbrannye proizvedeniya* (Moscow: Voenizdat, 1958), v. 2, p. 342.

45. Voroshilov, *Stat'i i rechi*, p. 445.

46. Frunze, *Izbrannye proizvedeniya*, v. 2, p. 268.

47. While czarist Russia spent 1.6 billion rubles in 1913, the Soviet Union spent .4 billion rubles in 1923 and .6 billion rubles in 1926 on defense. See Politicheskoe Upravlenie PKKA, *1918-1928 let krasnoi armii-albom diagram* (Moscow: Voenni Vestnik Izdate'stvo, 1928). By 1925 Poland was spending almost four times as much on defense per capita as the Soviet Union. See Frunze, *Izbrannye proizvedeniya* v. 2, p. 284.

48. Mashatov stated at the Tenth Party Congress in 1921, "The truth is that our [party] cadre is afraid to be commanders and many among them have great merit but they are afraid to have stripes on their arms." See Desyatyi s'ezd RKP (b), *Stenograficheskii otchet* (Moscow: Partizdat, 1933), p. 302.

49. As Voropaev and Iovlev have observed, "The low level of general education, weak knowledge of mathematics, physics, and chemistry created for the military cadres enormous difficulties in mastering complicated military technique." See their *Bor'ba KPSS za sozdanie voennkh kadrov*, pp. 80, 89, 129, 132. The situation was little better among army Communists, 80 percent of whom had a primary school education or less in 1921. See G. K. Ordzhokidze, *Stat' i rechi* (Moscow: Politizdat, 1956), v. 1, p. 239.

50. While in the 1922-26 period a tiny 1.7 percent of the graduates of the naval academy were of proletarian origin, by 1929 76 percent of the graduates of the Military Technical Academy were of nonproletarian, nonpeasant origins. See Voropaev and Iovlev, *Bor'ba KPSS za sozdanie voennykh kadrov*, p. 129.

51. Berkhin, *Voennaya reforma v SSSR*, pp. 258-259.

52. Bubnov, *O krasnov armii*, p. 142.

53. *Izvestiya*, February 23, 1923.

54. Voropaev and Iovlev, *Bor'ba KPSS za sozdanie voennykh kadrov*, pp. 113-114.

55. *V. I. Lenin i sovetskie vooruzhennye sily* (Moscow: Voenizdat, 1967).

56. *KPSS i stroitel'stvo vooruzhennykh sily SSSR*, p. 274.

57. For the Futien Mutiny, see Donald Klein and Anne Clark, *Biographic Dictionary of Chinese Communism* (Cambridge: Harvard University Press, 1971), v. 1, p. 729. For the Huangpo plot, see Jerome Ch'en, *Mao and the Chinese Revolution* (New York: Oxford University Press, 1967), p. 164.

58. Thomas Robinson, *A Politico-Military Biography of Lin Piao* (Santa Monica, Calif.: Rand Corporation, 1971), pp. 79-80.

59. This is not to ignore the internal conflicts and differences within the Chinese army. Mao denounced the tendency toward autonomous "mountaintopism" during the civil war, but these differences and conflicts were far less severe than in the Red Army.

60. Robinson, *A Politico-Military Biography of Lin Piao*, p. 110.

61. Only 10 percent of the Soviet officers had received their training exclusively in the Red Army. See Trotsky, *Kak vooruzhalas' revoliutsiya*, v. 3, P. 2, p. 277. By contrast, in our group of elite Chinese officers, sixteen had graduated from the army academy at Juichin and Yenan, eleven had attended the quasi-revolutionary Whampoa Academy, and only eleven attended traditional military schools.

62. The *voenspets* formed 75 percent of the officer corps in 1918 but only 34 percent in 1920. See Petrov, *Partiinoe stroitel'stvo v sovetskoi armii i flote*, p. 39, and Voropaev and Iovlev, *Bor'ba KPSS za sozdanie voennykh kadrov*, p. 41.

63. C. Martin Wilbur, "The Ashes of Defeat," *China Quarterly*, no. 18 (April/June 1964): 3-54.

64. William W. Whitson, *The Chinese High Command* (New York: Praeger, 1973), p. 503. By contrast, key Soviet commanders and their units were repeatedly moved from one to another. Budenny's First Cavalry Army played a role in the campaigns against Denikin, Poland, Wrangel, and Makhno.

65. A majority of the elite officers in our group (twenty-nine of forty-six) joined the Chinese army at its inception in 1927, and an overwhelming majority (thirty-seven of forty-six) had joined the army by 1930.

66. See Davis Bobrow, "The Political and Economic Role of the Military in the Chinese Communist Movement" (Ph.D. diss., MIT, 1962), p. 714.

67. Key officers are defined as future marshals (ten named in China in 1955, eight named in the Soviet Union in 1935 and 1940), commander in chief, chief of staff, navy commander, and air force commander in the Soviet Union in 1921 and China in 1950. Key officers are counted if they were either full or alternate members of the Central Committee elected in the Soviet Union in 1921 and in China in 1945 (and still sitting in 1950).

The Russian Comunist party Central Committee, elected at the Tenth Party Congress in 1921, numbered forty full and alternate members. The Chinese Communist party Central Committee, elected at the Seventh Party Congress in 1945 and still serving in 1950, numbered seventy-seven full and alternate members.

For the Soviet data, see Desyatyi S'ezd RKP (B), Mart, 1921, *Stenograficheskii Otchet*. For the Chinese data, see Klein and Clark, *Biographic Dictionary of Chinese Communism 1921-1965*.

68. An army representative is defined as a man who occupied a full-time position in the army (generally in a command, staff, political work, or administrative position) at the time he was elected to the Central Committee. For the sources, see note 62.

69. Andrew Nathan, "A Factionalism Model for CCP Politics," *China Quarterly* no. 48 (January/March 1973): 58.

70. Despite the fact that both armies reached a roughly similar 5 million man size by the end of the civil war, the Soviet army had only 278,000 Communists compared to 1.2 million Communits in the Chinese army. See Politicheskoe Upravlenie RKKA, *1918-1928 let krasnoi armii—albom diagram*, p. 42, and John Gittings, *The Role of the Chinese Army* (London: Oxford University Press, 1967), p. 111.

71. For Eastern Europe, see Zbigniew Brzezinski, *The Soviet Bloc* (Cambridge: Harvard University Press, 1960), pp. 91, 119-120, 155.

72. For Yugoslavia, see Bogdan Denitch, *The Legitimation of a Revolution: The Yugoslav Case* (New Haven: Yale University Press, 1976) pp. 7, 129. For Cuba, see Edward Gonzalez, "Castro and Cuba's New Orthodoxy," and Jorge I. Dominguez, "Cuba's Maturing Revolution," *Problems of Communism* 36, no. 1 (January/February 1976): 1-19, 68-73.

Two Decades After The Civil Wars

chapter 4

RUSSIAN AND CHINESE ARMY/PARTY RELATIONS

In the last three chapters we have seen that the Russian and Chinese armies and their officer corps emerged in sharply differing conditions from their civil wars. As a weak, divided, and somewhat unreliable force by the end of its civil war, the Russian army was scarcely a prime contender for power in the 1920s. Furthermore, dominated by a mass of apolitical (if not hostile) peasant soldiers and noncommissioned officers and an elite of *voenspets*, the army was perceived as a potential threat to the party. It was further weakened by the massive demobilization of the early 1920s and the relatively small military expenditures of the 1920s. Even by 1929 it was considered at best capable of rebuffing only a Polish attack. Although its capabilities and legitimacy improved dramatically in the 1930s, it remained isolated from party and society. As it had been the passive beneficiary of the massive industrialization of the 1930s, so too was it to be the passive object of the Great Purges.

By contrast, the Chinese army had emerged from its civil war as a strong, effective force, closely fused with the party. This revolutionary legitimacy would enable it to play a key role during major campaigns for the revolutionary transformation of society. Its effectiveness would be a major asset for the party. It would retain 50 percent of its manpower in the post-civil war period, compared to only 10 percent for the Russian army. During the Korean War, it would oust the American army from North Korea and even Seoul and later stalemate it around the 38th parallel. In 1962 it would decisively destroy the Indian army before making a unilateral withdrawal. In 1969 it would engage the Soviet army with some success on the Ussurri River.

Only in the campaign over the Taiwan Straits in 1958 would it demonstrate minimal fighting ability, this time in the air. Overall, though, the continuing power and legitimacy of the PLA, especially in a hostile international environment, would help ensure it a major politicial role.

Furthermore, the civil wars helped shape the overall political environment in which the armies functioned in the two decades after the civil wars. The protracted nature of the Chinese revolution created a relatively homogeneous elite grouped into three major institutions (army, party, and government) functioning under the overall guidance of Chairman Mao. By contrast, in Russia, the secret police, as a frequent army substitute and force compensating for the lack of the mass peasant base existing in China, emerged as a powerful and legitimate institution. Furthermore, the governmental bureaucracy, lacking a gestation period as in China and filled with old czarist *chinovniki* ("civil servants") and bourgeois specialists, was not a major political force in Russia. The bitter party struggles, which culminated in Stalinist dominance by 1927, reflected not only the death of the original leader in 1924 but also the relative diverse factions and heterogeneous nature of the party leadership. These had arisen from the sudden ascension to power in the October Revolution.

In this context, it was hardly surprising that the PLA exerted far greater political influence in the policymaking area than the Red Army in the two decades after the civil wars. Similarly, it seems logical that the Chinese Communist party relied far less on coercive means of control over its army than did the Russian Communist party over the Red Army in this period.

FORMAL INDICATORS OF POWER

A comparative analysis of formal indicators of power—army representation in the Politburo and Central Committee and army participation in the party congresses—illuminates the sharp differences in the role of the armies in the Soviet Union (1921-40) and China (1950-71). Table 7 shows the far greater army representation in the Chinese Politburo than in the Soviet Politburo. Despite remarkable changes in the technology and officer corps of the Red Army, the war commissar remained the only army representative in the Soviet Politburo throughout the 1921-40 period. By contrast, army representation among the full and alternate members of the Chinese Politburo surged from one member in 1950 (9 percent) to six members in 1956 (27 percent) and twelve members in 1969 (48 percent) and then sharply declined after the Lin Piao affair to six members in late 1971 (31 percent).

Table 7   Army Representation in the Russian Communist Party Politburo (1921-40) and the Chinese Communist Party Politburo (1950-71)—Full and Alternate Members[1]

Congress	Russia	China	Congress
(10) 1921	13% (1/8)	9% (1/11)	1950 (7)[2]
(11) 1922	10% (1/10)	17% (2/12)	1953
(12) 1923	9% (1/11)	23% (3/13)	1955
(13) 1924	15% (2/13)	27% (6/23)	1956 (8)
(14) 1925	7% (1/14)	23% (6/26)	1958
(15) 1927	6% (1/17)	22% (5/23)	1965
(16) 1930	7% (1/15)	52% (13/25)	1969 (9)
(17) 1934	7% (1/15)	37% (7/19)[3]	1971
(18) 1939	9% (1/11)		

Sources: Boris Levytsky, *The Soviet Political Elite*, Donald Klein and Anne Clark, *Biographic Dictionary of Chinese Communism 1921-1965.*

[1] An army representative is defined as a man who served in a full-time position (command, staff, administration, or political work) in the army at the time that the Politburo was selected.
[2] The Seventh Party Congress was held in 1945.
[3] The figure is for the period after the demise of Lin Piao and his associates.

Sharp differences also pervaded the nature of the army representatives. The lone Soviet army representative, War Commissars Trotsky (1921-25), Frunze (1924-25), and Voroshilov (1925-40), possessed neither professional military training nor military experience before the civil war. All three men were professional revolutionaries, who served as key party representatives in the army. Despite the existence of a number of talented party career commanders, such as Yakir and Tukhachevsky, in the 1921-40 period not a single career soldier sat in the Politburo. By contrast, while only one of eight Soviet marshals was chosen for the Politburo in the 1921-40 period, all ten of the Chinese marshals were selected for the Politburo in the 1950-71 period. Nearly all the Chinese marshals, career soldiers despite their revolutionary past, occupied key command and staff posts in the army.

The striking separation of army and party elites in the Soviet Union was seen in the fact that not a single civilian Politburo member in the 1921-40 period had served as an officer in the civil war! The minority of civilian Politburo members who had served in the army during the civil war, such as Stalin, Kirov, and Kuibyshev, had been commissars and party representatives on various Revolutionary Military Committees, but, they were in the army, not of it. As soon as the civil war came to a close, they moved on to other party assignments. By contrast, army and party elites were so close in China that Defense Minister Lin Piao could be Mao's designated successor in the 1966-71 period. And several civilian party members in the Politburo, such as Mao and Li Hsien-nien, possessed extensive military backgrounds.

Table 8 shows a pattern similar to Politburo representation for Central Committee representation. Soviet army representation on the Central Committee was so minimal that it never exceeded 13 percent of all seats and dipped as low as 3 percent in 1927. By sharp contrast, Chinese army representation was very substantial. It fluctuated from 50 percent in 1950 to 37 percent in 1956 and 45 percent in 1969. During the 1930s, Soviet army representation rose modestly from 3 percent in 1930 to 10 percent in 1939.

These figures do conceal a change in the nature of the men who represented the army in the Central Committee. During the 1920s five of the six army representatives on that body—Trotsky, Frunze, Voroshilov, Bubnov, and Unshlikht—were old revolutionary party representatives in the army. In the 1930s a whole new generation of career military men, including the eight marshals named in 1935 and 1940, were appointed to the Central Committee. In China the military representatives were more a product of the army throughout the period.

Finally, the party congresses also reflected the striking isolation of the Soviet army elite from the party elite and the close interaction of

Table 8   Army Representation in the Russian Communist Party Central Committee (1921-40) and the Chinese Communist Party Central Committee (1950-71)—Full Members[1]

Congress		Russia	China	Congress
(10)	1921	13% (4/30)	50% (22/45)	1950 (7)[2]
(11)	1922	11% (3/27)		
(12)	1923	7% (3/40)		
(13)	1924	8% (4/53)		
(14)	1925	5% (3/63)	37% (34/91)	1956 (8)
(15)	1927	3% (2/71)		
(16)	1930	3% (2/71)		
(17)	1934	4% (3/71)		
(18)	1939	13% (9/71)	45% (77/170)	1969 (9)[3]

Sources: Boris Levytsky, The Soviet Political Elite; Nikolai Galay, "The Soviet Armed Forces and the Twenty-Second Party Congress," Bulletin-Institute for the Study of the USSR, p. 7; Donald Klein and Anne Clark, Biographic Dictionary of Chinese Communism, 1921-1965; William Whitson, ed. The Military and Political Power in China in the 1970s, pp. 62, 118, 520-521.

[1]An army representative is defined as a man who served in a full-time position (command, staff, administration, or political work) in the army at the time that the Central Committee was selected.

[2]The Seventh Party Congress was held in 1945.

[3]Other authors have offered different figures for military representation in China in 1969. Elegant has calculated 56 percent representation and Powell has calculated 47 percent representation for the army. See Robert Elegant, Mao's Great Revolution, p. 456, and Ralph Powell, "The Party, the Government and the Gun," Asian Survey, 10 (June 1970): 45.

the Chinese army and party elites. As Table 9 shows, Soviet army men gave only 0 to 5 percent of all speeches made at the party congresses in the 1921-40 period. By contrast Chinese army leaders gave 14 percent and 38 percent of the published speeches at the Eighth and Ninth Party Congresses in 1956 and 1969. During the 1920s the isolation of the Soviet army leadership was so pronounced that army men made only 0 to 2 percent of all speeches made at four congresses which we analyzed. Furthermore, at these four congresses, four of the five marshals named in 1935 did not speak even once while the remaining marshal, War Commissar Voroshilov, made a single speech. The very existence of these key military leaders was ignored. At these four congresses the names of future Marshals Blyukher and Yegorov were never mentioned even once. The name of Marshal Tukhachevsky merited one lone passing reference with regard to the 1920 battle for Warsaw. Only Marshals Budenny and Voroshilov, Stalin's supporters in the 1920s, received frequent mention. Although participation by key Red Army leaders rose markedly in the congresses held in the 1930s, it still remained at a low level. Furthermore, the records of all congresses surveyed in the 1922-39 period revealed that, with the exception of ritualistic remarks, military speakers totally avoided nonmilitary topics.

Table 9   Army Representation in Russian Communist Party Congresses 1922-39

Year	Party Congress	No. of Military Speeches[1] / No. of All Speeches	Pages of Military Speeches / Pages of all Speeches
1922	11	1.5% (2/139)	.8% (4/556)
1923	12	2.0% (3/150)	.8% (5/668)
1924	13	0.0% (0/51)	0.0% (0/595)
1927	15	.6% (1/175)	1.5% (21/1426)
1934	17	3.0% (4/137)	2.6% (17/655)
1939	18	4.6% (6/132)	6.0% (40/646)

Sources: For the Eleventh Party Congress, see Odinnadtsatyi S'ezd RKP(B), Marta-2 Aprel', 1922, Stenograficheskii Otchet; For the Twelfth Party Congress, see Dvenadtsatyi S'ezd RKP(B), 17-25 Aprelya, 1923, Stenograficheskii Otchet; For the Thirteenth Party Congress, see Trinadtsatayi S'ezd RKP(B), Mai, 1924, Stenograficheskii Otchet; For the Fifteenth Party Congress, see Pyatnadtsatyi S'ezd VKP(B), Dekabrya, 1927, Stenograficheskii Otchet; For the Seventeenth Party Congress, see KPSS, XVII S'ezd, 26 Yanvarya-10 Fevralya, 1934, Stenograficheskii Otchet; For the Eighteenth Party Congress, see KPSS, XVIII S'ezd, 10-21 Marta, 1939, Stenograficheskii Otchet.

[1]A military speech was a speech delivered by a member of the Red Army, on either a military or nonmilitary subject, to the Congress.

However, in China army leaders played prominent roles in the congresses held in 1956 and 1969. At the Eighth Party Congress in 1956, Marshal Chu Teh and Marshal P'eng Teh-huai delivered the fifth and sixth speeches. Overall, PLA men delivered 14 percent

(4/29) of the publicized speeches at the congress and their words filled 12 percent of the published pages. Furthermore, unlike the Red Army leaders, the Chinese army leaders also spoke on nonmilitary topics. Marshal Chu Teh, for example, spoke broadly about the general problems facing the party and country. The PLA played a significant, but far from dominant, role at the Congress.[1]

This situation changed dramatically at the Ninth Party Congress in 1969. The very sketchy available information has indicated the major role played by Defense Minister Lin Piao, then Mao's designated heir, at the congress. Lin Piao delivered the major speech, and at least five (and perhaps six) of the thirteen reported speeches at the three short plenary sessions were made by PLA men.[2]

Thus, all the formal indicators of power indicate a strong and oscillating political role for the PLA and a weak and isolated position for the Red Army.

INFORMAL POLITICAL INDICATORS

During the interwar period the Soviet army exercised little political power in decision-making. Indeed, the bulk of the army was basically isolated from the party. Table 10 shows that, with the brief exception of 1934, party membership in the army fluctuated between a low of 7 percent in 1921 to a high of 15 percent in 1930 and a final figure of 14.3 percent in 1940. This was scarcely surprising in view of the fact that the ranks in developing Russia were filled, especially in the 1920s, with peasants scarcely enthusiastic about the urban-oriented radical Bolsheviks. As Table 11 shows, as late as 1929, 66 percent of all soldiers were peasants. A second key element, noncommissioned officers, was also heavily peasant in origins and highly apolitical.

Finally, the bulk of the officers were not involved in politics. As Table 12 shows, even by the end of the 1920s, despite great improvement from the 20 percent party membership of 1921, fully one-half of the officers did not belong to the party. During the 1930s roughly one-third of the officers did not join the party. Many of those who did join the party emulated the professional apolitcal ethos of Marshal Shaponshnikov. Among the minority of officers actively involved in political affairs, only a smaller number were Stalinists. Consisting

largely of civil war associates of Stalin at Tsaritsyn and in the First
Cavalry Army, the Stalinist faction, including Budenny, Voroshilov,
Timoshenko, Shchadenko, and Kulik, played a prominent role in the
Red Army.[3] Notably unsympathetic toward modern mechanized
warfare, this faction served as a "transmission belt" for Stalin's
control over the army rather than as an independent faction influencing Stalin. It faithfully and servilely implemented the Stalinist line at all
times, even during the Great Purges.

Table 10   Communist Party Membership in the Overall Red
Army 1921-40

Year	Communist Party	Komsomol	Communist Affiliation
1921	7.0%	0.0%	7.0%
1922[1]	7.5%	0.0%	7.5%
1923[2]	10.0%	0.0%	10.0%
1924	10.0%	6.0%	16.0%
1925	12.0%	11.0%	23.0%
1926	14.0%	16.0%	30.0%
1927	15.0%	22.0%	37.0%
1928	12.8%	14.5%	27.3%
1929[3]	10.0%	30.0%	40.0%
1930	15.9%	18.4%	34.3%
1932	—	—	59.4%
1934	24.2%	23.9%	48.1%
1935	—	—	50.0%
1936	14.1%	23.3%	37.4%
1937	10.7%	28.8%	39.5%
1938	9.8%	32.0%	41.8%
1939	11.3%	39.9%	51.2%
1940	14.3%	32.8%	46.1%

Sources: K. E. Voroshilov, Stat'i i Rechi, pp. 343, 521, 574, 611; *Dvenadsati S'ezd
RKP(B), Stenograficheskii otchet,* p. 53; D. A. Voropaev and A. M. Iovlev, *Bor'ba
KPSS za sozdanie voennykh kadrov,* p. 68; and *KPSS i stroitel'stvo vooruzhennykh
sil SSSR (1918-June, 1941),* p. 220; *Voennyi vestnik* #30, October 25, 1930; XIV S'ezd,
VKP(B) *Stenograficheskii otchet,* p. 70; St. Ivanovich, VKP(B) *Desiat' let kommunis-
ticheskoi monopolii,* pp. 149-151; KPSS, XVII S'ezd, 26 January-10 February, 1934,
Stenograficheskii otchet, p. 232; J. Stalin et al., *From the First to the Second Five
Year Plan,* p. 360; Yuri Petrov, *Partiinoe stroitel'stvo v sovetskoi armii i flote (1918-*

1961), pp. 228, 230, 242, 244, 246, 248, 321, 323; *Istoriya velikoi otechestvennoi voiny sovetskogo soyuza*, v. 1, p. 98; Michel Berchin and Eliahu Ben-Horin, *The Red Army*, p. 54.

[1]The data are for March 1922.
[2]The data are for April 1923.
[3]The data for this year are particularly unreliable.
Notes
For a number of these years, other figures exist which differ from those cited in the table. An official publication of PUR gives the following alternative data for the 1921-28 period:

For membership in the Communist party,

	1921	4.7%
	1922	4.6%
	1923	10.3%
	1924	9.2%
	1925	10.3%
	1926	12.9%
	1927	13.9%
	1928	16.0%

For membership in Komsomol,

	1925	7.7%
	1926	13.2%
	1927	15.8%
	1928	16.1%

See Politicheskoe Upravelenie RKKA, *1918-1928 let krasnoi armii—albom diagram*, p. 33. For 1924, Berkhin has given yet a different figure of 8 percent membership in the Communist party. See I. B. Berkhin, *Voennaya reforma v SSSR (1924-1925)*, p. 401. Finally, Voroshilov has given an alternate figure for Komsomol membership in 1936— 33 percent of all Red Army men. See K. E. Voroshilov, *Stat'i i rechi*, p. 611.

A loose group of officers, noted for their appreciation of modern mechanized warfare, was centered around Marshal Tukhachevsky. This group, which supported such favorable Stalinist policies as industrialization and modernization but did not exclude the possibility of opposition to Stalin, included such leading military figures as Yakir, Garkavy, Uborevich, Dubovoy, Alksnis, Yegorov, and Gamarnik.[4]

Major attempts by army elements to influence policymaking in nonmilitary areas all met resounding defeats in the interwar period. During the early 1920s a loose Trotskyite faction, consisting of War Commissar Trotsky, the head of the Political Administration, Antonov-Ovseenko, and the commander of the vital Moscow garri-

Table 11   Communist Party Membership Among Red Army
Commanders During the 1921-36 Period

Year	Communist Party	Komsomol	Communist Affiliation
1921	20.0%	—	20.0%
1922	22.5%	—	22.5%
1923[1]	29.5%	—	29.5%
1924	30.6%	1.2%	31.8%
1925	41.0%	2.0%	43.0%
1926	46.0%	4.0%	50.0%
1927[2]	49.6%	5.8%	55.4%
1928	—	—	55.0%
1929	—	—	52.7%
1930	52.5%	4.1%	56.6%
1932	—	—	61.0%
1933[3]	67.8%	4.0%	71.8%
1934	67.8%	4.0%	71.8%
1935	68.0%	—	—
1936	64.1%	5.9%	70.0%

Sources: Yuri Petrov, Partiinoe stroitel'stvo v sovetskoi armii i flote (1918-1961), p. 179; D. A. Voropaev and A. M. Iovlev, Bor'ba KPSS za sozdanie voennykh kadrov, p. 106; KPSS i stroitel'stvo vooruzhennykh sily SSSR (1918-June, 1941), p. 274; K. E. Voroshilov, Stat'i i rechi, pp. 153, 230, 374, 612; A. S. Bubnov et al., Grazhdanskaya voina 1918-1921, v. 2, p. 108; D. A. Voropaev and A. M. Iovlev, Bor'ba KPSS za sozdanie voennykh kadrov, pp. 89, 106; K. E. Voroshilov, Oborona SSSR, pp. 148, 151; B. Tal, Istoriya krasnoi armii, pp. 190-191; A. Gernomius, Partiya i krasnaya armiya, p. 166; A. A. Grechko, Vooruzhennye sily sovetskogo gosudarstva, p. 203; V. I. Lenin i sovetskie vooruzhennye sily, p. 289; J. Stalin et al., From the First to the Second Five Year Plan, p. 360; KPSS i stroitel'stvo vooruzhennykh sily SSSR, p. 274; V. I. Lenin i sovetskie vooruzhennye sily, p. 289; KPSS, XVII S'ezd, 26 Yanvarya 10 Fevralya, 1934, Stenograficheskii otchet, p. 232; Michel Berchin and Eliahu Ben-Horin, The Red Army, p. 55; 50 Let vooruzhennykh sil SSSR, p. 213.

[1]For 1923, Berkhin cites 22.9 percent of the commanders belonging to the party. See I. B. Berkhin, Voennaya reforma v SSSR (1924-1925) p. 263.

[2]For 1927, Shatagin and Prusanov have cited 48.1 percent of the commanders belonging to the party, while another Soviet source has claimed that 54 percent of the commanders belonged to the party. See N. I Shatagin and I. P. Prusanov, Sovetskaya armiya—armiya novogo tipa, p. 107, and Boevoi put' sovetskykh vooruzhennykh sil, p. 211.

[3]For 1933, the same Soviet source has claimed that 59 percent of all commanders belonged to the Communist party or Komsomol. See Boevoi put' sovetskykh vooruzhennykh sil, p. 212.

Table 12   Social Origins of the Overall Red Army
1921-39

Year	Working Class	Peasantry	Other
1921	18.0%	71.0%	11.0%
1923	17.9%	70.8%	11.3%
1925[1]	11.0%	82.0%	7.0%
1926[2]	18.0%	71.0%	11.0%
1927	18.8%	63.4%	12.8%
1928	21.0%	67.0%	12.0%
1929	24.0%	66.0%	10.0%
1930	31.2%	57.9%	10.9%
1932	39.0%	—	—
1933	43.0%	47.0%	10.0%
1934	45.8%	42.5%	11.7%
1937	45.0%	—	—
1939	43.0%	47.0%	10.0%

Sources: N. F. Kuz'min, *Krushenie poslednova pokhoda a antanty,* p. 185; K. E. Voroshilov, *Stat'i i rechi,* pp. 170, 173, 283, 445, 573, 611; *V. I. Lenin i sovetskie vooruzhennye sily,* p. 119; *Krasnaya zvezda,* no. 297, January 1, 1925; St. Ivanovich, *VKP(B)-Desiat' let kommunisticheskoi monopolii,* p. 146; *50 Let vooruzhennykh sil SSSR,* p. 193; *Boevoi put' sovetskikh vooruzhennykh sil,* p. 211; N. I. Shatagin and I. P. Prusanov, *Sovetskaya armiya—armiya novogo tipa,* p. 117; KPSS, XVII S'ezd, 26 January-10 February, 1934,*Stenograficheskii otchet,* p. 233; N. V. Piatnitsky, *Krasnaya armiya SSSR,* v. 1, p. 15.

[1]For 1925, War Commissar Frunze has stated that peasants formed 84.7 percent of the army, workers formed 11.0 percent and others 4.3 percent of the army. See *Russian Review* 3, no. 13 (July 1925): 275. Also for 1925, Bubnov has claimed that peasants formed a phenomenal 90 percent of the army. See A. S. Bubnov, *O krasnoi armii,* p. 128.

[2]For 1926, another Soviet source has given figures of 15.3 percent for the working class, 79.5 percent for the peasantry and 5.2 percent for others. See Politicheskoe Upravlenie RKKA, *1918-1928 Let krasnoi armii—albom diagram,* p. 41.

son, Muralov, held key posts in the army. However, this base must not be exaggerated. While Stalinist and Zinovievite followers also sat on the Revolutionary Military Council, many army commanders, especially *voenspets*, adopted a position of professional neutrality. Most army party officers, angered by Trotsky's arrogant behavior during the civil war, his extensive use of *voenspets*, and his opposition to the "proletarian military doctrine," were indifferent to his fate. Although he refrained from taking his case to the army, his followers, notably Antonov-Ovseenko, did so openly. In December 1923 the Political Administration of the army, without Central Committee approval, issued Circular No. 200 which allowed open discussion of political issues in the army. The result, as Soviet historian Petrov has asserted, was that "Factional struggle in the army took an extremely sharp form."[5] Only in Moscow, where the Trotskyites controlled the party organization of the staff of the Moscow Military District and one-third of the party cells of the garrison, was some success achieved. Elsewhere the Stalinist faction reigned supreme and crushed the Trotskyites.[6] Within a year Antonov-Ovseenko and Trotsky lost their posts, the Political Administration was radically reshaped, and the army's top command was Stalinized.

During 1927 some army leaders did not stay totally aloof from the party struggle with the Left Opposition. In that year Yakir, Putna, and other commanders evidently signed some form of confidential defense of the opposition.[7] Also, during that same year future Marshals Blyukher and Tukhachevsky and other top military leaders opposed the Stalinist line on China.[8] Neither attempt met with any success.

The final major attempt to influence the party came at the August 1936 plenum of the Central Committee, which was held after the Zinoviev-Kamenev trial. At this plenum roughly three-fourths of the Central Committee supported Bukharin and opposed Stalin over the purges and liquidation of opponents. Only Marshals Budenny and Voroshilov, both Stalinist stalwarts, supported Stalin while the other seven military members of the Central Committee—Yakir and Gamarnik (members), Marshals Yegorov, Blyukher, and Tukhachevsky, and Bulin and Uborevich (candidates)—opposed Stalin.[9]

This military participation was extremely defensive in nature. There is no evidence that the military leaders led the opposition to Stalin at the plenum. They voted in roughly the same proportion as the far more numerous civilian members of the Central Committee. The army opposition to Stalin occurred under the most severe imaginable circumstances—the threat of massive purges which would be highly detrimental both to the institutionalized interests of the army and to the health and well-being of the top military leaders.

Yet, this intervention too was unsuccessful. Within a year the Great Purges would completely liquidate the non-Stalinist military elite and a significant part of the officer corps.

However, if the military leaders were excluded from the fundamental political decisions, their input was still needed on military matters. As the importance and complexity of military affairs grew with the industrialization and modernization of the country and the increasing foreign threat in the 1930s, the role of the military leaders grew concurrently. The power of the military leaders was enhanced not only by their military expertise but by the great growth of military industries and military-related industries. Furthermore, the importance of the military factor (as oposed to the military sector) in the 1930s provided the top army leadership with frequent, even daily, contact with Stalin. This access to the top political leadership was a key source of army influence.

In military-related matters the leaders often played an important role in the interwar period. In 1930, after a number of *voenspets* were arrested by the secret police on charges of conspiring to annihilate the leadership of the Ukrainian army, Yakir and Dubovoy went to Moscow and obtained the release and rehabilitation of most of them.[10] In 1933 future Marshal Blyukher evidently obtained the abolition of compulsory levies and the partial restoration of the New Economic Policy in the Far East on the grounds of military necessity.[11] Similarly, in the Ukraine, military commanders Yakir and Dubovoy, together with several important party *obkom* secretaries, obtained a halt in the further delivery of bread shipments from the famine-starved Ukraine.[12]

By sharp contrast, the Chinese army, having emerged from its civil war as an effective and legitimate force fused with the party, played a significant although varying role in military and party affairs in the 1950-71 period. Nearly all officers were party members as were a large stratum in the ranks. Its record of intervention in nonmilitary areas was marked by a number of failures as well as some successes. During the 1950-54 period the army/party fusion continued to function on a diminished level. The army played a crucial role in exercising key governmental and even party functions at the provincial and local level, and in providing many key cadres for the party and government.[13] During the 1950-52 period military commanders served as chairmen of the Military Administrative Committees for four of the six huge regions into which the country was then divided.[14] Although the actual participation of the army in party affairs probably declined in the middle 1950s due to the end of military rule and the stress on army modernization, the army did increase its representation in the Politburo. In 1956 seven of the ten marshals were elected to the Politburo. The far smaller demobilization of the Chinese army than that of the Russian army in the decade after the end of the civil war reflected the continuing importance of the Chinese army.[15] The army functioned in a role greater than that of an interest group. Table 13 shows that, despite increased army representation in the Politburo, military expenditures declined from 23.6 percent of the budget in 1954 to 15.1 percent in 1958, indicating the army's role as a key actor in the political system in the 1954-58 period.[16]

Table 13   Military Expenditures of the Chinese Army 1950-59

Year	Military Expenditures (in billions of dollars)	Percent of Budget
1950	—	38.8
1951	—	48.0
1952	—	—
1953	6.2	28.1
1954	5.8	23.6
1955	—	22.1
1956	6.1	20.0
1957	5.5	18.9
1958	5.0	15.1
1959	5.8	11.2

Sources: Current Background, no. 214, October 1, 1952, p. 3; Eighth National Congress of the Communist Party of China v. 2, p. 28; S.C.M.P., no. 1724, March 5, 1958, p. 9; Current Background, no. 336, July 14, 1955, p. 5; S.C.M.P., no. 1584, August 6, 1957, p. 10; E.C.M.M., no. 46, August 7, 1956, p. 12; Alice Hsieh, Communist China's Strategy in the Nuclear Era, p. 150.

The Great Leap Forward in 1958 created a considerable strain on army/party relations. The movement of the PLA toward a modern, professional army on the Soviet model had greatly enhanced the power and number of professional commanders in the army. The Great Leap Forward, by rejecting the Soviet model of societal development, put into grave question the future course of army development. Its failings must have reinforced the desire of those who supported the Soviet model of army development to oppose any change in direction for the army.

In July 1959 at the Lushan Plenum, Defense Minister P'eng Teh-huai challenged Mao on a wide range of military and nonmilitary issues. He was supported by a number of key military leaders—including the chief of staff—although not actively by any of the other six marshals on the Politburo. Several civilian party leaders also supported him.[17] P'eng blisteringly scored the "petty bourgeois fanaticism" of the Great Leap Forward which "renders us liable to commit 'leftist' mistakes." He attacked the communes, the backyard steel program, and the lack of reality in the Great Leap Forward. He even directly attacked Chairman Mao and his "cult of the individual." He alleged that "If the Chinese workers and peasants were not as good as they are, a Hungarian incident would have occurred in China and it would have been necessary to invite Soviet troops in." Finally, he clearly opposed the rejection of the Soviet model of army development.[18]

Mao felt sufficiently threatened that at a meeting in July 1959 he dramatically proclaimed that, "If we deserve to perish then I will go away, go to the countryside to lead the peasants and overthrow the government. If you the Liberation Army don't follow me, I'll go to find a Red Army. I think the Liberation Army will follow me."[19] Mao did garner sufficient support to achieve a "soft" purge of Defense Minister P'eng Teh-huai, Chief of staff Huang K'o-cheng, and several other army leaders.[20] Mao successfully gained support for an end to the alliance with the Soviet Union and reliance on the Soviet model of development for either the army or society. The new army leaders, Lin Piao as defense minister and Lo Jui-ching as chief of staff, realigned the army with the thinking of the Maoist faction in the party.

However, the results of the Lushan Plenum demonstrated several factors different from Soviet purges. The defeated army faction led by P'eng had possessed sufficient legitimacy to raise nonmilitary issues that could not have been raised by Soviet officers, especially after the 1924-26 purges, without incurring charges of army interference in civilian affairs. The treatment of the purged men was far less severe in China than in Russia. Thus, the army in China even at this point was capable of positive but limited intervention in the political system as a political actor.

Furthermore, the power of the army began to grow considerably under Defense Minister Lin Piao in the early 1960s. In the extended "Learn From the PLA" campaign the army was frequently evoked as a societal model. By the time of the Cultural Revolution in 1966, Defense Minister Lin Piao had already become Mao's designated successor.

As the chaos of the Cultural Revolution mounted and the party and governmental institutions disintegrated below the central level, the army emerged as a major Maoist power base and key force in maintaining order. Especially below the central level, the army exercised decisive political influence.[21] The People's Liberation Army was instrumental in setting up the new revolutionary committees, which temporarily ruled China at the provincial level at the end of the Cultural Revolution. Even by the end of 1968, three-fourths of the chairmen and one-half of the members of the standing committees of these revolutionary committees in the twenty-nine administrative areas of China were army men.[22] At the Ninth Party Congress in 1969 army men occupied twelve of twenty-five Politburo seats while Defense Minister Lin Piao, Mao's designated successor, gave the principal address. In words which would have been considered heretical in the Soviet Union, a 1969 Chinese editorial ignored the role of the party and stressed the centrality of the army's political role by declaring,

Military power is the heart of state power. The army as the main factor in the dictatorship of the proletariat is the mighty pillar of the dictatorship. In the acute and complicated struggle between the bourgeoisie . . . and the proletariat the army is the most important factor. Provided the army does not change color and is in the hands of genuine Marxists, the proletariat is not afraid of the emergence of revisionism in other fields and rebellion by the bourgeoisie.[23]

The Lin Piao Affair in 1971 illustrated the great difficulty in dislodging the army from its extensive involvement in political affairs. In his speech at the Tenth Party Congress, Chou En-lai recounted the protracted nature of the conflict which lasted from 1969 to 1971. He labeled it the tenth major struggle in Chinese Communist history.[24] Given the fact that five key army Politburo members and numerous other army and party leaders were affiliated with the Lin Piao faction, the struggle was fierce. Only through the mobilization of civilian party, government, and some military leaders was Lin Piao ultimately defeated. The power of the army declined sharply in the aftermath of the mysterious deaths of Lin Piao and his Politburo allies and the purge of his followers. However, the lack of an institutionalized army/party relationship was reflected graphically in the fact that the key posts of defense minister, chief of staff, and political commissar remained unfilled from 1971 until 1975! And, even then, within a year the defense minister (Yeh Chien-ying) and the chief of staff (Teng Hsiao-p'ing) left their posts. In short, we have seen that army/party relations were much more fluid and the army played a far greater role in party affairs in China than in the Soviet Union.

Unlike the Soviet officers, nearly all Chinese officers not only joined the party but also actively participated in political affairs. Especially at the elite level, nearly all officers were old revolutionaries. No large and identifiable element in the Chinese officer corps stood apart from the dominant party stratum. Indeed, both during the 1950-54 period of military rule in the provinces and the 1967-71 period of the Cultural Revolution and its aftermath, army commanders played an important role in party and governmental affairs, especially below the central level. This was also reflected in the large and active party stratum in the ranks. While 30 percent to 40 percent of the ranks belonged to the party in the 1950s, the figure probably increased even further in the 1960s under the leadership of Defense Minister Lin Piao.[25]

PARTY CONTROLS

Given the frequency of military coups in underdeveloped countries, such as Russia and China in this period, both party leaderships were naturally anxious to ensure party control over the military. The accusations of Bonapartism hurled against War Commissar Trotsky in the early 1920s and Marshal Tukhachevsky and his fellow officers in 1937 in the Soviet Union were paralleled by the attack on Defense Minister P'eng Teh-huai in 1959 and the campaign against Defense Minister Lin Piao in 1971 in China. However, sharp differences existed in the nature of party controls over the military in the two countries in the two decades after the civil war. As the Russian army emerged from the civil war as a weak and unreliable force, the party developed an elaborate network of coercive measures, reinforced in the 1930s by major utilitarian measures. By contrast, the Chinese party felt far less need to use such measures with regard to the effective and reliable PLA and depended extensively on normative measures and incorporation of the army in the policymaking process.

Purges represented the most important coercive measure. The principle similarity between Soviet and Chinese army purges was that both parties ultimately managed to contain possible army challenges to party control. The differences were far greater. Interestingly, the Soviet army was virtually exempt from most of the purges which recurrently swept the party in the 1921-40 period. Thus, while in 1921, 25 percent and, in 1929, 11.7 percent of all Communists were purged, only 10 percent and less than 5 percent respectively of all army Communists were purged. Similarly, while in 1933 and 1934, 17 percent and 25 percent of all Communists were purged, only 4.3 percent and "far fewer" army Communists were purged.[26] The two major purges—1924-26 and 1937-41— were, by contrast, deep and decisive in molding and reaffirming the army's rigid noninvolvement in politics. Their initial impetus possibly may have come from defensive political moves made by army Communists against the dominant Stalinist faction in the party. In both cases army resistance to the decisive purges was minimal or nonexistent.

Although the party was increasingly dominated by the Stalinist faction in the early 1920s, power in the army remained at least nominally in the hands of a loose Trotskyite faction. This faction included War Commissar Trotsky, Moscow garrison commander Muralov, and Political Administration head Antonov-Ovseenko. While Trotsky acknowledged the apolitical nature of the army by refusing to involve the army in his struggle for power, Antonov-Ovseenko took the struggle into the army in December 1923. Nonetheless, noted earlier, the Stalinists easily defeated the Trotskyites and purged them from the army. In their place came Stalinists such as Voroshilov, who served as war commissar from 1925 until 1940. While the Political Administration was sharply reduced in size, stripped of its power, and directly subordinated to the Central Committee, Special Sections (00) of the secret police were established within the army. A number of *voenspets* were purged, the post of commander in chief of the army was abolished and the Revolutionary Military Council was reorganized and packed with Stalinists.[27]

Similarly, after the majority of army representatives had opposed the extension of the purges at the August 1936 plenum of the Central Committee, the Stalinist faction launched the massive purges within the army. The toll included 3 of 5 marshals, 14 of 16 Class 1 and 2 army commanders, all 8 admirals, 60 of 67 corps commanders, 136 of 199 divisional commanders, and 221 of 397 brigade commanders. All seven of the military representatives on the Central Committee who had opposed Stalin were purged and shot. All eleven vice commissars of defense were shot as well. The massive purges liquidated 15,000 to 35,000 officers.[28]

These extensive purges destroyed any possible resurgence of army political involvement and ended the possible use of the army as a check on Stalinism. The army's positive involvement in political struggles had long ago ceased; and the certain amount of independence and autonomy in military affairs, the self-legitimation, and the self-confidence of key officers gained from their civil war exploits were crushed by the Great Purges.[29] The removal of almost an entire generation of civil war leaders allowed the rise of the surviving Stalinists, such as Budenny, Timoshenko, and Kulik, to positions of great power and the rapid promotion of a new generation of younger officers to key positions.

In contrast to the thorough and decisive purges in the Soviet army, most army purges in China were partial and indecisive in institutionalizing army/party relations. Furthermore, army political power actually grew in the aftermath of the 1959 (P'eng Teh-huai), 1965 (Lo Jui-ching), 1967 (Ho Lung), and 1968 (Yang Cheng-wu) purges. The softness of most purges was evident in the fact that Defense Minister P'eng Teh-huai, purged in 1959, actually retained his Politburo seat for several years thereafter.[30] None of these four purges involved the use of physical violence. The purges were often so limited in scope that in 1959, 1965, and 1968 they in each case involved the removal of less than five officers and commissars, albeit important ones as the chiefs of staff. The 1971 purge of the Lin Piao faction, which presaged a sharp reduction in army power in party affairs, differed sharply from the other purges. Not only did Defense Minister Lin Piao and five other army Politburo colleagues die under mysterious circumstances in an airplane crash in Mongolia, but nearly 100 central military leaders, many air force officers, and perhaps as many as 35 provincial-level party secretaries were purged.[31] However, even this hard, widespread, and probably violent purge failed to institutionalize army/party relations. The key posts of defense minister, chief of staff and head of the General Political Department remained vacant until 1975. However, the ability of civilian party leaders, together with some military leaders, to withstand and destroy a powerful challenge mounted by such key army leaders as the defense minister, air force commander, navy commissar, and chief of staff, showed the limits of army influence in the policymaking process.[32]

The secret police formed a second potent mechanism of coercion. In Russia the secret police created a highly complex, centralized, and pervasive network of informers in the army. This produced, in Brzezinski's words, "an overwhelming sense of fear of possible arrest and prosecution" which tended "to limit most effectively any overt acts of opposition to Soviet power."[33] Furthermore, during the 1921-40 period special secret police troops, operating independently of army control, were estimated to number at least 250,000 men.[34] Possessing airplanes, tanks, and heavy artillery and having first choice of prospective army recruits, these forces formed a potent counterforce to any independent action by the army.[35] By contrast, in testimony of numerous refugees, there does not seem to have been an extensive police network in the Chinese army. Furthermore, for the majority of the 1950-71 period the PLA directly subsumed Chinese secret police troops under its own control.

The role of the commissars differed in the two armies. In Russia, given the unreliability of the officer corps (and especially the *voenspets*, the commissars were used as an openly coercive force which could countermand the orders of the officers and even arrest them during the civil war. In the interwar period the role of the commissars (who ultimately numbered 34,000 by 1939) oscillated between sharing command functions with officers and being clearly subordinated to them.[36] In China, given the nearly universal party membership of the officers during the civil war, the commissars possessed more of an educative function than a coercive one in the two decades after the civil wars.

Both armies made use of psychological coercion of the soldiers and officers isolated in the barracks. However, the thin party stratum and lack of mass peasant support made this an unreliable instrument in the Soviet Union. By contrast, the lengthy gestation period, large party stratum, and strong peasant support of the revolution enabled the Chinese army to provide leadership at the crucial primary unit level. A study by Kirkpatrick and Uliassi found that the PLA had created an "effective" method of motivating even passive officers and men through an intricate network of psychological pressures.[37]

Finally, a key method of coercive control was the massive renewal (and expansion) of the officer corps. Given the highly unsatisfactory state of the officer corps at the end of the civil war, the Russian party proceeded to purge and demobilize thoroughly the bulk of army officers during the 1920s. The officer corps was reduced from 130,000 commanders in 1921 to 48,000 commanders in 1928.[38] The first to be ousted were the 14,400 voenspets who had served in the White armies before joining the Red Army. The ongoing dismissal of voenspets reduced their numbers from 35 percent of all officers in 1921 to only 10.6 percent of the officer corps in 1930.[39] Although men of proletarian and peasant origins were poorly educated and often poorly equipped for military command, the party consistently promoted such reliable men to key positions.[40] As Table 14 shows, men of working-class origin were 12 percent of all officers in 1921, 29.4 percent of all officers in 1929, and a striking 46 percent in 1934. Overall, during the 1925-37 period 135,000 men graduated from military schools and 13,000 men graduated from military academies.[41] As Table 15 shows, the proportion of officers who belonged to the party also rose significantly. While 41 percent of regimental commanders and 45 percent of divisional commanders belonged to the party in 1924, 78 percent and 93 percent respectively did so by 1937. Thus, by the middle 1930s a new officer corps had emerged in the Soviet Union.

Table 14   Social Origins of Red Army Commanders 1921-34

Year	Working Class	Peasantry	Other
1921	12.0%	67.0%	21.0%
1923	13.6%	52.7%	33.7%
1924	—	—	25.0%
1925	12.3%	56.0%	23.7%
1926	16.0%	57.2%	26.8%
1927[1]	22.4%	56.0%	21.6%
1928	28.0%	50.0%	22.0%
1929	29.4%	—	—
1930	31.2%	—	—
1932	40.0%	—	—
1933	42.3%	—	—
1934	46.0%	—	—

Sources: V. I. Lenin i sovetskie vooruzhennye sily, pp. 288, 290; K. E. Voroshilov, *Stat'i i rechi*, pp. 153, 230, 445, 521, 613; *KPSS i stroitel'stvo vooruzhennykh sily SSSR (1918-June, 1941)*, p. 274; D. A. Voropaev and A. M. Iovlev, *Bor'ba KPSS za sozdanie voennykh kadrov*, pp. 89, 106, 145; A. S. Bubnov et. al., *Grazhdanskaya voina 1918-1921*, v. 2, pp. 105, 109; I. B. Berkhin, *Voennaya reforma v SSSR (1924-1925)*, p. 262; *Russian Review* 3, no. 13 (July 1925): 275; J. Stalin et. al., *From the First to the Second Five Year Plan*, p. 360; Malcolm Mackintosh, *Juggernaut*, p. 76.

[1] Yuri Petrov has given somewhat different figures for 1927. He has quoted figures of 18.1 percent for the working class, 71.3 percent for the peasantry, and 10.6 percent for other. See Yuri Petrov, *Partiinoe stroitel'stvo v sovetskoi armii i flote (1918-1961)*, p. 244.

By contrast, no such renewal occurred in China. The top military leaders at the end of the civil war period still occupied key military posts throughout the 1960s. This reflected the effectiveness and legitimacy of the army both during the civil war and in such actions as the Korean War and the Indian incursion.

Utilitarian measures also differed between the two armies. During the early and middle 1920s the spartan life of a Red Army officer included low pay, unheated barracks, and no personal servants, officers' mess, or officers' club. In the 1926-39 period these utilitarian aspects became important, and the officer corps was transformed into an elite and privileged element in Soviet society. Officers were given villas, personal discount stores, separate officers' messes and clubs, theaters, and even a sanitorium at Sochi. In 1935 personal ranks and titles were introduced. The officer corps became one of the best paid groups in society. Thus, all of these measures promoted identification with the Soviet system. On the other hand, there was far less emphasis on such aspects in the Chinese army. Ranks and titles, introduced in 1955, were abolished again in 1965.

The Chinese army relied far more heavily on normative measures than the Russian army. The fusion of army and party during the civil war and the long party membership of top army officers allowed considerable reliance on normative appeals and the close friendships of top army and party officials. The lack of such conditions in Russia retarded the use of such appeals and ties. Both armies made extensive use of the political indoctrination of recruits.

Table 15   Communist Party Membership Among Higher Red Army Commanders During the 1924-37 Period

Year	Regimental Commanders	Divisional Commanders	Corps Commanders
1924	41%	45%	85%
1926	51%	55%	85%
1933	88%	93%	100%
1934	—	90%	100%
1935	72%	90%	100%
1937	78%	93%	96%

Sources: Yuri Petrov, Partiinoe stroitel'stvo v sovetskoi armii i flote (1918-1961), p. 180; K. E. Voroshilov, Stat'i i rechi, pp. 153, 374; N. F. Kuz'min, Krushenie poslednovo pokhoda a antanty, p. 185; Michel Berchin and Eliahu Ben-Horin, The Red Army, p. 55; Istoriya velikoi otechestvennoi voiny sovetskogo soyuza, v. 1, p. 95.

A final traditional means of garnering army support has been through the supply of new modern weaponry to the military. During the 1920s this was an insignificant factor in Russia given the low state of military expenditures and the pitifully low level of military technology. Lacking native-designed tanks and airplanes and possessing a mere 2.6 horsepower/soldier in 1929, the Red Army "was much weaker than the army of the strongest imperialist powers."[42] The massive industrialization of the 1930s, however, created a completely new Red Army which by the end of the 1930s received thousands of new tanks and airplanes each year. As Table 16 shows, military expenditures skyrocketed from 1.6 billion rubles in 1929 to 34 billion rubles in 1938 and a phenomenal 56.7 billion rubles in 1940. The army leaders were very appreciative. At each of the three party congresses in the 1930s they praised Stalin and echoed War Commissar Voroshilov's words at the Eighteenth Party Congress in 1939 that "The Red Army was and is the special object of care . . . personally of Stalin."[43]

The Chinese army underwent no such transformation in its two decades after the civil war. During the 1954-58 period of emulation of the Soviet model and receipt of Soviet aid, the PLA did undergo considerable technological improvement. However, after the withdrawal of Soviet military aid by 1960, the PLA, given low military appropriations, fell further behind in the development of military technology. Only in the area of nuclear weapons was considerable progress made. Overall, by the early 1970s the PLA functioned at the technological level of the late 1950s.

ISSUES AND CONFLICTS

The formative revolutionary period had a significant impact on the kinds of issues and conflicts which arose in the post-revolutionary period and on the mechanisms of conflict resolution and adjustment. As Whitson has cogently observed, the Chinese as early as 1937 had begun to evolve a stable system of regionally based field armies. The particularistic loyalty of commanders to their field army, especially in times of crisis as even Parish concedes, has been significant in the two decades after the end of the civil war.[44] By contrast, no such regional loyalty emerged in the Soviet army in the 1921-40 period.

Table 16   Military Expenditures and Manpower of the Red
Army 1923-40[1]

Year	Military Expenditures (billions of rubles)	Manpower (millions of men)
1923[2]	.4	.6
1926	.6	.6
1929	1.6	.6
1934	5.0	.9
1936	14.8	1.3
1938	34.0	1.5
1940	56.7	3.0

Sources: Politicheskoe Upravlenie RKKA, 1918-1928 let krasnoi armii—albom dia-
gram, p. 14; I. B. Berkhin, Voennaya reforma v SSSR (1924-1925), p. 450; K. N.
Plotnikov, Biudzhet sovetskogo gosudarstva, pp. 71, 79; 50 let vooryzhennykh sil
SSSR, p. 198; A. G. Zverev, O gosudarstvennom biudzhete SSSR na 1945, p. 7; F. S.
Tyusin, Bor'ba kommunisticheskoi partii za ukreplenie voennogo mogushestva
SSSR, p. 59.

[1] Due to inflation in the 1923-40 period, the growth in real military expenditures was
actually somewhat less in real terms than that indicated by Table 6.
[2] The table begins with 1923 as it marked the first year after the full demobilization of
the Red Army at the end of the civil war.

Indeed, as we have seen, the relative weakness of the Red Army
precluded the creation of an effective field army system in the civil
war. The few effective commanders and their army units were
rushed from one front to another as the military situation dictated.

Instead of revolving around field armies, key Soviet army loyalties
revolved around three groups in the 1921-40 period—the Stalinist
clique, the loose Tukhachevsky faction, and the group of apolitical
officers under Shaposhnikov. These divisions reflected two salient
facts: the rise of Stalin and the nature of the civil war. Mao had helped
to create the Chinese Red Army in 1927 and had been a paramount
political and military leader for over two decades by his ascension to
power in 1949. All field armies and top military commanders
acknowledged his authority. The last openly anti-Maoist political and
military leaders (such as Chang Kuo-tao) had been purged by 1938.
On the other hand, Stalin's situation was vastly different. Even by the

end of the civil war, he was only one of the lesser members of the Politburo, eclipsed by Lenin, Trotsky, and Zinoviev. His military role had been minimal compared to that of War Commissar Trotsky or a large number of top commanders (and even a few commissars). Thus, his authority was suspect in the army. Since the army acknowledged party control over itself, it led to a strong role for the small Stalinist clique (including Voroshilov, Budenny, Shchadenko) that had been associated with him at Tsaritsyn in the civil war. A considerably larger group of talented officers were grouped around future Marshal Tukhachevsky. While supporting Stalinist measures which favored the military, this group did not rule out (as in 1936) the possibility of opposing Stalin. The conflict between the Stalinist and Tukhachevsky factions was reinforced by sharply divergent views over the nature of modern warfare. Finally, the existence of a large apolitical element, absent in the Chinese case, testifies to the powerful role of the *voenspets* and nonparty commanders in the civil war and afterwards.

The differences between the Russian and Chinese civil wars can also help explain the prolonged salience of the "red" versus the "expert" argument in China and its relative absence in Russia. In China a relatively primitive, infantry army, based on substantial peasant support and often utilizing guerrilla tactics, had successfully smashed a stronger and technologically superior enemy. Given the stringent budgetary restraints of an underdeveloped China in the 1950-71 period, it was hardly surprising that a significant element of poorly trained Communist officers preferred to continue with the predominantly red orientation which had proven so successful in the rural, pre-modern civil war setting. Other military leaders, including those trained in the Soviet Union, such as Liu Po-cheng and younger, more professional officers, naturally preferred a more expert approach. This conflict also spilled over into the party.

By contrast, there was no significant red faction in the Soviet army. The Russian army had no great successful history as the Chinese army and lacked active support from the peasants. The army had been too weak to participate effectively in mass work. Undisciplined guerrilla activity had often been unsuccessful and even disastrous in the civil war. Both Lenin and Trotsky had often attacked *partizanshchina*. All agreed on the need to dissolve the army in 1921 and to reconstitute a regular, modern army, oriented toward defense of the country from powerful Western capitalist countries. The military and party leadership, although somewhat divided over the proper tactics of modern warfare, were united in their support for the massive technological transformation of the Red Army in the 1930s. The new officer corps was highly supportive of this vast expansion of the capabilities of the army in the 1930s. Thus, the civil war legacy combined with societal transformation and political changes to affect the nature of issues and cleavages in the Russian and Chinese armies.

NOTES

1. *Eighth National Congress of the Communist Party of China* (Peking: Foreign Languages Press, 1956), v. 1-2. This role corresponded with the level of representation of the army on the Politburo and Central Committee.

2. *Ninth National Congress of the Communist Party of China*, Special Issue, *China Pictorial*, No. 7, 1969.

3. Many of the leaders of this faction, notably Budenny, Voroshilov, and Kulik, earned the dubious sobriquet of "Horse Marshals" for their lack of comprehension of modern mechanized warfare. Men, such as Voroshilov and Budenny, preferred to live in the glorious past of the civil war and continued to stress the importance of cavalry and "mass blow." The First Cavalry Army was an important source of recruitment. As Budenny has written, "From the ranks of the Cavalry Army have come not a few prominent men . . . . Former cavalrymen K. E. Voroshilov, S. K. Timoshenko, A. A. Grechko, A. I. Yeremenko, K. A. Meretshov, K. S. Moskalenko became Marshals of the Soviet Union and P. F. Zhigarev, S. I. Bogdanov, P. S. Rybalko, Ya. N. Fedorenko, A. I. Leonov—Marshals of the army." See S. M. Budenny, *Proidenny put'* (Moscow: Voenizdat, 1973), v. 3, p. 397. Ruslanov has observed that the men of this faction were largely men of lower educational and cultural achievements who had served as Czarist NCOs in World War I. They tended to group themselves around Marshal Budenny. See P. Ruslanov, "Marshal Zhukov," *Russian Review* 15, no. 13 (July 1956): 192.

4. Considerable secondary evidence exists to show the existence of such a faction. However, the precise definition of the members of such a faction remains incomplete. Dubovoy's wife has related that Yakir, Tukahchevsky, and Uborevich "always maintained close personal contact and

working connections" and in 1936 worked out a common plan for military preparations. In presenting this plan, they criticized other military leaders (generally from the Stalinist faction) as "old men for alloting first place to cavalry and mass blow." Marshal Bagramyan has recalled that "International questions ... strongly occupied Yakir" and that Yakir, Tukhachevsky, Yegorov and Sedyakin shared common military views. See *Komandarm Yakir: Vospominaniya druzei i soratnikov* (Moscow: Voenizdat, 1963), pp. 8, 112-113. Babenko has described the close relationship of Yakir, Garkavy, Alkulov, and Blyukher and the friendship of Yakir with Tukhachevsky, Uborevich, Baranov, Kotovsky, and Gamarnik. See P. Babenko, *I. E. Yakir* (Moscow: Politizdat, 1964), p. 7. Ruslanov has described a Tukhachevsky-Yegorov faction based on young professional military men of the czarist army with military education and culture. See P. Ruslanov, "Marshal Zhukov." Erickson has described a Tukhachevsky-Gamarnik faction as the major basis of potential opposition to Stalin. See John Erickson, *The Soviet High Command, A Military-Political History, 1918-1941* (London: Macmillan, 1962), p. 465. The very lack of agreement on the exact nature of the leadership of the faction shows that the faction was a loose coalition of similarly thinking men rather than a tight personalized following around one charismatic leader. All eight generals shot in June 1937—Tukhachevsky, Gamarnik, Yakir, Kork, Uborevich, Feldman, Eideman, Primakov, and Putna—belonged to this group. In Stalin's mind they evidently formed the potential nucleus of opposition to his regime.

5. Yuri Petrov, *Stroitel'stvo politorganov, partiinikh i komsomolskikh organizatsii armii i flota (1918-1968)*, (Moscow: Voenizdat, 1964), p. 143. However, the overall opposition outside of Moscow was minimal. In the aftermath of the struggle against both Trotskyism and later the Right Opposition, only a miniscule .19 percent of all army Communists were purged compared to 1 percent of all civilian Communists. See D. A. Voropaev and A. M. Iovlev, *Bor'ba KPSS za sozdanie voennykh kadrov* (Moscow: Voenizdat, 1960), p. 109.

6. Yuri Petrov, *Partiinoe stroitel'stvo v sovetskoi armii i flote (1918-1968)*, (Moscow: Voenizdat, 1964), p. 162 and Yuri Petrov, *Stroitel'stvo politorganov, partiinikh i komsomolskikh organizatsii armii i flota (1918-1968)*, p. 162. In addition to Trotsky and Antonov-Ovseenko, Deputy War Commissar Lashevich and Commander of the Navy Zof were eventually ousted from their posts in 1926.

7. Isaac Deutscher, *The Prophet Unarmed* (New York: Random House, 1959), p. 350.

8. A. Neuberg, *Armed Insurrection* (London: NLB, 1970), p. 20. Erich Wollenberg, who wrote this section of the book, was in charge of the military bureau of the Marx-Engels Institute in Moscow in the late 1920s.

9. Erickson, *The Soviet High Command*, p. 426.

10. *Komandarm Yakir: vospominaniya druzei i soratnikov* (Moscow: Voenizdat, 1963), pp. 94, 109-111; P. Babenko, *I. E. Yakir* (Moscow: Politzdat, 1964), p. 75.

11. Walter Krivitsky, *In Stalin's Secret Service* (New York: Harper & Row, 1939), p. 222.

12. *Komandarm Yakir: vospominaniya druzei i soratnikov*, pp. 111-112. Stalin was dissatisfied with the actions of Yakir and Dubovoy and according to Voroshilov asserted "They are not in cooperation. The military men must be concerned with their own matters and not talk about that which does not concern them" (p. 112). Perhaps it was no accident that the three military commanders who wrested concessions from Stalin—Yakir, Dubovoy, and Blyukher—all were shot during the Great Purges.

13. Ting Wang has concluded that the army furnished an "overwhelming majority" of governmental cadres in this period. See William Whitson, ed., *The Military and Political Power in China in the 1970s* (New York: Praeger, 1972), pp. 125-126. John Gittings has found that 30 percent of forty-three key officers surveyed went into party and governmental work during this period. See his *The Role of the Chinese Army* (London: Oxford University Press, 1967), p. 273. Such men as Li Hsien-nien and Yu Ch'u Liu left the army to become ministers in the government. In providing cadres for the party and government, the army was fulfilling Mao's directive of February 1949 that "We have to rely chiefly on the army to supply our working cadres." See Mao Tse-tung, *Selected Works* (Peking: Foreign Languages Press, 1967), v. 4, p. 338.

14. Only in the north and northeast regions was rule relinquished to civilian party cadres immediately after liberation. See William Whitson, *The Chinese High Command* (New York: Praeger, 1973), p. 521. Future Marshals Yeh Chien-ying, Liu Po-cheng, and Ch'en Yi served respectively as chairmen of the Military Control Committees for Peking, Nanking, and Shanghai. See Gittings, *The Role of the Chinese Army*, p. 265.

15. By 1958 the PLA had 2.5 million men, a level equal to 50 percent of its peak manpower during the civil war. See Gittings, *The Role of the Chinese Army*, p. 305. By contrast, in the late 1920s the Red Army had 562,000 men, a level barely equal to 10 percent of its civil war peak.

16. Parris Chang has suggested that the Chinese army functioned as an interest group in this period. See Parris Chang, "The Changing Patterns of Military Participation in Chinese Politics," *Orbis* 16, no. 3 (Fall 1972): 794. However, such an interest group would be primarily concerned with translating its political power into actions protective of its own interests. Table 13 shows that the army, despite its increased representation on the Politburo, functioned in exactly the opposite manner. Furthermore, such a concept of

interest groups implies the existence of a network of interest groups which help form a political system. China, however, as an underdeveloped country, lacked more than a few significant institutions and groups at this time. Finally, the army, given its past fusion with the party and continued interpenetration with it (especially at the elite level) could hardly function only in terms of its own narrow institutional interests.

17. His military supporters included the chief of staff, Huang Kuo-cheng, the directors of the General Training Department, General Political Department, and General Logistics Department, Hsiao K'o, Tan Cheng, and Hung Shueh-chih, a vice minister of defense, Li Ta, and the commander of the Northeast Military Region, Teng Hua. His civilian supporters included Chang Wen-tien, the vice minister of foreign affairs, and Chou Hsiao-chou, first party secretary for Hunan Province. For useful sources, see David Charles, "The Dismissal of P'eng Teh-huai," *China Quarterly*, no. 8 (October/December 1961): 69, 73; *S.C.M.P.* no. 4004, August 18, 1967, p. 1; Union Research Institute, *The Case of P'eng Teh-huai, 1959-1968* (Kowloon, Hong Kong: 1968), p. 39; and Alice Hsieh, *Communist China's Strategy in the Nuclear Era* (Englewood Cliffs, N. J.: Prentice-Hall, 1962).

18. URI, *The Case of P'eng Teh-huai, 1959-1968*, pp. 10, 11, 40, 171. Indeed, one 1967 attack on Marshal P'eng Teh-huai quoted him as having stated that "If it [the Great Leap Forward] were allowed to continue, chickens, ducks and pigs would go extinct and seeds would have to be imported from foreign countries" (p. 172). He scored the backyard steel program with its unrealistically high targets and a "habit of exaggeration" "which has done tremendous harm to the prestige of the Party" (pp. 11-12). A Cultural Revolution article alleged that he had called Mao's works "outdated and worthless" and queried "Aren't we studying them like we study the three character sentence in a children's classic book?" (p. 171).

19. URI, *The Case of P'eng Teh-huai, 1959-1968*, p. 421 (July 23, 1959 speech). During the Cultural Revolution various articles charged that P'eng was a "time bomb that had been planted in the Party and army," that he was "preparing a counterrevolutionary coup d'etat," and that "P'eng Teh-huai and company . . . were extremely dangerous" (pp. 130, 176-177, 142).

20. In addition to the principal figures of Defense Minister P'eng Teh-huai and Chief of Staff Huang K'o-cheng, only three other men—Tan Cheng, Chang Wen-t'ien, and Chou Hsiao-chu—were clearly purged from their posts in connection with this affair. Two other vice ministers of defense—Li Ta and Hsiao K'o—were transferred to important nonmilitary positions. Thus, only five (or seven) men were directly affected by the purge. Furthermore, in sharp contrast to the Kao Kang-Jao Shu-shih affair, all of the purged men were allowed to retain their party membership. Indeed, following a

Central Committee resolution to treat the purged with "great sincerity and warmth," they were even allowed to retain their Politburo and Central Committee seats. This action contrasted sharply with the harshness of treatment customary for purged men in the Soviet Union. For sources, see Charles, "The Dismissal of Marshal P'eng Teh-huai," pp. 69, 71; URI, *The Case of P'eng Teh-huai, 1959-1968*, p. 44; Hsieh, *Communist China's Strategy in the Nuclear Era*, p. 174; and Jurgen Domes, *The Internal Politics of China* (New York: Praeger, 1973), p. 112.

21. As early as March 1967, nearly every province, large municipality, and autonomous region was being run by a Military Control Committee, which assumed civilian administrative functions formerly performed by the party and government. These committees, already functioning at that time in twenty-three of twenty-nine administrative areas, served much the same function of representing temporary military rule until a satisfactory civilian political administration could be established as they had in the 1950-54 era. The mere fact that such a powerful institution could be resurrected thirteen years after the establishment of civilian rule in 1954 testified to the striking degree of continuity in Chinese politics.

22. Jurgen Domes, "Party Politics and the Cultural Revolution," in *Communist China 1949-1969: A Twenty Year Appraisal*, eds. Frank Trager and William Henderson (New York: New York University Press, 1970), p. 90. The exact figures are that 75.9 percent (22 of 29) of the chairmen, 49 percent 234 of 479) of the members of the standing committees and 45.7 percent (100 of 219) of the chairmen and vice chairmen of the Revolutionary Committees were army men.

23. *S.C.M.P.*, no. 4474, August 13, 1969, p. 11. Defense Minister Lin Piao at the Ninth Party Congress in 1969 declared that "The People's Liberation Army is the mighty pillar of the dictatorship of the proletariat. Chairman Mao has pointed out many times: 'From the Marxist point of view the main component of the state is the army'." See *Peking Review*, no. 18, April 30, 1969, p. 25.

24. While Lin Piao evidently characterized the struggle between his faction and its opponents as a "life and death struggle," Radio Lanchow on September 19, 1972, called it "the most serious and fierce line struggle" in the history of the party. See *Issues and Studies*, May 1972, p. 81 and *F.B.I.S.*, September 19, 1972, p. H1.

25. Defense Minister Lin Piao placed considerable emphasis on rebuilding and strengthening the party organization in the army. By 1961 party branches existed in all companies while 80 percent of all platoons and even 50 percent of all army squads had party cells. See J. Chester Cheng, ed., *The Politics of the Chinese Red Army: A Translation of the Bulletin of Activities of the People's Liberation Army* (Stanford; Hoover Institution, 1966), p. 595.

26. *KPSS i stroitel'stvo vooruzhennykh sily SSR (1918-Juin, 1941)* (Moscow: Voenizdat, 1963), p. 194; KPSS, SVII S'ezd, 26 Yanvarya-10 Fevralya, 1934, *Stenograficheskii otchet*, p. 232; Yuri Petrov, *Partiinoe stroitel'stvo v sovetskoi armii i flota (1918-1968)*, p. 226. Indeed, Yaroslavsky in 1929 wrote that "The examination of the Red Army and Fleet has demonstrated that here we have cells of the best composition.... From the Trotsky and Sapronov slander on the Red Army already a very long time ago nothing has remained...." See *Bolshevik* no. 20 (1929): 17.

27. Yuri Petrov, *Partiinoe stroitel'stvo v sovetskoi armii i flote* (1918-1961), pp. 239, 244, and *KPSS i stroitel'stvo vooruzhennykh sily SSSR (1918-Juin, 1941)*, p. 240.

28. For an extended treatment of the subject, see Robert Conquest, *The Great Terror* (New York: Macmillan, 1968). While Erickson has estimated that a minimum of 15,000 officers (from a total of 75,000 officers) were purged, Conquest and Krivitsky have placed the number as high as possibly 35,000 officers. See Erickson, *The Soviet High Command*, p. 406; Conquest, *The Great Terror*, p. 485; and Krivitsky, *In Stalin's Secret Service*, p. 232.

29. Marshals, such as Tukhachevsky and Blyukher, were "legendary figures" in the Soviet Union. Marshal Tukhachevsky, in particular, was "tremendously popular." See Erickson, *The Soviet High Command*, p. 401, and Alexander Weissberg, *The Accused*, trans. Edward Fitzgerald (New York: Simon and Schuster, 1951), p. 436. Most top military commanders were heroes of the civil war and did not owe their positions to Stalin. Furthermore, their role in the civil war had often been more visible than that of Stalin. What Azrael has written about the managers could be applied with even more force to the military leaders, "For all that they had surrendered to the general secretary, the red directors had not surrendered the right to be consulted on major policy questions, or the right to engage in a certain amount of meaningful criticism or the right to independent status as makers of history and custodians and interpreters of doctrine. And even if he could have abrogated these rights without provoking the managers to open opposition, Stalin could not reasonably assume that they would feel no sense of loss or abandon all hope of reclaiming what they took to be their due ... few of them were so completely lacking in self-respect and a sense of personal worth that they could be expected to accept the status of politically emasculated state serfs without some defiance of protest." See Jeremy Azrael, *Managerial Power and Soviet Politics* (Cambridge: Harvard University Press, 1966), p. 101.

30. URI, *The Case of P'eng Teh-huai*, p. 44.

31. Philip Bridgham, "The Fall of Lin Piao," *China Quarterly*, no. 55 (July/September 1973): 442-443.

32. The army remained, however, an important political actor, especially inasmuch as elements within it (regional military commanders and some central military leaders) were instrumental in securing the downfall of Lin Piao. Furthermore, the appointment of the seventy-six year old Marshal Yeh Chien-ying as Defense Minister in 1975 demonstrated the grave difficulties in resolving army/party tensions.

33. Zbigniew Brzezinski, ed., *Political Controls in the Soviet Army* (Ann Arbor: Edwards Brothers, 1954). As he further asserted, this "institutionalization of an all pervading atmosphere of terror," by creating a competition to prove loyalty to the regime, became "an important factor in the development of political loyalty to the regime" (p. 85).

34. These troops performed internal security and border defense duties. Their exact numbers are unknown but Wollenberg has suggested (and others have agreed) that they numbered 250,000 men while Keefe had suggested that in the early 1930s they numbered 750,000 men. See Erich Wollenberg, *The Red Army*, trans. Claud W. Sykes (London: Secker and Warburg, 1959), p. 213; Michel Garder, *A History of the Red Army* (London: Pall Mall Press, 1966), p. 79; D. Fedotoff White, *The Growth of the Red Army* (Princeton: Princeton University Press, 1944), pp. 197-198; and Erickson, *The Soviet High Command*, pp. 376, 390-391. For the latter figure, see Eugene Keefe et. al., *Area Handbook for the Soviet Union* (Washington, D.C.: Government Printing Office, 1971), pp. 143, 583.

35. Handpicked by secret police representatives who sat on all recruiting commissions, these troops were the best available men from a mental and physical viewpoint. Receiving higher pay, better rations, and better equipment than the regular army troops, they were organized into divisions and regiments replete with armor and airplanes. See Wollenberg, *The Red Army*, p. 213, and Malcolm Mackintosh, *Juggernaut* (New York: Macmillan, 1967), p. 86. The combination of large numbers of elite secret police troops and their networks within the army made them a very powerful force in the Soviet Union in the 1930s. One might hypothesize that the tremendous growth in the power and size of the secret police was rooted both in the legacy of the civil war (from which it emerged as an effective and legitimate organization) and from the needs of a revolutionary transformation from above.

36. They numbered 15,000 men in 1934 and 34,000 men in 1939. See KPSS XVIII S'ezd, 10-21 Marta, 1939, *Stenograficheskii otchet*, p. 200.

37. Thus, the elaborate use of such tools as indoctrination, self-criticism, mutual criticism, and surveillance within a well-structured primary group dominated by party cadres worked very well. See William Bradbury et al., *Mass Behavior in Battle and Captivity—The Communist Soldier in the Korean War* (Chicago: University of Chicago Press, 1967), p. 165.

38. Voropaev and Iovlev, Bor'ba KPSS za sozdanie voennykh kadrov, p. 106.

39. K. E. Voroshilov, Stat'i i rechi (Moscow: Politizdat, 1937), p. 445. While in 1921, 12,400 former White officers were demobilized, in 1924, 9,390 commanders and administrators were dismissed. Of those dismissed in 1924, 1,584 were ousted for having served in White armies, while 535 were dismissed for bad political qualities. See A. S. Bubnov et al., Grazhdanskaya voina 1918-1921 (Moscow: Gosizdat, 1930), v. 2, pp. 98, 102. A Soviet history describes the latter part of the 1920s, "In the 1926-1929 years the Party continued to purge the army of socially alien Trotskyite and other treasonous elements and in addition those unprepared and unable to resolve new tasks." See KPSS i stroitel'stvo vooruzhennykh sily SSSR (1918-June, 1941), p. 274.

40. While in 1928 a phenomenal 87 percent of those taken into military school had less than seven years of schooling, by 1932 the typical student sent by the party to military-technical school still had only seven years of education. As Soviet historians Voropaev and Iovlev have asserted, "The low level of general education, weak knowledge of mathematics, physics and chemistry created for the military cadres enormous difficulties in mastering complicated military technique." See Voropaev and Iovlev, Bor'ba KPSS za sozdanie voennykh kadrov, pp. 80, 129, 132.

41. 50 let vooruzhennykh sil SSSR (Moscow: Voenizdat, 1968), p. 213. During the 1929-41 period, 148,000 commanders, military engineers, and political workers graduated from military schools. See S. S. Lototsky et al., Sovetskaya armiya (Moscow: Voenizdat, 1970), p. 94. During the 1930s such future Marshals as Bagramyan, Fedorenko, Konev, Govorov, Malinovsky, Rotmistrov, Rybalko, Tolbukhin, and Yeremenko graduated from military academies.

42. Voropaev and Iovlev, Bor'ba KPSS za sozdanie voennykh kadrov, p. 121 and N. II Shatagin and I. P. Prusanov, Sovetskaya armiya—armiya novogo tipa (Moscow: Voenizdat, 1957), p. 109. In 1929 the Red Army possessed only 200 tanks and armored cars, a situation which War Commissar Voroshilov later claimed had "created enormous dangers for the defense of our country." See K. E. Voroshilov, Stat'i i rechi (Moscow: Partizdat, 1937), pp. 517, 569.

43. KPSS, XVIII S'ezd, 10-21 March, 1939, Stenograficheskii otchet, p. 203. Given the Great Purges which had just decimated the officer corps, there was a certain note of irony in Voroshilov's remarks. In general, though, the officer corps would have agreed with Marshal Meretskov who, in his autobiography, stated that in the 1930s "Every major task in industry and agriculture and in the field of Party, Government or social activity was tackled from the point of view of its impact on the Soviet Union's defense

capacity, the international situation, or the strength of the Red Army." *See* K. A. Meretskov, *Na sluzhbe narody: stranitsii vospominanii* (Moscow: Politizdat, 1968), p. 169.

44. William Parish, "Factions in Chinese Military Politics," *China Quarterly*, no. 56 (October-December 1973): 667-699.

chapter 5

RUSSIAN AND CHINESE ARMY/SOCIETY RELATIONS

Army/society relations in China and Russia in the two decades after the civil wars manifested several interesting features and raised certain questions. Why did the Russian army, unlike the Chinese army and many armies in developing countries, perform few societal functions outside the barracks? Why did the performance of such functions by the Chinese army show strong cyclical variations? And why did both armies strongly and successfully pursue societal tasks within the barracks?

SOCIETAL FUNCTIONS PERFORMED INSIDE THE BARRACKS

It is important to begin with the differentiation between societal functions performed inside the barracks ("school of communism," literacy, and skills) and societal functions performed outside the barracks (economic production, role model, and political leadership). Societal functions performed inside the barracks provided benefits for both army and society. They improved the quality of army manpower. They promoted party control of the army by increasing the size of the party stratum in the army and by politicizing nonparty soldiers. The army was one of the few relatively modern and cohesive institutions in an underdeveloped country which could provide a significant source of cadres to lead the revolutionary transformation of society, especially in the countryside. These functions of politicization and education of recruits, as Lucian Pye and Morris Janowitz have both stressed, are common to nearly all armies in developing countries—although to less intensive and explicit degree than in Communist countries.[1]

Furthermore, given the isolation of the Bolsheviks from the countryside, the party needed the army as a bridge to the countryside even more in Russia than in China. Bubnov asserted in 1925, "And when we say: face to the village, that slogan has for us permanent significance because through the army we most easily have turned to the village."[2] The continued weakness of the Red Army would further reinforce the party's desire to emphasize societal functions within the barracks.

Furthermore, both armies had successfully performed such functions in the barracks during the civil wars. This gave further impetus to the use of the army for these functions in the two decades after the end of the civil wars. While Marshal Tukhachevsky in 1921 declared that "The barracks have been made into a school of revolution, a school of defense . . . a working school of communism," Mao Tsetung declared in 1949, "The army is a school. Our field armies of 2,100,000 are equivalent to several thousand universities and secondary schools."[3]

Both armies successfully prepared large numbers of Communists and Communist sympathizers from among army recruits during the civil war. In 1921 Gusev plausibly estimated that 200,000 men had joined the party after they had entered the army.[4] This meant that fully 40 percent of all army Communists in the civil war were recruited only after they had joined the army. Similarly, the People's Liberation Army evidently prepared at least 300,000 and perhaps over 500,000 new Communists from among the recruits during its civil war.[5]

Both armies also made considerable progress in reducing illiteracy and promoting skills. As Soviet historians have observed, the Red Army devoted "great attention" to these functions for "the liquidation of illiteracy was the most important task of the party-political apparat."[6] By July 1920 the army operated 3,625 schools for literacy, 10,029 libraries, and perhaps 2,000 clubs.[7] The Red Army reduced the rate of illiteracy from over 34 percent of all soldiers in 1918 to 8.2 percent in May 1921. In 1919 and 1920 alone the army claimed to have educated 160,000 illiterates.[8] While no corresponding data are available for the People's Liberation Army, the army evidently made significant efforts to foster literacy. By 1950 Chinese commissar T'ao Chu could echo the early Soviet statement by declaring that "In the army's military, political, and cultural training, cultural training is currently the most important."[9]

It was, therefore, hardly surprising that both armies consistently and successfully pursued societal tasks in the barracks in the two decades after the civil wars. The Russian Communist party endeavored to make the Red Army "a school of Socialism for millions of peasants and workers," or, in Stalin's phrase, "a party-political school."[10] The Chinese Communist party similarly strived to make the PLA "a Socialist University" and "a great school of revolution."[11] Both armies, in seeking to create as many party members as possible in their role as "schools of communism," could subscribe to Gusev's words of 1921, "In the barracks where peasant youth in the course of two years separation from the countryside will be gathered, there is the possibility . . . to broadly fulfill the task of transforming the peasant into a Communist . . . . It is possible to bring up to 20 percent as "factory-made Communists."[12]

In Russia during the 1920s the Red Army fulfilled Gusev's prediction as perhaps 18 percent to 20 percent of each army levy or roughly 50,000 men, joined the party.[13] This was of particular significance in the countryside. During the stormy process of revolutionary transformation in the early 1930s, the pace of creating new Communists accelerated. The army levy of 1930 grew from a 27 percent party stratum on its entry to a phenomenal 67 percent party stratum on its demobilization.[14] Party recruitment plummeted during the purges in the 1934-38 period.[15] Indeed, despite a 60 percent growth in the size of the army, army party ranks declined from 231,000 members in 1934 to 147,500 members in 1938; but, in the 1938-40 period, army party ranks, increasing by over 350,000 members, more than trebled.[16]

Similarly, the PLA, whose party membership fluctuated around 30 percent to 40 percent of the army, may have prepared as many as 2 million new party members in the 1950s.[17] Tryon has calculated that in the 1955-57 period more than 50 percent of the Communists in Liaoning Province and 60 percent of the Communists in Hunan Province were former soldiers.[18] In the late 1950s, however, party membership declined to the point where more than one-third of the army's companies lacked a party branch.[19] While very little data exist for the 1960s, the increased emphasis on army party organizations and increased army role in politics under Defense Minister Lin Piao undoubtedly led to an increase in the recruitment of new Communists. In 1965 alone "hundreds of thousands" of soldiers joined the party and Komsomol.[20]

Furthermore, by breaking down the narrow one-village outlook of peasant soldiers and training them for leadership roles based on achievement, the armies, as "schools of communism," provided party and non party soldiers with "a schooling of extraordinary importance." In Russia in 1925 a Central Committee plenum declared that "The Red Army has already become the most important school of preparedness of Soviet workers, especially for the countryside."[21] In 1928 War Commissar Voroshilov disclosed that a phenomenal 66.7 percent of the chairmen of rural soviets in the Russian Republic were former Red Army men.[22] During the 1930s the increasing number of demobilized soldiers became in the words of one Soviet history "a reliable support of the party in the socialist transformation of the country."[23] In 1933 Kaganovich observed that most good collective farm leaders and workers were ex-Red Army men, and later a 1938 Pravda editorial claimed that "The Red Army yearly returns to the Homeland hundreds of thousands of Party and non-Party Bolsheviks.[24]

The PLA similarly prepared large numbers of soldiers for leadership roles in the revolutionary transformation of society. Demobilized soldiers formed "an important force" in the collectivization campaign of 1955.[25] During the 1950s several hundred thousand collectively demobilized servicemen performed "outstanding and brilliant deeds" in spearheading production and construction work in frontier, coastal, and land reclamation areas.[26] During the Great Leap Forward in 1958 the former soldiers played a sufficiently "important" role that a Jen Min Jih Pao editorial even called them "the force to rely on in the socialist construction effort in our country."[27] Table 17 shows that in the 1956-58 period at least one-third of all demobilized servicemen (often at least one-half) served as basic-level cadres. In Kiangsu, Shantung, and Hupeh provinces, 54 percent, 40 percent, and 38 percent respectively of all demobilized

RUSSIAN AND CHINESE ARMY/SOCIETY RELATIONS

Table 17 Percent of Demobilized Servicemen Occupying Posts of Basic-Level Cadres in China

Percent	Area	Year
64	21 *hsien* (6 provinces)	1965
61	Chinghua *hsien*	1956
54	Kiangsu Province	1957
54	P'an *hsien* (county)	1963
40	Shantung Province	1954-56
38	Honan Province (22 hsien and cities)[1]	1956
38	Hupeh Province	1957
36	Hsingping *hsien*[1]	1957
35	Taian *hsien*	1957
33	Shantung Province	1957
33	Hopei *hsiang*	1958
10	Changehih *hsiang* (district)	1957

Sources: S.C.M.P., no. 1470, February 14, 1957, p. 5; no. 1471, February 15, 1957, p. 4; No. 1504, April 4, 1957, p. 13; no. 1588, August 12, 1957, pp. 13, 18; no. 1628, October 10, 1957, p. 34; no. 1653, November 18, 1957, p. 30; no. 1714, February 17, 1958, p. 22; no. 1786, June 6, 1958, p. 5; no. 3150, January 30, 1964, p. 6; F.B.I.S., *Daily Report-Far East,* January 16, 1957, p. BB3.

[1]These two items are not strictly comparable because for Honan Province the statistic included models and for Hsingping *hsien* the statistic included people's deputies to congresses. Furthermore, there is some overall problem of comparability inasmuch as the statistics represent units of widely varying populations (from provinces to *hsiangs*) and do not all correspond to the same time period.

soldiers served as basic-level cadres in the middle 1950s. Many "models" and "activists" arose from their ranks.[28] In Hupeh Province in 1958 no less than 30 percent of all ex-PLA men were "models" or advanced workers."[29] Numerous articles and speeches, in praising their "high degree of political consciousness" and "outstanding work style," have stressed their "hard core" role in the countryside.[30] Many speakers have echoed Vice Premier Tung Pi-wu's description of them as "a really valuable and positive force" in society.[31] Although data is much scarcer for the 1960s, it seems likely, given the prominent role of the PLA in politics, that the former soldiers continued to play "an important role in Chinese villages" and elsewhere.[32] In Shantung Province in 1963 no less than 30 percent of all rural basic-level cadres and 60 percent of such cadres in old revolutionary base areas were demobilized soldiers.[33]

While both armies played key roles as a "school of communism" in preparing party and nonparty leaders for the revolutionary transformation of society, they also fostered literacy among masses of often uneducated and poorly educated soldiers. While Stalin spoke of making the Red Army "not only an armed force" but also "a serious school . . . a school of literacy," Chinese commissar T'ao Chu spoke in 1950 of abolishing illiteracy and making "the raising of the army's cultural level the core of military training."[34] In fostering literacy, the army not only benefited society but aided its own programs of technical modernization and preparation of party and nonparty cadres. Janowitz has observed that "There can be no doubt that the military has a capacity for education in fundamental literacy.[35] This task was important given the fact that as many as 80 percent of PLA soldiers in the early 1950s were illiterate.[36]

Both armies, aided by societal campaigns against illiteracy, achieved success in liquidating illiteracy in their ranks. The Red Army claimed to have educated 361,900 illiterates in the 1921-27 period.[37] War Commissar Voroshilov later asserted that after 1924 no Red Army man had ever been demobilized as an illiterate.[38] While repeated PLA claims about the liquidation of illiteracy in the 1950s cast doubt on the exact nature of success in this area, there is little doubt of general Chinese achievements in this area.[39] By the end of the 1950s, the army sought to demobilize soldiers at the educational level of junior middle school.[40] This effort continued in the 1960s.

Finally, both armies stressed the development of skills consonant with the technical modernization of the army and general economic development. Lucian Pye has observed that "those who have been trained with it [the army] learn skills and habits of mind which would be of value in other industrial organizations."[41] While little data are available for either country, in Russia by the 1930s the Red Army demobilized yearly "tens of thousands" of skilled men.[42] During the 1950-57 period the Chinese army demobilized more than 600,000 trained soldiers (10 percent of the total); by 1960 demobilized soldiers were "mostly technicians with knowledge of a special skill."[43]

In short, isolated in barracks, subjected to military discipline, submerged in a pervasive community atmosphere for two or three years, the recruits were ideal subjects for the extensive political, cultural, and technical programs of the two armies. Table 18 shows that in the Red Army spending on culture and enlightenment rose from a modest 2.2 million rubles in 1924 to 72 million rubles in 1934 and 250 million rubles in 1939. The expenditure per capita rose from roughly 4 rubles in 1924 to 131 rubles in 1939. Table 19 reflects the "vast" work done in the army.[44] While in 1927 the Red Army had 36 Red Army houses (a building for cultural activities), 719 clubs, and 5,278 Lenin corners (specific rooms in Red Army Houses for cultural purposes), by 1939 it had 276 Red Army houses, 1,900 clubs, and 27,435 Lenin corners.[45] Political instruction, supplemented by literacy classes, continued two hours a day for two years in the Red Army.[46] Although War Commissar Voroshilov may have exaggerated somewhat in his 1928 claim that "The Red Army after the civil war became more similar to a political-enlightenment school for Red Army men than to a military organization," his statement reflected the extent to which the Red Army, as well as the PLA, successfully performed extensive societal functions within the barracks.[47]

Table 18   Red Army Expenditures on Culture and Enlightenment (1924-39)

Year	Rubles (millions)	Rubles/ Soldier
1924	2.2	4
1928	3.3	6
1930	8.3	14
1934	72.0	77
1939	250.0	131

Sources: Politicheskoe Upravlenie RKKA, *1918-1928 let krasnoi armii—albom diagram*, pp. 61, 63, 73; K. E. Voroshilov, *Stat'i i rechi*, p. 614; *Istoriya velikoi otechestvennoi voiny sovetskogo soyuza*, v. 1, p. 99; Sergei Kournakoff, *Russia's Fighting Forces*, p. 60.

Table 19   Red Army Cultural, Educational, and Political
Institutions (1923-39)

Year	Red Army Houses	Clubs	Lenin Corners
1923	4	894	—
1927	36	719	5,278
1931	97	855	8,930
1934	142	1,336	15,091
1939	276	1,900	27,435

Sources: Politicheskoe Upravlenie RKKA, *1918-1928 let krasnoi armii—albom diagram*, pp. 61, 63, 73; K. E. Voroshilov, *Stat'i i rechi*, p. 614; *Istoriya velikoi otechestvennoi voiny sovetskogo soyuza*, v. 1, p. 99; Sergei Kournakoff, *Russia's Fighting Forces*, p. 60.

SOCIETAL FUNCTIONS PERFORMED
OUTSIDE THE BARRACKS

Similarly, the extensive Chinese army role and minimal Russian army role in societal functions performed outside the barracks (economic production, role model, political leadership) in the two decades after the civil war had roots in the civil war periods. It is striking to note that near the end of the civil war, the Bolsheviks used the Red Army for economic production and role model; but, in both cases, the party was soon dissatisfied and discontinued the use of the army for these functions.

In 1920 the Red Army, utilizing four labor armies numbering by various estimates 159,000 to 400,000 men, became extensively involved in simple mass production tasks.[48] Despite continued calls for economic production into 1921, the labor armies were soon discontinued because of "meager results" and "negligible productivity."[49] The Ninth Congress of Soviets in 1921 adopted a resolution that "economic work of the Red Army . . . is not able to be developed on account of the needs of military instruction, education, and fighting capabilities of the army."[50]

Similarly, at the end of the civil war the Russian army was briefly used as a role model and then decisively rejected. Early in 1920 War Commissar Trotsky called for the militarization of labor, and Lenin declared that "What has been organized in the Red Army must also be created on all the fronts of labor."[51] At the same time the party's Central Committee called for the militarization of some industrial branches and declared that "The methods of the army (with all necessary changes) must be applied in the field of labor organization, with the direct utilization of the experience of those Party workers who will be transferred from military to economic work."[52]

However, by 1921, the end of the war communism (the official name for Soviet domestic policy during the civil war) and the advent of NEP made military methods seem regressive and irrelevant. Labor armies had failed. Features associated with a military model, such as discipline and compulsory labor, had proven counterproductive in the economy. The army was undergoing massive demobilization. The revolt of the Kornstadt sailors and general ineffectiveness of the army in crushing small peasant revolts in 1921 dealt a further blow to the use of the army as a model. It drew attention to the numerous negative features of the Red Army, such as dominance of the officer corps by *voenspets* and the ranks by passive and even hostile peasant soldiers, frequent treason, mass desertion, thin party stratum, and a general ineffectual nature. By January 1922, the same Lenin who less than two years earlier had strongly argued for the relevance of the army as a role model for economy and society, now declared that "military methods of operation are least of all applicable to the trade unions."[53] With the exception of the continued use of bourgeois specialists in governmental and economic work (which was patterned on the use of *voenspets* in the army), the army was specifically rejected as a model for society by the end of 1921.

Finally, the party did not use the army for political leadership during the civil war. The Russian army, plagued by numerous problems, was barely capable of performing its military tasks, let alone any civilian tasks.

The state of the Chinese army was sharply different from that of the Russian army at the end of the civil war. By contrast to the minimal and unsuccessful Russian army production effort, the Chinese army engaged in far more extensive and successful economic production by the end of the civil war. Responding to calls by the Common Program and Chairman Mao late in 1949 to "during peacetime systematically take part in agricultural and industrial production,"[54] the army in five of the six military regions claimed to have cultivated and reclaimed more than 500,000 acres of land in the first eight months of 1950. While in Russia less than 10 percent of all soldiers had engaged in economic production even at the peak of the effort, in China 40 percent to 60 percent of all soldiers were involved in ambitious economic projects. Although the advent of the Korean War forced the army to return to its primary military task, the PLA, unlike the Red Army, had become in the words of an official Chinese pamphlet, "an important factor in the effort to repair the ravages of war and lay the foundation for prosperity in the countryside." It further added that "The work of the PLA in production is a long-term affair."[55]

Similarly, in sharp contrast to the Red Army, the People's Liberation Army, especially in the 1949-52 period, performed extensive political leadership functions, particularly in newly liberated areas. The country was divided into six military regions, and although the civilian party elite in Peking maintained overall control, the military ruled the country at the provincial and local levels. This period of direct military rule in China demonstrated the legitimacy and effectiveness of the PLA and contrasted sharply with the lack of such a role for the Russian army.

Finally, the Chinese army was neither suggested nor rejected as a model for society by the end of the civil war. The Chinese Communist party, as it continued the same relatively moderate policies (which contrasted sharply with the radical war communism policies of the Russian Communist party) that led to a triumphant sweep of the army across China in 1948 and 1949, saw no need to utilize the army as a model for society. At the same time, by virtue of its demonstrated effectiveness, lengthy history of close association and even fusion with the party, and large party stratum, the PLA, in sharp contrast to the Red Army, remained a potential model for society.

A discussion of the state of army/society relations at the end of the civil wars would hardly be complete without at least a brief look at the sharply contrasting behavior of Russian and Chinese soldiers among civilians. The record of Red Army soldiers, even by the end of the civil war, was abysmal. Misbehavior by Red Army soldiers has been cited as a major cause of peasant revolts in 1920 and 1921. In January

1920 the troops in Rostov raped, murdered, and pillaged the local population. In the spring of 1920 Red Army soldiers in Daghestan were guilty of such "disorderly" behavior that the local population rose in a bloody revolt. Similarly, in May 1920, after crushing an Azerbaijani nationalist revolt, local Red Army units "looted and pillaged the city (Gandzha) for an entire week."[56] In the Polish campaign of 1920 the Red Army evidently engaged in barbaric pogroms and wreaked devastation in the countryside.

By contrast, the behavior of the Chinese soldiers towards the local population, especially in contrast with not only the poor behavior of the Russian soldiers but also that of the Kuomintang soldiers, was generally exemplary. The PLA basically followed "Three Main Rules of Discipline and Eight Points for Attention" which had been reissued in October 1947.[57] The strict discipline of the army included emphasis on never taking anything from the people, handing over all booty, and sleeping on sidewalks or standing in the rain to avoid intruding on people. Various Western observers and even PLA defectors have commented on the generally excellent behavior of Chinese soldiers toward the local population.[58] Thus, the positive behavior of the Chinese soldiers contrasted sharply with the frequently negative behavior of the Russian soldiers in society.

These sharp differences in the nature of the two armies and their performances of societal tasks by the end of the civil wars had profound implications for army/society relations in the post-civil war period. By the end of the civil wars, the 5 million man armies, possessing the instruments of violence and functioning as the only major integrated national organization besides the party, posed both a threat and an opportunity to the party. The high frequency of coups in developing countries would attest to the real threat which such large armies could pose any regime. Furthermore, in Communist developing countries, the army has always posed an especially serious potential threat to the claim of the party to a hegemony of power. In Russia, the army, alien from the party, dominated by *voenspets* and incapable of suppressing small revolts by itself, was weak and ineffectual. At times, as during the Kronstadt revolt and repeated mass desertions to enemies during campaigns to suppress troublesome revolts, the army actually posed a direct threat to the party. Furthermore, the potential threat posed by the army was magnified by the fact that its size (4.1 million soldiers in 1921) dwarfed that of the party (.6 million members).[59] Only through a massive demobilization of the army and renewal of the officer corps could a new, more reliable and effective force, one less of a drain on the economy, be created. During the interim period, protracted due to economic weakness and a poor industrial base, the army would not be able to perform any significant nonmilitary functions. Furthermore, its very poor record of performing such functions outside of the barracks in the civil war would reinforce the tendency to isolate the army within the barracks.

During the 1921-40 period, the party relied on independent secret police troops, commissars, and a secret police network within the army to control it. During the 1920s, the extreme weakness of the army, a legacy of the civil war era, precluded any major diversion of military effort to societal activities outside the barracks. A 1925 German military report dismissed the Red Army as a force of little consequence; as late as 1929 the Red Army was considered at best able to contain a Polish attack.[60] Furthermore, in the 1928-40 period, the Stalinist faction launched a massive campaign of revolutionary transformation of society from above (with profound roots in the civil war era) which entailed extensive violence directed against elements, such as peasants, heavily represented in the army. This fact, combined with the hostility of many elements in society, reinforced the desire of the party to insulate the army from the often unfriendly society, especially in the countryside. Furthermore, the great bulk of the commanders of the Red Army, while loyal to Stalin in most instances, were not members of the Stalinist clique (Budenny, Voroshilov, Shchadenko) in the army. During the 1930s the army, as all other institutions in society, was greatly expanded and modernized, isolated from society, and controlled by party and secret police elements. Peasant revolts, arising from collectivization and the elimination of kulaks as a class, were crushed mainly by expanded secret police units rather than by the army. The rising threat from German fascism and Japanese militarism was a final deterrent to any diversion of the efforts of the rapidly modernizing but still weak Red Army to any nonmilitary tasks.

It is in this context that we can best understand the relatively rigid mold of army/society relations in Russia in the 1921-40 period. Throughout the period the army, for political, economic, and military reasons, was excluded from performing any significant functions for society outside the barracks, largely by the dominant Stalinist faction. At the same time, those functions performed by the army within the barracks were generally not subjected to any sharp patterns of cyclical change but tended to be relatively constant features of army life.

This minimal use of the Red Army for societal functions outside the barracks was particularly striking as applied to economic production and role model. The economic production function is common to many armies in developing countries. The discipline, cohesion, and relative modernity of such armies have facilitated the use of the army for such tasks. Janowitz has written that army production projects "can be found throughout most new nations but, with some notable exception their importance is more symbolic than economic . . . the military seems to be used as a cutting instrument to undertake new, unconventional and dramatic projects rather than development in depth."[61]

However, despite the high frequency of the use of armies in developing countries for economic functions, exceptional emphasis placed on development of the Soviet Union, and severe economic and budget constraints, the Red Army refrained from almost any economic production in the 1921-40 period, except in the Far East. There, impelled by the growing Japanese threat in the 1930s, the Russians were forced to create a large army. A small indigenous population, very poor local production, and the enormous distance from European Russia hindered the development of the Special Red Banner Far Eastern Army under future Marshal Blyukher. The army created a special "Kolkhoz Corps" of perhaps 100,000 reservists and trained soldiers organized in divisional and regimental formations. Settled in collective farms along the lengthy and vulnerable Manchurian border, the soldiers worked as farmers on the kolkhozes (collective farms). Their produce helped feed the regular army troops and augmented the reserve supplies of the army. The soldiers engaged in part-time military training and were subjected to mobilization at any time.[62] This system provided needed production for the army and ensured the presence of 100,000 well-trained reservists in a remote and important part of the Soviet Union.

The major economic contribution of the army to society was, characteristically, a negative one. The multimillion man Red Army had been a major drain on economic resources by the end of the civil war.[63] Given the lengthy borders and continued hostility of powerful Western states during the 1920s, many military leaders, such as War Commissar Frunze, saw a 1.5 to 2 million man cadre army as an ideal size for the Red Army after the end of the civil war.[64] However, Berkhin has written,

But, the Soviet state was not then able to support such a big army . . . . The support of such an army would have placed an impossible burden on the state budget, on the shoulders of the workers of the country, would have blocked the cause of reconstruction of the national economy, taken many hundreds of thousands of people away from productive labor and so on. All this forced the Soviet government to reduce in 1924 the numbers of its own cadre armed forces to 600,000.[65]

In contrast to the Chinese army which remained at a level of 45 percent of peak manpower of the civil war era in the 1950s, the Russian army was reduced in the early 1920s to a level of only 10 percent of peak manpower in the civil war period. The 562,000 man cadre element in the Red Army permitted the army to function at a low level of budgetary expenditures. During the 1923-27 period the army received a scant 12.7 percent to 17 percent of the state budget.[66] The territorial cadre system, which minimized the army's impact on society by calling up peasant territorial soldiers for training in months they could be spared most easily, was abandoned only in 1938 in face of imminent war. Shatagin and Prusanov wrote about the territorial cadre system: "Such a system promoted, on one hand, the embracing of military preparation of the entire contingent of the drafted age group and did not take away men from productive labor and gave the possibility for the Soviet state to reduce expenditures on military needs."[67] Thus, the Red Army contribution to the economy, in lieu of any significant economic production, was the negative one of not imposing a great burden on extremely limited resources.

The situation was even less positive with regard to the two other major societal functions performed outside the barracks—political leadership and role model. Despite its glorification and even lionization in the 1930s, the Red Army played no political leadership role in society. As it had been the passive beneficiary of the massive industrial transformation of the 1930s, so too was the army the passive object of the Great Purges which decimated it in the late 1930s.

A similar pattern prevailed with the role model function. As we have seen, the Red Army had been briefly considered as a role model in the 1920-21 period and then had been rejected. In the 1920s the many negative features of the Red Army—technical primitiveness, poor battlefield capabilities, questionable reliability, continuing dominance in theoretical matters by *voenspets*, fluctuating command structure, poor grasp of military knowledge, and general apolitical stance—made it unsuitable as a societal model. Even in the 1930s, despite the great improvement in the state of the Red Army and the great militarization of Russian society, the army was not used as a role model. The political costs still outweighed any possible benefits. However, there did develop in the 1930s a "cult of the army" in Soviet society. Parallel to the growing external military menace and internal militarization of society, there arose a glorification of the army. This was expressed in numerous parades and songs and a cult of the uniform. The officer corps became one of the elite and prestigious elements in Soviet society. Nevertheless, the army remained apart from society.

By contrast to the Red Army, the PLA emerged from the civil war as an effective and highly legitimated force. Unlike the Red Army, it had successfully performed extensive societal functions not only within the barracks but also outside the barracks. It had a long history of performing such functions. The intimate interwining of army and party, absence of any major problems of desertion or treason, and the complete lack of any army revolts all served to minimize concern about any army threat to the party. Given the great tasks of economic reconstruction, governmental consolidation, and socialist development that faced the parties in both underdeveloped countries at the end of the civil wars, a strong and effective army, as the PLA, represented a major asset.

Furthermore, another legacy of the civil war, the strong military capabilities of the Chinese army (albeit at a relatively low level of military technology) were repeatedly manifested in the 1950-71 periods. The Chinese army performed effectively in the Korean War, Indian incursion, and Sino-Soviet border clashes. Only in the 1958 Taiwan Straits crisis did the PLA—primarily the air force—demonstrate a low military capability. Furthermore, the PLA resolutely crushed internal disorders, whether in the early 1950s, in Tibet in 1959 or during the Cultural Revolution. Further, unlike the Red Army, the PLA directly subordinated Public Security Forces (secret police troops) under its command in the 1950-58 and 1967-71 period.

At the same time, the Chinese army engaged extensively in economic production during the 1950-71 period. The economic production activities of the PLA have manifested a cyclical tendency with peaks of intensity reached during the most difficult campaigns for a revolutionary transformation of society, e. g., the Great Leap Forward and the Cultural Revolution. The amount of economic production performed by the Chinese army has been largely a political issue. Such factors as the state of the campaign for revolutionary transformation of society, the struggle between reds and experts in the army and factions in the party, and the renewed level of external threat to China all combined to determine the level of army economic production. During the 1950-56 period, the Korean War (1950-53), the pursuit of the professional model of the Soviet army, and the relatively successful party efforts to transform society limited army production activities to a relatively minimal, symbolic level. In 1954 a *Jen Min Jih Pao* editorial called on the PLA to "aid local work in leisure time."[68] In 1956 army involvement in economic production activity was a paltry 4 million uncompensated work days, or less than 2 days a year for each soldier.[69] Most of the army production work consisted of large projects carried out by specialized units, such as the PLA Railway Corps and the PLA Sinkiang Production and Construction Corps.

When the party abandoned the Soviet model of development and launched the Great Leap Forward in the 1958-60 period, the party overrode the evidently vigorous opposition of military professionals to escalate sharply army production activity. Table 20 illustrates the dramatic changes. By engaging in 59 million days of production in

1958, 44 million days in 1959, and 46 million days in 1960, the army contributed an average of 18 to 24 days of uncompensated labor per soldier per year. By doing such work, and by shifting its efforts from sector to sector in response to party needs, the army aided the economy, contributed its visible approval and revolutionary legitimation to the Great Leap Forward, and signified its rejection of the Soviet model of a professional army apart from society.

Table 20   PLA Economic Production Activity (1956-64)

Year	Millions of Man Days	Days/ Soldier
1956	4.0	1.7
1957	20.0	8.7
1958	59.0	25.7
1959	44.0	19.2
1960	46.0	20.0
1961	22.8	9.9
1962	—	—
1963	8.0	3.5
1964	5.0[1]	2.2

Sources: S.C.M.P., no. 1619, September 27, 1957, p. 19; no. 1724, February 18, 1958, p. 11; no. 1937, January 20, 1959, p. 20; no. 2174, January 12, 1960, p. 13; no. 2430, February 2, 1961, p. 2; no. 2682, February 3, 1962, p. 16; no. 3153, February 4, 1964, p. 17; no. 3391, February 5, 1965, p. 7.

[1] The figure is for rural communes.

During the early 1960s, when economic retrenchment set in and the Great Leap Forward was partially abandoned, the role of the army in economic production declined drastically. As the table shows, while the army engaged in 46 million days of uncompensated labor in 1960, it engaged in only 22.8 million days in 1961 and a paltry 5 million days in 1964. In 1962 the army was asked to devote only "odd" moments to agriculture while in 1964 it allocated only "spare time" to production.[70] The sharp decline in production reflected the weakened state of the army which precluded diversion from militar tasks, the elevation of the Liuist faction to dominance in the party and the retreat from the Great Leap Forward which lessened the need for the army to demonstrate its support for the party.[71]

However, the revival of the power of the Maoist, faction led to the launching by 1966 of the Cultural Revolution, the next great campaign for the revolutionary transformation of society. The army responded to Mao's May 1966 directive which declared that "Each army unit should engage in one or two of the three fields of activity—agriculture, industry, and mass work.... In this way our army of several million will be able to play a very great role indeed."[72] In 1966 most army units achieved self-sufficiency in meats and vegatables, a level unattained since the major production effort of 1959.[73] In 1967 army production registered a sharp 50 percent increase in the harvest of grain and "great" increases in the output of vegatables, meat, and edible oil; and in 1968 army units produced a surplus of meat and vegetables.[74] In 1969 increasing army production reached an "all-time height," as self-sufficiency extended to such areas as salt, coal, and medicine.[75] In 1970 the campaign for army production reached its peak with a considerable (40 percent) increase in total food output over 1969, while in 1971 output rose only slightly (10 percent) over 1970.[76] Thus, output increased yearly during the 1966-71 period, which also coincided with the rising power of Defense Minister Lin Piao.

Economic production performed by the army served a multitude of economic, military, and political functions. Economically, it reduced the burden of the army on the state, increased the standard of living of the army, developed remote areas (such as Sinkiang), and overcame difficult obstacles in the path of economic development. Militarily, the economic production function permitted the stationing of large forces in remote strategic areas. Politically, it promoted a new labor and revolutionary consciousness in the army, identified the army with its revolutionary tradition, and committed it to the party's program of societal development.

Nevertheless, the costs of economic production in terms of military training, esprit de corps, enhanced political visibility of the army, and possibly questionable economic benefits precluded the use of the army for such activities in Russia and restricted intensive use of the army for such purposes in China to periods of difficult revolutionary campaigns to change society. The essentially political nature of army economic production was clearly demonstrated in the early 1960s. During this period of severe economic difficulties, the amount of economic production performed by the army sharply declined. The economic production function thereby reflected the state of the struggles within the army and party (e.g., Maoists v. Liuists), the perceived degree of external threat, and the state of the campaign for the revolutionary transformation of society.

A similar state prevailed with regard to the political leadership function. The PLA played a major role, especially in critical periods. Despite its heavy involvement in the Korean War, the PLA exercised broad governmental authority below the central level in the 1950-54 period. It played a leading role in land reform in the period. In those areas where the party was weak, the army acted as a party substitute. Marshal Nieh Jung-chen has written about the 1950-54 period, "In the newly liberated areas it [the army] has taken part in the glorious tasks of mobilizing the people for completion of democratic reforms, and to consolidate the people's democratic dictatorship."[77] Similarly, during the 1955 collectivization campaign, the army played a role, albeit a smaller one, in political leadership.[78] Evidently due to substantial military opposition (which later surfaced at the Lushan Plenum), the army had only a minor and corrective role in the aftermath of the Great Leap Forward.[79] In the early 1960s, in the partial retreat from the Great Leap Forward, the political role of the army remained at a low but conscious level. In this period the army maintained regular contacts with more than 450 communes, brigades, and production teams.[80]

During the Cultural Revolution, the army, as the principal Maoist power base under Lin Piao and as the only force with revolutionary legitimation capable of holding together a disintegrating society, greatly expanded its political leadership functions. It became the major organization discharging political leadership roles, including even party and government roles. By 1967 hundreds of thousands of PLA propaganda teams spread Mao's thought "to every corner of the country."[81] A 1968 Army Day editorial expounded on the role of the army, "To do propaganda among the masses, organize them, arm them and help them to establish revolutionary political power— this is Chairman Mao's consistent thinking on army building; these are the PLA's basic tasks and our army's glorious traditions since the period of the Chingkan Mountains."[82] During this period Defense Minister Lin Piao himself was Mao's declared heir apparent. Only with the reconstruction of the party and governmental institutions after the end of the Cultural Revolution and the subsequent demise of Lin Piao and his five army Politburo colleagues did the political leadership role of the PLA diminish greatly. In short, the PLA, in contrast to the Red Army, performed extensive political leadership roles in society, especially during periods of party weakness and campaigns for societal transformation. The intensity of the role depended on the capabilities of the party, the scope of the campaign, the extent of the difficulties encountered in the campaign, and internal policy disputes within the army and party.

The positive qualities of the PLA in the 1950-71 period—high degree of revolutionary legitimation, excellent battlefield performance, large party stratum, close ties with the party elite—made the Chinese army a logical candidate for the role of model for society. However, the concept of the army as role model had troublesome implications for army/party relations, for its use as role model suggested that the army was viewed as a repository of virtues, values, and traditions, a role customarily reserved for the party in Communist countries. This attitude implied that the PLA, unlike armies in most Communist countries, might not be considered a direct subordinate of the party. Rather it might be a junior partner or even a potential rival to the party.

The first use of the army as a role model, during the "Everyone a Soldier" campaign in the midst of the Great Leap Forward in 1958, was of uncertain benefit to the army. The campaign sought to transform 220 million people into an "ocean of soldiers" capable of conducting a people's war. A national conference in October 1958 declared that

when the whole nation was organized "army style" and did their work like military operations as well as living collectively, it would greatly strengthen the revolutionary will of the people and cultivate the Communist style of work among them. They would conquer nature and accelerate the socialist construction of the motherland with the same heroism as the whole PLA.[83]

However, the use of the army as a model may actually have diluted the political power of the military by shattering the army's monopoly on weapons and devaluing the need for a strong institution devoted to military needs.

In the early 1960s, after the extensive politicization conducted in the army by Defense Minister Lin Piao, it again became a possible model for the future revolutionary society. During 1963 there emerged a massive emulation campaign in honor of a single army hero, Lei Feng. In 1964 the party unfolded an extensive program of "Learning From the PLA," during which the political work system of the army became a model for emulation by civilian party, state, and economic departments.[84] In the period before the Cultural Revolution, Mao increasingly turned to the army both as a revolutionarily legitimated political ally and as a means for rejuvenating the party and other elements in society. The emulation of the PLA reached dizzying heights during the Cultural Revolution. One August 1966 editorial at the onset of the Cultural Revolution glowingly described the army as a model for society,

> To learn from the PLA is not an expedient measure but a plan for a century and ten centuries. It is a major question with a bearing on the unlimited promotion of the revolutionary spirit of the millions upon millions of cadres and workers, a major question bearing on whether the socialist enterprise will forever follow the socialist direction. For this reason learning from the PLA is not a matter for one or two years. Rather we must learn from it repeatedly, continuously, on a long-term basis, forever . . . . [85]

This campaign of setting forth the PLA as a model continued in a relatively intense manner throughout the 1966-67 period. A typical April 1967 editorial declared, "proletarian revolutionaries should positively and humbly learn from the PLA. . . . Salute to the great PLA! Learn from the great PLA!"[86] Furthermore, throughout the Cultural Revolution, and especially during its latter phases, the army produced a seemingly endless number of "heroes" for public emulation.[87] By the end of the Cultural Revolution, and particularly after the demise of Lin Piao and his army colleagues in 1971, the army frequently ceased to be put forth as a role model for society.

In summary, while the Red Army played no role as a model for society, the PLA played such a role during and immediately preceding the two most difficult campaigns for the revolutionary transformation of society—the Great Leap Forward and the Cultural Revolution. In so doing the army was viewed as a repository of revolutionary values. By serving as a role model, the army both aided the party in carrying out these campaigns by lending them its support and revolutionary legitimation and also reaped great symbolic prestige, especially relative to the party.

Thus, the legacy of the civil war era played an important role in determining the parameters of army/society relations in Russia and China in the two decades after the civil war.

NOTES

1. Lucian Pye, "Armies in the Process of Political Modernization," in *The Role of the Military in Underdeveloped Countries*, ed. John Johnson (Princeton: Princeton University Press, 1962), pp. 82-83; Morris Janowitz, *The Military in the Political Development of New Nations* (Chicago: University of Chicago Press, 1964), p. 81.

2. A.S. Bubnov, *O krasnoi armii* (Moscow: Voenizdat, 1958), p. 144.

3. M.N. Tukhachevsky, *Izbrannye proizvedeniya* (Moscow: Voenizdat, 1964), v. 1 (*1919-1927*), p. 95; Mao Tse-tung, *Selected Works*, (Peking: Foreign Languages Press, 1967), v. 4, p. 338.

4. S.I. Gusev, *Grazhdanskaya voina i krasnaya armiya* (Moscow: Voenizdat, 1958), pp. 142-143. Official Soviet sources have estimated that 260,000 Communists were sent to the front in the civil war while 500,000 Communists fought in the war. While a certain percentage of the remaining 240,000 Communists may have volunteered and gone off to fight, the great bulk, or perhaps 200,000 Communists, were probably prepared in the army. Many of them probably joined during the open enrollment during "Party Week" in October 1919. For the figures, see A.A. Grechko, *Vooruzhennye sily sovetskogo gosudarstva* (Moscow: Voenizdat, 1974), p. 345, and Yuri Petrov, *Partiinoe stroitel'stvo v sovetskoi armii i flote (1918-1961)* (Moscow: Voenizdat, 1964), p. 110.

5. As the PLA possessed .3 million Communists in 1945 and 1.2 million Communists in 1950, many, if not most, must have been prepared in the army. See Davis Bobrow, "*The Political and Economic Role of the Military in the Chinese Communist Movement*" (Ph. D. diss., MIT, 1962), p. 217.

6. *KPSS i stroitel'stvo vooruzhennykh sily SSSR (1918-June, 1941)* (Moscow-Voenizdat, 1959), p. 211; Yuri Petrov, *Stroitel'stvo politorganov, partiinikh i komsomolskikh organizatsii armii i flota (1918-1968) (Moscow: Voenizdat, 1971), p. 180.*

7. N. I. Shatagin and I. P. Prunsanov, *Sovetskaya armiya—armiya novogo tipa* (Moscow: Voenizdat, 1957), p. 60.

8. Politicheskoi Upravlenie RKKA, *1918-1928 let krasnoi armii—albom diagram* (Moscow: Voennyi vestinik, 1928), p. 60.

9. Ying-mao Kao, *The People's Liberation Army and China's Nation Building* (White Plains, N.Y.: International Arts and Sciences Press, 1972), p. 165.

10. *KPSS o vooruzhennykh silakh sovetskogo soyuza* (Moscow: Voenizdat, 1969), p. 304; K. E. Voroshilov, *Stat'i i rechi* (Moscow: Partizdat, 1937), p. 574.

11. *Survey of China Mainland Press,* no. 896, September 25, 1954, p. 15; *S.C.M.P.,* no. 3754, August 5, 1966, p. 2.

12. Gusev, *Grazhdanskaya voina i krasnaya armiya,* pp. 171-172.

13. The 1924 army levy entered with a 10 percent membership and graduated with a 28 percent party membership in 1926. The 1926 army levy entered with a 20 percent party membership and graduated with 40 percent in 1928. See Voroshilov, *Stat'i i rechi,* p. 574.

14. Ibid., p. 574.

15. Petrov, *Partiinoe stroitel'stvo v sovetskoi armii i flote (1918-1961),* p. 242.

16. *Istoriya velikoi otechestvennoi voiny sovetskogo soyuza* (Moscow: Voenizdat, 1960), v. 1, p. 98; Petrov, *Partiinoe stroitel'stvo v sovetskoi armii i flote (1918-1961),* pp. 242, 246, 321, 323.

17. Bobrow, "The Political and Economic Role," pp. 216, 714-716; Ying-mao Kau, *The People's Liberation Army and China's Nation Building,* p. 168.

18. Carol Tryon, "The Role of Demobilized Soldiers in the People's Republic of China," Columbia University East Asia Certificate Essay (New York, 1969), p. 42.

19. Union Research Institute, *Documents of the Chinese Communist Party Central Committee* (Kowloon, Hong Kong: 1968), v. 1, p. 385.

20. *S.C.M.P.,* no. 3700, May 18, 1966, p. 13.

21. *KPSS i stroitel'stvo vooruzhennykh sil SSSR (1918-June 1941),* p. 260.

22. Voroshilov, *Stat'i i rechi,* p. 171.

23. *Istoriya velikoi otechestvennoi voiny sovetskogo soyuza,* v. 1, p. 39.

24. J. Stalin et al., *From the First to the Second Five Year Plan*, (Moscow-Leningrad: Politizdat, 1933), p. 221; *Pravada*, February 16, 1938.

25. *S.C.M.P.*, no. 1166, November 8, 1955, p. 15.

26. *S.C.M.P.*, no. 2108, October 2, 1959, p. 10.

27. *S.C.M.P.*, no. 1823, July 31, 1958, p. 8; *S.C.M.P.*, no. 1786, June 6, 1958, p. 3.

28. *S.C.M.P.*, no. 1071, June 17, 1955, p. 13; *S.C.M.P.*, no.1794, June 18, 1958, p. 5.

29. *S.C.M.P.*, no. 1786, June 6, 1958, p. 3.

30. For a sample of such articles, see *S.C.M.P.*, no. 1713, February 14, 1958, p.28; *S.C.M.P.*, no. 1780, May 27, 1958, p. 11; and *S.C.M.P.*, no. 2108, October 2, 1959, p. 18.

31. *S.C.M.P.*, no. 2020, May 6, 1959, p. 3. Defense Minister P'eng Teh-huai lauded their "outstanding achievements" in 1956 while Interior Minister Hsieh Chueh-tsai praised them as "a strong force in our nation's socialist construction." See *S.C.M.P.*, no. 1420, November 29, 1956, p. 9, and F.B.I.S., *Daily Report—Far East*, January 2, 1957, p. BB4.

32. *S.C.M.P.*, no. 3511, August 5, 1966, p. 8.

33. *S.C.M.P.*, no. 2915, February 8, 1963, p. 10.

34. Voroshilov, *Stat'i i rechi*, p. 574; Robert Rigg, *Red China's Fighting Hordes* (Harrisburg, Pa.: Military Service Publishing Co., 1952), p. 147.

35. Janowitz, *The Military in the Political Development of New Nations*, p. 81.

36. Ying-mao Kao, *The People's Liberation Army and China's Nation Building*, p. 173.

37. Illiteracy was reduced from 8.2 percent of the army in May 1921 to 1 percent in October 1926. See Politicheskoe Upravlenie RKKA, *1918-1928 let krasnoi armii—albom diagram*, p. 60.

38. Voroshilov, *Stat'i i rechi*, pp. 574, 612.

39. In 1952, 1957, and 1958 the army claimed to have essentially "wiped out" illiteracy in its ranks. See *S.C.M.P.*, no. 404, August 28, 1952, p. 12; *S.C.M.P.*, no. 1234, February 24, 1956, p. 5; and *S.C.M.P.*, no. 1817, October 23, 1957, pp. 24-25.

40. *S.C.M.P.*, no. 2388, September 15, 1960, p. 1.

41. Pye, "Armies in the Process of Political Modernization," in *The Role of the Military in Underdeveloped Countries*, ed. Johnson p. 82.

42. *Istoriya velikoi otechestvennoi voiny sovetskogo soyuza*, v. 1, p. 99.

43. *S.C.M.P.*, no. 1828, August 8, 1958, p. 10; *S.C.M.P.*, no. 2219, March 18, 1960.

44. Erich Wollenberg, *The Red Army*, trans. Claud W. Sykes (London: Secker and Warburg, 1959), p. 181.

45. The Red Army Houses came replete with theaters, auditoriums, cinemas, lecture rooms, libraries, exhibit halls, and game rooms. The Lenin corners had books, magazines, radios, and political material.

46. Voroshilov, *Stat'i i rechi*, p. 170.

47. Ibid., p. 169.

48. A.S. Bubnov et al., *Grazhdanskaya voina 1918-1921* (Moscow: Gosizdat, 1930), v. 2, p. 89; V.S. Vladimirtsev, *Partiya-organizator razgroma kontrrevoliutsii na yuge* (Moscow: Voenizdat, 1971), pp. 213, 219.

49. *The Trotsky Papers* trans. Anya Bostock, 2 vols. (The Hague: Mouton, 1964, 1971), v. 2, p. 840; F.I. Dan, *Dva goda skitanii* (Berlin: 1922), p. 26.

50. I.B. Berkhin, *Voennaya reforma v SSSR (1924-1925)* (Moscow: Voenizdat, 1958), p. 44.

51. V.I. Lenin, *Collected Works* (Moscow: Politizdat, 1969), v. 30, p. 346.

52. Lev Trotsky, *Khozyaestvennoe stroitel'stvo sovetskoi respublikii* (Moscow: Gosizdat, 1927), pp. 107-114.

53. Lenin, *Collected Works*, v. 33, p. 193.

54. John Gittings, *The Role of the Chinese Army* (London: Oxford University Press, 1967), p. 31.

55. *The Chinese People's Liberation Army* (Peking: Foreign Languages Press, 1950), pp. 57, 61.

56. Richard Pipes, *The Formation of the Soviet Union* (Cambridge: Harvard University Press, 1954), p. 228.

57. Mao Tse-tung, *Selected Works*, v. 4, p. 155.

58. See Adele and Allyn Rickett, *Prisoners of Liberation*, rev. ed. (Garden City, N.Y.: Doubleday, 1973) and Derk Bodde, *Peking Diary—A Year of Revolution* (New York: Henry Schuman, 1950).

59. Politicheskoe Upravlenie RKKA, *1918-1928 let krasnoi armii-albom diagram*, p. 6.

60. John Erickson, *The Soviet High Command* (London: Macmillan, 1962), p. 291.

61. Janowitz, *The Military in the Political Development of New Nations*, p. 77.

62. N. Suntsov, *Krasno-znamennyi dal'ne vostochnyi* (Moscow: Voenizdat, 1971).

63. The state plan for 1920 assigned to the Red Army 100 percent of the tobacco, 90 percent of the male shoes, 60 percent of the meat, fish, and sugar, and 40 percent of the soap and cotton fabric collected by state organs. See V.S. Vladimirtsev, *Partiya—organizator razgroma kontrrevolyutsii na yuge* (Moscow: Voenizdat, 1971), p. 212.

64. M.V. Funze, *Izbrannye proizvedeniya* (Moscow: Voenizdat, 1967), v. 1, p. 438.

65. Berkhin, *Voennaya reforma v SSSR (1924-1925)*, p. 77.

66. Politicheskoe Upravlenie RKKA, *1918-1928 let krasnoi armii—albom diagram*, p. 14.

67. N.I. Shatagin and I.P. Prusanov, *Sovetskaya armiya—armiya novogo tipa* (Moscow: Voenizdat, 1957), p. 107.

68. *S.C.M.P.*, no. 750, February 18, 1954, p. 3.

69. *S.C.M.P.*, no. 1619, September 27, 1957, p. 19.

70. *S.C.M.P.*, no. 2682, February 3, 1962, p. 16; *S.C.M.P.*, no. 3391, February 5, 1965, p. 7.

71. A secret army bulletin spoke of the "disaster" of the Great Leap Forward which caused "unrest" in the army and potentially a "very dangerous" situation. See J. Chester Cheng, ed. *The Politics of the Chinese Red Army: A Translation of the Bulletin of Activities of the People's Liberation Army* (Stanford: Hoover Institution, 1966), pp. 11, 14.

72. *S.C.M.P.*, no. 4092, January 4, 1968, p. 28.

73. *S.C.M.P.*, no. 3937, May 11, 1967, p. 13.

74. While army farms reclaimed 53,000 hectares of former wasteland, all army men in 1967 also helped in the spring plowing and production of the communes. See *S.C.M.P.*, no. 3893, March 7, 1967, p. 10; *S.C.M.P.*, no. 4092, January 4, 1968, p. 28; and *S.C.M.P.*, no. 4361, February 20, 1969, p. 15.

75. During 1969 the PLA claimed "tremendous successes in agricultural and sideline production." See *S.C.M.P.*, no. 4574, January 12, 1970, pp. 108-109.

76. The annual army report spoke of "greater development in agricultural and sideline production than in the previous year." See *S.C.M.P.*, no. 4829, February 2, 1971, p. 40; and *S.C.M.P.*, no. 5075, February 14, 1972, p. 29.

77. *S.C.M.P.*, no. 896, September 25, 1954, p. 13.

78. *S.C.M.P.*, no. 1468, February 12, 1957, p. 9.

79. *Current Background*, no. 579, May 25, 1959, p. 2.

80. *S.C.M.P.*, no. 3282, August 19, 1964, p. 4.

81. *S.C.M.P.*, no. 4102, January 8, 1968, p. 12.

82. *S.C.M.P.*, no. 4233, August 7, 1968, p. 15.

83. *E.C.M.M.*, no. 150, October 1, 1958, *S.C.M.P.*, no. 1881, October 24, 1958.

84. There exists a secondary literature in the area. See John Gittings, "The 'Learn From the PLA' Campaign," *China Quarterly*, no. 18 (April/June 1964): 153-157.

85. *S.C.M.P.*, no. 3762, August 17, 1966, p. 9.

86. *S.C.M.P.*, no. 3932, May 4, 1967, p. 20.

87. The list seemed especially endless during 1968, when the power of the army seemed to reach its peak.

chapter 6

CONCLUSION

Before we proceed to an analysis of the key differences in army/party and army/society relations in Russia and China, it might be well to summarize the similarities which validate the comparison between the two armies. During the civil wars, the two parties created huge multimillion man armies to fight over vast territories. The two armies, as avowedly revolutionary forces in underdeveloped countries, functioned in similar environments. Operating at quite primitive levels of military technology, both armies lacked modern arms industries, significant quantities of technologically sophisticated military weaponry (ships, tanks, airplanes) and commanders experienced in the use of modern weaponry. Relying heavily on captured and "inherited" weapons, both the Red Army and the PLA heavily utilized an inadequate number of simple infantry weapons.[1] Masses of poorly educated peasants dominated the ranks and the noncommissioned officer positions in both armies. As avowedly class-conscious revolutionary armies, both the Red Army and the PLA abolished symbols of rank and authority, promoted egalitarian pay and living conditions, rejected traditional armies as organizational models, and excluded alien class elements. The party played a key role in the functioning of both armies.

By the end of the civil wars, both parties faced the crucial tasks of economic reconstruction and socialist construction. They needed to create viable government in those parts of the country occupied relatively late in the civil wars. As Communist countries, both Russia and China faced a very real threat of foreign intervention by powerful, hostile enemies, which necessitated the maintenance of a minimal credible deterrence. Given the underdeveloped state of both countries, the parties sought to carry out revolutionary transformations of societies. In this difficult endeavor, the party in both countries sought successfully to transform the barracks into a "school of communism" that would turn out skilled, literate, cultured Communists or Communist sympathizers capable of aiding the revolutionary transformation of society.

Nevertheless, despite similarities in such key areas as the hostility of the international political environment in the two decades after the end of the civil wars and the low level of development and military technology at the end of the civil war, the Russian and Chinese armies differed sharply in their relationship to party and society. The Chinese army has played a greater role in party affairs than the Russian army in the two decades after the end of the civil wars. In terms both of formal representation in the party (Central Committee, Politburo) and participation in the policymaking process, the Chinese army has tended to become a major political actor vis-à-vis the party. At the Ninth Party Congress in 1969, it even achieved almost a majority of the seats on the Politburo. At certain times, as in the 1950-54 and 1967-71 periods, the army has exercised considerable governmental power and helped to construct (or reconstruct) the party apparatus in certain areas. The power of the PLA was symbolized by Defense Minister Lin Piao, Mao's designated successor in the 1966-71 period, who delivered the main speech at the Ninth Party Congress in 1969. Not only did most of the key army officers also hold important party positions, but nearly all of the Chinese army representatives in the bodies of the party elite were old revolutionary career soldiers.[2] The party has relied on the normative commitment of the old revolutionary military leaders, personal ties of army and party leaders, an intricate political system, congruence of army and societal modernization, large party stratum in the army, benefits to the army of modernization, and a system of dual control to guarantee army loyalty to the party.

By contrast, the Russian army never achieved more than a relatively minimal representation (generally less than 10 percent of all Central Committee seats) in key party bodies. No professional career soldier ever sat on the Politburo in the 1921-40 period, much less was considered an "heir apparent." Especially in the 1920s, nearly all army representatives in key party bodies were party representatives in the army. The Russian army never became a major political actor in the policymaking process in the two decades after the end of the civil war. Indeed, during the Great Purges, it failed even to protect its own institutional integrity from the devastation wrought in the officer corps. Given the alienation and distance of the army elite from the party elite (in the early 1920s, neither the commander in chief nor the chief of staff of the Red Army even belonged to the party), the party relied by necessity to a much greater extent than in China on coercive and utilitarian measures to elicit the support of the army for the system. Confined largely to military affairs and trapped in a network of coercive pressures, the army never exercised any governmental functions nor played an important role in party affairs.

Similarly, sharp differences existed in army/society relations between the two countries. The Chinese army often performed extensive societal functions outside of the barracks. Especially during campaigns for the revolutionary transformation of society, the PLA performed some combination of extensive political leadership, economic production, and role model functions for society. By contrast, with the sole exception of economic production performed by the "Kolkhoz Corps" in the Far East in the 1930s, the Russian army performed virtually no civilian functions outside of the barracks. Furthermore, considerable differences existed between the two armies in the nature of military functions. The Chinese army successfully performed both external defense and internal protection functions while the Russian army shared these tasks with rival secret police and border troops and performed them less well.

Second, army/party and army/society relations were far more institutionalized and rigid in Russia than in China during the two decades after the end of the civil wars. In Russia, despite enormous changes in the nature of the army and society, a certain pattern of army/society relations conducted largely within the barracks ("school of communism") emerged in the early 1920s and remained essentially unchanged throughout the 1921-40 period. At the same time, a basic pattern of army/party relations (or perhaps army/dominant Stalinist faction relations), with minimal army involvement in and influence over party affairs, was established in the early 1920s.

The two major purges, in the 1924-26 and 1937-41 periods, strongly reaffirmed the basic army/party pattern of the army's exclusion from the policymaking process in all areas except those of purely military significance. The relatively stable army representation at a low level in key party bodies throughout the entire period reflected the relatively rigid nature of army/party relations in Russia.

On the other hand, in China, army/party and army/society relations have been far more volatile and changing over time. The army's role in society, as seen in such areas as economic production, political leadership, and role model, has fluctuated sharply from a very intense to a minimal involvement. Intense involvement has tended to occur during periods of campaigns for a revolutionary transformation of society. Similarly, the army's role in the policymaking process has fluctuated dramatically. During the 1950-54 and 1967-71 periods, the army exercised major governmental powers while at other times it has withdrawn from the performance of such functions. Army representation on the CCP Politburo has ranged all the way from one member (1950) to twelve members (1969) to six members (fall 1971). Lesser but still considerable variations have existed over time for army representation in the Central Committee. Thus, army/party and army/society relations have been far more volatile and uninstitutionalized in China than in Russia in the two decades after the end of the civil wars.

The third major difference concerns the use of force, or the threat thereof, between the army and party. Given the great tensions involved in the conduct of any revolutionary transformation of society and the common use of violence by armies in underdeveloped countries, the use of force would hardly be surprising. Different patterns emerged between the two countries. In Russia, the party successfully utilized devastating force to decimate virtually the entire officer corps (especially in its upper ranks) during the Great Purges of the late 1930s. Furthermore, despite fabricated charges of a coup attempt by Marshal Tukhachevsky, there was no known attempt or threat by Russian officers—even in the face of the Great Purges—to use force against the policies or leaders of the party. In China, however, the situation was quite different. Despite numerous purges of army officers (1959, 1965, 1967, 1968, and 1971), the party never—

with the possible exception of the Lin Piao affair—used violence against army officers.[3] Indeed many key PLA officers purged during the Cultural Revolution, such as Yang Chen-wu (acting chief of staff) and Hsiao Hua (director of PLA GPD), far from being shot as in Russia, were evidently reinstated in high military positions by 1974! Moreover, also unlike Russia, there is evidence that, both in the Wuhan Incident in 1967 and in the Lin Piao affair in 1971, top military officers either used, or threatened to use, force against the policies and even the leaders of the party.

The civil war periods were the most important, although hardly the only, cause of the differences between the two armies. Often neglected by scholars, they were critically important formative periods for the future development of Russia and China. The civil wars played a key role in shaping the mentality and attitudes of the party leaders in both Russia and China in the two decades after the end of the civil wars. The prominence of the civil war generation in Russia and the Yenan syndrome and Long March veterans in China in the two decades after the end of the civil war reflected this fact. Furthermore, during the civil war period in both countries the crucial instruments of governance—army, secret police, government, and other institutions—were formed, and the nature of the party was transformed.

Many key events in the two decades after the end of the civil wars in Russia and China cannot be fully understood without reference to the wars themselves. In Russia, the Great Purges, with the repeated charges of treason and foreign conspiracies to dismember the country, are considerably more explainable in terms of the experiences of the party in the civil war. In that period the Bolsheviks were continually plagued by treasonous activities by many supposed allies (Left-SRs, Muraviev, Grigoriev, Makhno, Kronstadt sailors, Lundquist), and the active intervention by many Allied countries against the Bolsheviks (French sailors at Odessa, Japanese troops in Siberia, American troops at Archangel). The acute sense of "capitalist encirclement" also developed as a consequence. The radical transformation of society in the 1930s had its roots in the radical war communism policies of the civil war period. The methods used to repress peasant revolts in the 1930s—Chekist terror, armed detachments of workers, and mobilizations of reliable units and Communists—bore striking resemblance to the methods used in the civil war.

Furthermore, the Bolshevik desire to impose collectivization on the peasantry, with force if necessary, in the 1930s had its origins in the civil war. The numerous peasant uprisings and their mass desertion from the Red Army in the civil war convinced the Bolsheviks, already anti-peasant in orientation, of the basic incompatibility of the peasantry and socialism. Stalin stated in 1919, "I must say that those elements, non-worker elements, who constitute the majority of our army—the peasantry—will not voluntarily fight for socialism."[4] The need for extensive coercion to suppress peasant uprisings, to requisition food from the countryside, and even to prevent desertion from the army during the civil war removed inhibitions about the use of force against the peasantry in the 1930s.[5] Bukharin, in "Letter of an Old Bolshevik," directly drew the parallel between the early 1930s and the civil war period by speaking of "the end of 1932 when the situation in the country was similar to 1921—the time of the Kronstadt rebellion.[6]

The civil war period was equally formative in China. The Maoist concept of "mass line" had its origins in the 1927-49 period.[7] During this period the Communists either had to gain the active support of the people or face extinction. The Maoist belief in voluntarism stemmed from the fact that over a lengthy time and against tremendous obstacles the Communists had persevered and triumphed. The radical militant and military-style egalitarianism so evident in the Great Leap Forward had its origins in the more than a decade spent by the party leadership in Yenan during the civil war period.

The civil war period was also the most crucial formative time for the future development of army/party and army/society relations in the two decades after the end of the civil wars. The most important aspect of the civil wars was that the Bolsheviks won theirs largely without, and at times in spite of, the Red Army. At the same time, the Chinese Communists won their civil war largely because of the People's Liberation Army.

The lack of a gestation period for the army before the civil war and the limited appeal of the Bolsheviks to the peasantry[8] severely crippled the peasant-dominated Red Army in the civil war. Furthermore, the very small urban proletarian base of the revolution helped limit the key party stratum within the army to only a small 5 percent of the army. Lacking any experienced Communist officers, the army was forced to rely heavily on such divisive, alien, and vacillating elements as *voenspets*, partisans, atamans, and non-Bolshevik radicals. Hindered by frequent treason in the officer corps and mass desertion in the ranks by disaffected peasants, the Red Army lurched from crisis to crisis. Possessing minimal mobilization capabilities and low fighting ability, the multimillion man Red Army was often routed by such weak foreign armies as the Polish in 1920. It even found it extremely difficult to rebuff attacks by small White forces. The small army of Yudenich (15,000 to 25,000 men) was able to threaten Petrograd seriously before the tide was turned with considerable external help given to the numerically superior Red Army. Indeed, the Red Army could not even suppress small-scale revolts by often poorly armed men (the Tambov, Makhno, and Kronstadt revolts) without major external help and without often becoming a threat to the regime through mass desertion to the enemy. Major political concessions (e.g., NEP), extensive Chekist coercion, and the mobilization of contingents of *kursanti*, Communists, Komsomolites, Chekists, and reliable army units were usually necessary before the Red Army could prevail over its enemies. Such events as the Kronstadt revolt further demonstrated the lack of reliability of even the more radical elements in the army. Aside from a few elite units (as the First Cavalry Army), the fighting ability of the Red Army was abysmal. It is little wonder that Lenin speculated in October 1921 that, despite the creation of a 5.5 million man Red Army, "Perhaps they (the Whites) would have crushed us had any of the capitalist states that were fighting us mobilized a few army corps in time."[9]

By contrast, the PLA, possessing a lengthy gestation period (1927-46) and popular appeal to the peasantry (agrarian reform and nationalism), was both an effective and revolutionary legitimated force. The gestation period permitted the army to create a large party stratum and institutionalize and perfect its mechanisms of control. As a consequence, the PLA, plagued in its early days (1927-35) by treason and desertion, had very little treason and desertion in the 1946-49 period. Over time the army built up a large, cohesive, and experienced officer corps. The PLA demonstrated a very substantial battlefield mobilization capacity. Unlike the Red Army, the PLA staged a triumphal march across the huge land mass of the country at the end of the civil war. In the Korean War, despite serious technological deficiences, the Chinese army pushed the powerful forces of the United Nations out of North Korea and then proceeded to stalemate them around the 38th parallel. Furthermore, given the army/party fusion of the civil war period, the PLA emerged from the civil war as an effective and revolutionary legitimated fighting force.

These differences had major implications for army/party and army/society relations in the two decades after the end of the civil war. By 1921 the Red Army had been tried and rejected as a production force and as a role model for society. By contrast, the People's Liberation Army successfully performed extensive societal functions outside of the barracks, including economic production and political leadership. Similarly, the Russian army elite, largely alien and isolated from the party elite, had only relatively minimal representation in the bodies of the party elite. Even those men tended to be almost exclusively party representatives in the army. By contrast, in 1950, the Chinese army elite was intimately intertwined with the party elite.

Given the great tasks of economic reconstruction and socialist construction which faced the parties in underdeveloped Russia and China at the end of the civil wars, a strong effective army could be a major asset for the party. Especially if such a force were closely tied to the party—and thereby not apt to become a threat to the party—then such an army, as the PLA, could play a major role in party and societal affairs. By contrast, a large, weak, and ineffectual army, largely alien from the party, and incapable of suppressing revolts without often becoming a threat to the party, would represent a threat to the party. Such an army, as the Red Army, would need to undergo massive demobilization and prolonged renewal of its officer corps in order to create a new, more effective force. In the interim period, the army could hardly play an important role in party or societal affairs. Thus, the civil war period would have had a major impact on the role of the army in the two decades after its end.

Furthermore, one could postulate that the party, given the enormous difficulties involved in conducting the revolutionary transformation of society, would need an agent, necessarily highly reliable, effective, and revolutionarily legitimated, to maintain order and repress all opposition to the transformation. The choice of such an agent depends upon the heritage of the civil war, the nature of the revolutionary transformation of society, and the relation of the agent to the dominant party faction. In Russia, the dominant Stalinist faction in the late 1920s and 1930s unleashed a massive, forced-draft bureaucratic revolutionary transformation of society, which entailed collectivization, industrialization, and modernization of society. The accomplishment of these difficult tasks necessitated, in Barrington Moore's words, "using terror as a major instrument to create and then consolidate a new social system, or else letting power go by default." Furthermore, the consolidation of the personal rule of Stalin meant that "terror had to be used within the Party itself, again to consolidate the power of the top leadership, perhaps essentially that of only one man, Stalin himself."[10]

The Stalinist faction relied on the secret police and not the army as its principal agent of force for several key reasons. The army, dominated even in 1930 by apathetic peasants in the ranks and noncommissioned officer positions, could not be considered a reliable force to suppress peasant revolts against collectivization and dekulakization. In this manner the Red Army was reflective of Soviet society as a whole. The party stratum in the army was quite small and consisted largely of commissars, political workers, commanders, and students in the military academies and schools. The officer corps, dominated in its upper ranks by *voenspets* and largely non-Stalinist commanders, was not a part of the dominant Stalinist group. The rise of serious military threats to the Soviet Union in the 1930s further argued for the relatively weak army to focus all of its attention on purely military affairs. The creation of forced-labor camps, the wide-scale shooting and terrorizing of civilians, and the "application ... of massive and sharp forms of repression"[11] would have been a task antithetical to the burgeoning professionalism in the army.[12] Instead, the elite, carefully selected secret police troops, reliable and effective, could be utilized in conjunction with other forces (as armed detachments of workers) to carry out the necessary repression. Furthermore, the secret police leadership formed an intimate part of the Stalinist faction. At the same time, these large secret police forces, both through their very existence and the maintenance of a secret network within the army, could effectively crosscheck any tendency of the army, already isolated from party and society affairs, to attempt to interfere with the transformation of society.[13]

The roots of this crucial choice lay in the civil war period. During the civil war the Russian army, dominated by apathetic and even hostile peasant masses in the ranks and *voenspets* in the officer corps, plagued by mass desertion and frequent treason, had been markedly ineffective and at times a threat to the regime. Instead, the party relied heavily on political concessions, Chekist coercion, and mobilization of *kursanti*, Communists, Komsomolites, and reliable army units. The secret police had functioned, especially after June 1918,[14] as an elite, select, and somewhat independent force which carried out extensive liquidation of enemies as well as penetration of enemy organizations.[15] The "Red Terror" may have claimed upwards of 50,000 victims.[16] As we have seen in Chapter 3, the secret police played a crucial role in the suppression of such uprisings as the Tambov and Makhno revolts and an important auxiliary role in the suppression of the Kronstadt revolt. The leader of the Cheka, Felix Dzerzhinsky, was a highly admired man and the bulk of the leadership of the Cheka consisted of old Bolsheviks of long revolutionary standing. Created even before the Red Army, the secret police emerged from the civil war as an effective and revolutionary legitimate force, intimately connected with the party elite.[17] When the time came to, in some aspects, "renew" the civil war in the 1930s, the secret police leadership now part of Stalin's faction, was a logical instrument to entrust with the task of carrying out the necessary repression.

By contrast, in China, army and party had been fused during a lengthy civil war in the countryside. As the army had developed into an effective and revolutionary legitimate force by the time of the decisive civil war (1946-49), no independent secret police force arose as its rival. Especially after the rejection of the Soviet model of development implicit in the Great Leap Forward, the Maoist faction, beginning in the early 1960s, increasingly turned to the army as a base of support. During the Cultural Revolution, the Maoists turned to the army both as a base of support and as a crucial agent for the maintenance of order. The revolutionary transformation embodied in the Cultural Revolution necessitated not mass repression but rather the use of a politicized force, capable of reconciling political factions, maintaining order, conducting propaganda, and rebuilding the party at the local level. The army, with its high degree of revolutionary legitimation from the civil war era and its general popularity and demonstrated effectiveness, was such a force. During the Cultural Revolution it also subordinated the smaller, possible rival, public security troops, under its command (as they had been in the 1950-58 period).

In both Russia and China during the revolutionary transformations of society—the 1930s in Russia, the Cultural Revolution in China—the primary organization in charge of the important instruments of force—the Russian secret police and the Chinese army—gained great power. Both the Russian secret police and the Chinese army underwent repeated purges during this period.[18] At the same time, both organizations dramatically increased their power. In Russia, the secret police, having suppressed the peasant uprisings and conducted the great purges, possessed its own armed forces, penetrated all other institutions with its network of spies, and created, especially in Siberia, a vast empire of millions of men in forced labor camps. Given the atrophy of key party institutions, the power of the secret police increased greatly, although under the ultimate control of Stalin. In China, during the Cultural Revolution, the PLA became the dominant institution in the vacuum created by the disintegration of party and government. Providing the essential order for society and reconciling various factions, the PLA soon gained a near majority on the Politburo and Central Committee. Defense Minister Lin Piao became Mao's "heir apparent" and the army, below the central level, ruled China through the Military Control Committees and later through the military-dominated Revolutionary Committees.

However, in both countries, a point came when the newly resurgent party sought to reassert its "normal" dominance over the agent in control of the key force. This point generally came after the essential completion of the revolutionary transformation of power when the importance of force was considerably lessened. In both countries, the organization (or at least its head) made a bid for power, lost, and then was sharply downgraded. Its leader generally was shot and his associates liquidated. In Russia, after Stalin's death,

Beria, the secret police chief, made a major bid for power, failed, and was shot. In the aftermath, the power of the secret police was sharply curtailed and several of Beria's associates (despite the new tendency toward leniency in dealing with opponents) were shot. In China, in the aftermath of the Cultural Revolution, with the resurgence of the civilian party apparatus and the lessened importance of force, Defense Minister Lin Piao and his associates faced a loss in the privileged position of the army. Defense Minister Lin Piao and his key military associates made a bid for power, lost, and died under mysterious circumstances in an air crash in Mongolia in 1971. In the aftermath, a sweeping purge swept the army, and its power was sharply downgraded.

Thus, in both countries, the party was displaced as the locus of decision-making during key periods of revolutionary transformation of society (1930s in Russia, Cultural Revolution in China). In its place power accumulated in the hands of a key party faction (Stalinist faction in Russia, Maoist faction in China) and its key instrument of force (secret police in Russia, army in China). The choice of the instrument of force was directly connected to the legacy of the civil war and the nature of the transformation of society. Eventually, after the agent of force had achieved great power, a resurgent party, under extremely tense and dangerous circumstances, sought to reassert its power over the organization in control of the crucial instruments of violence. In reaction to this attempt, the organization, making an unsuccessful bid for power, was sharply reduced in its power.

We have seen the great importance of the civil war as a formative period for future army/party and army/society relations. However, we should also consider other factors, especially important in determining the state of army/party and army/society relations at a given period. These factors include the nature and state of the process of transformation of society, the political struggles within the army and party, the degree of perceived external threat and the capabilities of the army. In Russia, the Stalinist faction controlled the party for the great majority of the 1921-40 period. In the 1920s, the great technical weakness of the army, its small party stratum, its domination by apathetic and poorly educated peasants in the ranks and *voenspets* in the upper ranks of the officer corps, all contributed to the weak role of the army in party and society affairs. During the 1930s, although the army underwent technological transformation, it remained apart from and isolated by the Stalinist faction and its agent, the secret police. The increasingly serious nature of the external threat in the 1930s, further precluded any serious diversion of military effort to societal activities outside of the barracks.

By contrast, the Chinese army emerged from the civil war as a legitimate and effective actor, capable of exercising governmental functions in the 1950-54 period. In the 1950-57 period, due to the serious external threat (Korean War), the emulation of the Soviet expert model, and the relative success of party policies, the army was called upon to exercise relatively minimal societal functions outside of the barracks. The elevation of six of the ten PLA marshals to the Politburo in 1956 reflected the importance of the army in the policymaking process. After the rejection of the Soviet model, embodied in the Great Leap Forward, the army and party have repeatedly been split by struggles between various factions over the proper strategy for development. During major campaigns for the revolutionary transformation of society from below—the Great Leap Forward and the Cultural Revolution—the Maoist faction has generally been in the ascendancy and discounted the seriousness of any external threat. The army has been called upon to aid the campaign by performing extensive and visible societal functions outside of the barracks. The degree to which the army has participated in such functions has depended on the nature of the dominant faction in the army. During the Great Leap Forward, the army, under the direction of Defense Minister P'eng Teh-huai (who was opposed to army involvement in such functions) participated extensively in economic production but only minimally in political leadership functions. Under Defense Minister Lin Piao, a leader of the Maoist faction in the army, the PLA participated extensively in economic production, political leadership, and role model functions. During periods of lulls or retreats from these campaigns—when the non-Maoist faction has often been in control of the party and even the army—the army has generally withdrawn from active participation in societal functions.[19] This tendency was accentuated by the possible existence of a serious external threat. Similarly, the power and role of the army expanded greatly during the Cultural Revolution and declined in its aftermath.

While the Soviet writer Malukhin has exaggerated in calling China in the late 1960s a "military dictatorship," nevertheless we have seen the existence of a far greater role for the Chinese army than the Russian army in party and societal affairs.[20] In this work we have pointed to the considerable importance of the formative civil war periods and the nature of the revolutionary transformation of society as key factors in explaining these differences.[21] It is only through the study of such somewhat neglected factors that the relatively dynamic and revolutionary politics of such Communist states as Russia and China in the two decades after the end of the civil wars can best be understood.

NOTES

1. In Russia the Red Army "inherited" large stocks of the military supplies of the czarist Army, while in China the PLA in 1945 "inherited" large quantities of weapons left behind by the Imperial Japanese Army.

2. The word "career" is used here to refer to the fact that most army leaders received some formal military training, entered the PLA while in their twenties and devoted the rest of their lives to military service.

3. The Lin Piao affair still remains a somewhat murky matter. In March 1966, though, Lo Jui-ching, purged chief of staff, did unsuccessfully try to commit suicide. Even he, however, was reinstated to a military post by 1975.

4. J. V. Stalin, *Works* (Moscow: Gosizdat, 1946-51), v. 4, p. 250.

5. The repressive policies of White regimes, the fear of a Czarist restoration, and the dread of a return of the landlords enabled the Bolsheviks to prevent the peasantry from openly or actively backing the Whites during the civil war.

6. Boris I. Nicolaevsky, "The Letter of an Old Bolshevik" *Power and the Soviet Elite*, ed. Janet Zagoria (New York: Praeger, 1965), p. 29.

7. The civil war period in one sense included the 1927-49 period.

8. The urban-oriented Bolsheviks, with few peasant members, had alienated the peasants by their food requisitioning squads, their social experimentation, and their often rapacious conduct in the countryside.

9. V. I. Lenin, *Collected Works* (Moscow: Progress Press, 1964), v. 33, p. 67.

10. Barrington Moore, *Terror and Progress—USSR* (New York: Harper & Row, 1954), p. 11.

11. Stalin and Molotov used this phrase in a May 8, 1933, secret directive. See Sergei Gordeyev, "Kollektivizatsiya sel' skogo khozyaistvo v Smolensk oblast' v period 1929-1934," p. 285.

12. The army, furthermore, as a relatively representative body, especially in the ranks, would have found it difficult to carry out such tasks.

13. The army also gained enormously from the transformation in terms of its massive technological transformation in the 1930s.

14. In June 1918, a contingent of Chekists under the command of Left Socialist Revolutionary, Popov, participated in the unsuccessful Left SR uprising in Moscow. After this event, the Cheka was purged and became a thoroughly reliable force.

15. Yakov Peters, who briefly headed the All-Russian Cheka in 1918, stated that "In its activities, the Cheka is completely independent, carrying out searches, arrests, shootings, afterwards making a report to the Council of People's Commissars and the Soviet Central Executive Committee." See Merle Fainsod, *How Russia Is Ruled* (Cambridge: Harvard University Press, 1965), p. 427.

16. Indeed, Chamberlin considers 50,000 victims to be a conservative estimate of the victims of the "Red Terror." See William Chamberlin, *The Russian Revolution 1917-1921* (New York: Grosset & Dunlap, 1935), v. 2, p. 79.

17. Among leading Chekists in the civil war were Abakumov, Agranov, Antipov, Bakayev, Bokiy, Chugurin, Dizhbit, Dukis, Dzerzhinsky, Eyduk, Fomin, Kadomtsev, Kedrov, Kolsnikov, Latzis, Mantsev, Menzhinsky, Nikifonov, Pavlunovsky, Peters, Rekstyn, Rusanov, Tulupov, and Yurovsky. Almost all of them were old revolutionaries, with the median date of joining the party being 1906. Thus, the Chekist leaders, in great contrast to the army leaders, had belonged to the party for as long as the top leaders in the party elite. This conferred on the Cheka a degree of trust and legitimation lacking in the army. The Cheka was formed in December 1917 while the army was created in 1918.

18. In Russia, both Yezhov and Yagoda were purged in the latter part of the 1930s and a thoroughgoing purge of the secret police was conducted in the late 1930s. In China, during the Cultural Revolution (which came after the purge of Lo Jui-ching), many officers were purged in January 1967 together with Ho Lung and in 1968 Yang Cheng-wu and associates were purged.

19. During the 1960-65 period, for example, the Liuist faction dominated the party. Although the Lin Piao faction was at least nominally in control of the army during the 1960s, the military professionals, whose ranks and power had been greatly expanded during the 1950s, remained a potent force. It seems that they used their position to obtain a reduction in army participation in societal functions outside of the barracks in return for support for other aspects of Lin Piao's program.

20. A Malukhin, *Militarism—Backbone of Maoism* (Moscow: Novosti, 1970) p. 16.

21. Given the importance of the civil wars in shaping the context and nature of Russian and Chinese politics, it is striking how little of value has actually been written on the civil war periods. This is particularly remarkable in the case of Russia. Considerable material now exists with which to write a competent work which would treat the civil war period both in comparative perspective with other civil wars and with its formative character.

APPENDIX A

THE SOVIET AND CHINESE OFFICER CORPS DURING THE CIVIL WARS

SOVIET OFFICER CORPS

Senior voenspets: F. Afanasyev, V. Alt'fater, I. Blazhevich, M. Bonch-Bruyevich, G. Eykhe, A. Gekker, V. Gittis, V. Glagolev, V. Grendal, N. Kakurin, D. Karbyshev, S. Kamenev, A. Kolenkovsky, A. Kork, F. Kostayev, P. Lebedev, A. Nemitts, A. Neznamov, F. Novitsky, V. Olderogge, N. Petin, A. Samoilo, B. Shaposhnikov, V. Shorin, A. Snesarev, N. Sollogub, A. Svechin, P. Sytin, I. Vatsetis, K. Velichko, A. Yegorov, and V. Yegoryev.

Junior voenspets: I. Dzevaltovsky, L. Galler, F. Kalnyn, N. Kashirin, A. Kondratyev, N. Kuibyshev, M. Levandovsky, G. Malandin, S. Mezhenikov, S. Pugachyov, G. Razilevich, V. Triandafilov, M. Tukhachevsky, and M. Viktorov.

Temporary junior officers: K. Avksentyevsky, Y. Balakhanov, M. Demichev, I. Dubovoy, R. Eideman, I. Fedko, I. Garkavy, Y. Gaylit, M. Germanovich, I. Grayazhov, Y. Kovtyulenev, G. Khakhanyan, V. Khripin, V. Levichev, L. Petrovsky, V. Putna, Y. Sablin, I. Uborevich, and G. Zinovyev.

NCOs: I. Belov, V. Blyukher, S. Bogdanov, S. Budenny, V. Frolov, O. Gorodovikov, M. Kalmykov, V. Kniga, I. Kutyakov, Y. Latsis, R. Malinovsky, K. Rokossovsky, S. Timoshenko, A. Todorsky, and G. Zhukov.

New revolutionary commanders: B. Parsky, V. Chuikov, B. Feldman, A. Grechko, K. Kalinovsky, I. Khalepsky, A. Lapin, K. Meretskov, A. Sedyakin, N. Voronov, I. Yakir, M. Yefremov, A. Yeremenko, M. Zakharov, and D. Zhloba.

Old revolutionary commanders: V. Antonov-Ovseenko, P. Baranov, R. Berzin, P. Bybenko, Y. Fabritsius, M. Frunze, G. Gai, T. Khvessin, G. Kotovsky, K. Mekhonosin, N. Muralov, N. Podvoisky, V. Primakov, F. Raskolnikov, A. Sergeyev, Y. Shchadenko, E. Skylansky, L. Trotsky, K. Voroshilov, and A. Znamensky.

Partisans: I. Apanesenko, M. Elinov, V. Chapayev, N. Grigoriev, N. Kalan-darishvili, Y. Kazansky, A. Kravchenko, S. Lazo, N. Makhno, A. Makrou-sov, F. Mironov, A. Parkhomenko, P. Shchetinkin, N. Shchors, and Y. Yakovenko.

CHINESE OFFICER CORPS

Chang Ai-p'ing, Chang Ching-wu, Chang Kuo-hua, Chang Ta-chih, Chang Tsung-hsun, Ch'en Hsi-lien, Ch'en I, Ch'en Keng, Ch'en Shih-ch'u, Ch'in Ch'uang-ch'eng, Chou Shih-ti, Chu Teh, Ho Lung, Hsiao Ching-kuang, Hsiao Hua, Hsiao K'o, Hsieh Fu-chih, Hsu Hsiang-Ch'ien, Hsu Kuang-ta, Hsu Shih-yu, Huang K'o-ch'eng, Li K'o-nung, Li Ta, Liao Han-sheng, Lin Piao, Liu Po-ch'eng, Liu Ya-lou, Lo Jung-huan, Lo Jui-ch'ing, Nieh Jung-chen, P'eng Shao-hui, P'eng Teh-huai, Su Yu, Teng Hua, T'eng Tai-yuan, Ulanfu, Wang Chen, Wang Cheng, Wang En-mao, Wang Shu-sheng, Yang Li-san, Yang Te-chih, Yang Yung, Yeh Chien-ying, and Yeh Fei.

Source: The list of 130 Soviet officers and 45 Chinese officers is meant to be illustrative rather than definitive. The names of the Chinese officers were culled from Donald Klein and Anne Clark, *Biographic Dictionary of Chinese Communism* (Cambridge, Mass.: Harvard University Press, 1971). The names of the Soviet officers were obtained from the Institute for Study of the U.S.S.R., *Who's Who in the USSR, 1961/1962* (Munich: Intercontinental Book and Publishing Company, 1962), *Who Was Who in the USSR* (Metuchen, N.J.: Scarecrow Press, 1972), and Boris Levytsky, *The Soviet Political Elite* (Stanford: Hoover Institution, 1969). The imbalance in numbers of Soviet and Chinese officers reflects the relative paucity of Chinese data and greater stability of the Chinese officer corps. All direct comparisons between the two officer corps were conducted at specific times and ranks.

APPENDIX B

The question of the involvement of the army in societal tasks, especially outside of the barracks, struck at the root of the question of the nature of the army. Although probably all Communist armies would naturally prefer to be both red and expert, the reality of very limited resources in Russia and China forced a "leaning to one side." An expert army, which with some modifications has existed in various Western countries, would be a modern, professionalized army, aloof and isolated from party and society, apolitical and passive. A red army, as the PLA in the civil war period, would be an important revolutionary modernizing political force, intimately involved with party and society.

The expert model offered several major advantages. Given the existence of powerful enemies hostile to the new Communist state, it stressed the focusing of all efforts on the creation of a powerful, technologically strong, and capable modern army. It thereby appealed to the natural desire of leaders in developing countries to try to match in a short time the standards of advanced Western countries. The model emphasized the removal of the army from politics. In Communist countries this could be modified into army subordination to the party. Finally, the model fit into a development strategy with emphasis on division of labor, functionality, and rationality. During the 1921-40 period in Russia and during the 1950-57 period in China, the Communist armies, with some modifications, have tended to move toward this model.

However, this model possessed several deficiencies, particularly troublesome in China. First, an expert model for the army represented a severe disjunction from the largely red model of the 1927-50 period. Pursuit of this model required a substantial reconstruction of the PLA. Second, such a model involved a sacrifice of the revolutionary legitimation acquired by the army in the pre-state period. Given the difficulties inherent in a revolutionary transformation of society, the party could use the help of an army with as much revolutionary legitimation and demonstrated effectiveness as the PLA. Third, the maintenance of a large, modern professional army represented a serious drain on the severely limited resources available to the state for economic development. Fourth, a modern, powerful army, aloof from society and party, represented a possible threat to the power of the party. If the campaigns for the revolutionary transformation of society should fail or go badly, the army, bearing no responsibility for the campaigns might become, as in many underdeveloped countries, a logical candidate to assume power. Finally, no matter how expert the PLA might become, it could never hope to match the military technology of the two superpowers, the United States and the Soviet Union.

These deficiencies were much less important in Russia than in China. For the Red Army, emerging in a weakened state from the civil war, possessed very little revolutionary legitimacy or capabilities of use to the party. Indeed, the primary desire of the party throughout the 1920s and early 1930s was the technical reconstruction of the army and the extension of party control over this alien and potentially dangerous institution. The party (or dominant Stalinist faction) reacted to the deficiencies of the expert model through the creation of a powerful network of coercive controls (which culminated in the massive purges in the late 1930s) within the army. The party sought to minimize the size of the Red Army and utilize a territorial cadre system until the threat of Japanese and German militarism forced a sharp rise in military expenditures in the 1930s. The successful modernization of the Soviet Union in only a decade limited the period in which the army was aloof from a society undergoing revolutionary transformation.

The red model, plausible thereby only in the Chinese model, offered potential solutions to many of the deficiencies of the expert model; but it also suffered from certain important problems. As demonstrated by the Korean War, modern warfare requires a high level of sophisticated weaponry and expertise. The red model, to the degree that it is primarily compatible only with a relatively primitive level of technology, does not answer the needs of modern warfare. Second, such a red model does not differentiate between the army and the party. While the army and party had been fused during the pre-1950 period, the development of the country required a certain division of labor between the two institutions. The red model, in the extreme, would leave the army without a *raison d'être* independent of that of the party. During the 1958-71 period, the PLA, largely under Defense Minister Lin Piao (1959-71) sporadically adopted various aspects of the red model while retaining some aspects of the expert model.

The PLA has tended to oscillate between these two models. During periods of revolutionary transformation of society, the army has tended, under pressure from the party, to move toward a red model with substantial participation in society. These periods have tended to coincide with the domination of the Maoist faction in the party. There have also been periods in which the external threat was downgraded so that diversion of military efforts into nonmilitary tasks seemed possible. During periods of lulls and retreat in the transformation of society, the army, under pressure from military professionals, has generally withdrawn from participation in societal functions outside the barracks and emphasized the expert model.

BIBLIOGRAPHY

The following represents a compilation of the principal materials used in the preparation of this work. It is not intended in any way to be a complete bibliographic survey of the military or any other subjects treated here.

SOVIET MATERIALS

Individual Memoirs (Also Collected Speeches and Writings)

Aralov, I. *Lenin vel nas k pobede*. Moscow: Gosizdat, 1962.

Bagramyan, I. *Tak nachinalas' voina*. Moscow: Voenizdat, 1974.

Blyukher, V. K. *Stat'i i rechi*. Moscow: Voenizdat, 1963.

Bonch-Bruyevich, M. *From Tsarist General to Red Army Commander*. Moscow: Progress Publishers, 1971.

Budenny, S. M. *Proidenny put'*. 3 vol. Moscow: Voenizdat, 1973.

Frunze, M. V. *Izbrannye proizvedeniya*. 2 vols. Moscow: Voenizdat, 1967.

Kamenev, S. S. *Zapiski o grazhdanskoi voine i voennom stroitel'stve*. Moscow: Voenizdat, 1963.

Meretskov, K. A. *Na sluzhbe narodu: stranitsii vospominanii*. Moscow: Politizdat, 1968.

Ordzhonikidze, G. K. *Stat'i i rechi*. Moscow: Politizdat, 1956. Vol. 1 (*1920-1926*).

Samoilo, A. *Dve zhizni*. Leningrad: Voenizdat, 1963.

Trotsky, Leon. *My Life*. Translation. New York: Charles Scribner's Sons, 1930.

The Trotsky Papers. Edited by Jan M. Meyer. 2 vols. The Hague, Netherlands: Mouton and Company, 1964, 1971.

Tukhachevsky, M. N. *Izbrannye proizvedeniya*. vol. 1 (*1919-1927*). Moscow: Voenizdat, 1964.

Voroshilov, K. E. *Stat'i i rechi*. Moscow: Partizdat, 1937.

Yakir, Petr. *Detstvo vo turme*. London: Macmillan, 1971.
Zhukov, G. K. *Vospominaniya i razmyshleniya*. Moscow: Novosti, 1969.

Works of Lenin and Stalin

Lenin, V. I. *Collected Works*. Translation. Moscow: Progress Publishers, 1964.
_____ . Polnoe sobranie sochinenii. 5th ed. Moscow: Politizdat, 1967-1970.
Stalin, I. V., et al. *From the First to the Second Five Year Plan: A Symposium*. Translation. Moscow-Leningrad: Politizdat, 1933.
_____ . *History of the Communists Party of the Soviet Union (Bolsheviks) Short Course*. New York: International Publishers, 1939.
_____ . *Sochineniya*. Moscow: Gosizdat, 1946-1951.
_____ . *Works*. Translation. Moscow: Foreign Languages Publishing House, 1953-1955.

Biographies

Babenko, P. *I. E. Yakir*. Moscow: Politizdat, 1964.
Bychevsky, V. B. *Marshal Govorov*. Moscow: Voenizdat, 1970.
Dushenkin, V. *Ot soldata do marshala*. Moscow: Politizdat, 1961.
Geroi grazhdanskoi voiny. Moscow: Molodaya Gvardiya, 1963.
O. I. Gorodovikov—vidni sovetskii voenachalnik. Vologograd: Elista, 1971.
Kardashov, V. *Rokossovsky*. Moscow: Molodaya Gvardiya, 1972.
Komandarm krylatkh—zhizn Ya. I. Alksnisa: sbornik vospominanii. Riga, Latvia: Liesma, 1967.
Komandarm Yakir: vospominaniya druzei i soratnikov. Moscow: Voenizdat, 1963.
Kondratev, N. D. *Yan Fabritsius*. Moscow: Voenizdat, 1957.
Kramarov, G. *Soldat revoliutsii o Sergei Ivanovich Gusev*. Moscow: Politizdat, 1964.
Kuznetsov, P. G. *Marshal Tolbukhin*. Moscow: Voenizdat, 1966.
Lipkina, A. G.; Muratov, Kh. I.; and Vostretsova, A. K. *Stepan Sergeevich Vostretsov*. Ufa: Bashkirskoe Knizhnoe Izdatel'stvo, 1966.
Popov, A. S. *Trud, talant, doblest'*. Moscow: Politizdat, 1972.
Roitman, N. D., and Tsetlin, V. L. *Polkovodets-kommunist*. Kishiniev: Kartya Moldovenyaske, 1967.
Rostunov, I. I. *General Brusilov*. Moscow: Voenizdat, 1964.

Sabostyanov, V., and Yegorov, P. *Komandarm pervogo ranga (I. P. Uborevich)*. Moscow: Politizdat, 1966.
Todorsky, A. I. *Marshal Tukhachevsky*. Moscow: Politizdat, 1963.

Party Congresses and Conferences

Vos'moi S'ezd RKP(B), Mart, 1919, *Protokoly*. Moscow: Partizdat, 1933.
Vos'maya Konferentsiya RKP(B), Dekabr', 1919, *Protokoly*. Moscow: Gosizdat, 1961.
Devyatyi S'ezd RKP(B), Mart-Aprel', 1920, *Stenograficheskii otchet*. Moscow: Partizdat, 1934.
Desytatyi s'ezd RKP(B), Mart, 1921 goda, *Stenograficheskii otchet*. Moscow: Partizdat, 1933.
Odinnadtsatyi S'ezd RKP(B), Mart-Aprel', 1922, *Stenograficheskii otchet*. Moscow: Partizdat, 1936.
Dvenadtsatyi S'ezd RKP(B), Aprel', 1923, *Stenograficheskii otchet*. Moscow: Politizdat, 1968.
Trinadtsatyi S'ezd RKP(B), Mai, 1924, *Stenograficheskii otchet*. Moscow: Gosizdat, 1963.
Pyatnadtsatyi S'ezd VKP(B), Dekabrya, 1927, *Stenograficheskii otchet*. Moscow: Gosizdat, 1961.
XVI S'ezd VKP(B), 26 Iyuna-13 Iyulya, 1930, *Stenograficheskii otchet*. Moscow: Partizdat, 1935.
KPSS, XVII S'ezd, 26 Yanvarya-10 Fevralya, 1934, *Stenograficheskii otchet*. Moscow: Partizdat, 1934.
KPSS, XVIII S'ezd, 10-21 Marta, 1939, *Stenograficheskii otchet*. Moscow: Gosizdat, 1939.

Military History

Nineteenth Century

Beskronyi, L. G. *Russkaya armiya i flot v XIX veke*. Moscow: Nauka, 1973.

Civil War

Bubnov, A. S.; Kamenev, S. S.; Tukhachevsky, M. N.; and Eidemann, R. P., eds. *Grazhdanskaya voina 1918-1921*. 3 vols. Moscow: Gosizdat, 1930.
Danilevsky, A. F., *V. I. Lenin i voprosy voennogo stroitel'stva na VIII s'ezde RKP(B)*, Moscow: Voenizdat, 1964.

Direktivi glavnogo kommandovaniya krasnoi armii (1917-1920): sbornik dokumentov. Moscow: Voenizdat, 1969.

Gusev, S. I. *Grazhdanskaya voina i krasnaya armiya.* Moscow: Voenizdat, 1958.

Istoriya grazhdanskoi voiny v SSSR (1917-1922). 5 vols. Moscow: Gosizdat, 1959.

Kakurin, N. *Kak srazhalas' revoliutsiya.* Vol. 2 *(1919-1920).* Moscow: Gosizdat, 1926.

Klyatskin, S. M. *Na zashchite oktyabrya.* Moscow: Nauka Izdatel'stvo, 1965.

Kratkaya istoriya grazhdanskoi voiny v SSSR. 2nd ed. Moscow: Gosizdat, 1962.

Kuz'min G. V. *Grazhdanskaya voina i voennaya interventsiya v SSSR.* Moscow: Voenizdat, 1958.

Kuz'min N. F. *V. I. Lenin vo glave oborony sovetskoi strany (1918-1920).* Moscow: Voenizdat, 1958.

V. I. Lenin i sovetskie vooruzhennye sily. Moscow: Voenizdat, 1967.

Lipitsky, S. V. *Voennaya deyatel'nost TSK RKP(B) 1917-1920.* Moscow: Politizdat, 1973.

Olikov, S. *Dezertir'stvo v krasnoi armii i bor'ba s nim.* Moscow: Voennoi Tipografii Upravleniya, 1926.

Partiya v period inostrannoi voennoi interventsii i grazhdanskoi voiny (1918-1920): dokumenti i materiali. Moscow: Gosizdat, 1962.

Petrov, Yuri. *KPSS—rukovoditel' i vospitatel' krasnoi armii (1918-1920).* Moscow: Voenizdat, 1961.

Petrovsky, D. A. *Voennaya shkola v gody revoliutsii.* Moscow: Voenizdat, 1924.

5 let krasnoi armii: sbornik statei (1918-1923). Moscow: Vyshii Voenni Redaktsionni Soviet, 1923.

Trotsky, Lev. *Kak vooruzhalas' revoliutsiya.* 3 vols. Moscow: Vyshii Voenni Redaktsionni Soviet, 1924.

Vladimirtsev, V. S. *Partiya—organizator razgroma kontrrevoliutsii na yuge.* Moscow: Voenizdat, 1971.

Vlasov, I. I. *V. I. Lenin i stroitel'stvo sovetskoi armii.* Moscow: Voenizdat, 1958.

Soviet Union (1917-1920)

Berkhin, I. B. *Voennaya reforma v SSSR (1924-1925).* Moscow: Voenizdat, 1958.

Boevoi put' sovetskikh vooruzhennykh sil. Moscow: Voenizdat, 1960.

Boevoi put' sovetskogo voenna-morskogo flota. Moscow: Voenizdat, 1967.

Grechko, A. A. *Vooruzhennye sily sovetskogo gosudarstva.* Moscow: Voenizdat, 1974.

Istoriya velikoi otechestvennoi voiny sovetskogo soyuza, 1941-1945. Vol. 1. Moscow: Voenizdat, 1960.

Kalashnik, M. *Na strazhe mirnogo truda.* Moscow: Novosti, 1969.

Kiryaev, N. M., and Tsygankov, V. P. *Voennye voprosy v kurse istorii KPSS.* Moscow: Voenizdat, 1960.

KPSS i stroitel'stvo vooruzhennykh sily SSSR (1918-June 1941). Moscow: Voenizdat, 1959.

KPSS o vooruzhennykh silakh sovetskogo soyuza: dokumenti 1917-1968. Moscow: Voenizdat, 1969.

Korablev, Yu. *V. I. Lenin i sozdanie krasnoi armii.* Moscow: Nauka, 1970.

Komsomol—boevoi drug DOSAAF. Moscow: DOSAAF Izdatel'stvo, 1958.

Lototsky, S. S., et al. *Sovetskaya armiya.* Moscow: Voenizdat, 1970.

Milovsky, M., et al., *Til' sovetskoi armii.* Moscow: Voenizdat, 1968.

Petrov, Yuri. *Partiinoe stroitel'stvo v sovetskoi armii i flote (1918-1961).* Moscow: Voenizdat, 1964.

————. *Stroitel'stvo politorganov, partiinikh i komsomolskikh organizatsii armii i flota (1918-1968).* Moscow: Voenizdat, 1971.

50 let vooruzhennykh sil SSSR. Moscow: Voenizdat, 1968.

Pitersky, N. A., et al. *Boevoi put' sovetskogo voenno-morskogo flota.* Moscow: Voenizdat, 1964.

Politicheskoe Upravlenie RKKA. *1918-1928 let krasnoi armii—albom diagram.* Moscow: Voenni Vestnik Izdatel'stvo, 1928.

Shatagin, N. I., and Prusanov, I. P. *Sovetskaya armiya—armiya novogo tipa.* Moscow: Voenizdat, 1957.

Suntsov, N. *Krasno-znamennyi dal'ne vostochnyi.* Moscow: Voenizdat, 1971.

Tal', B. *Istoriya krasnoi armii.* Moscow: Voenizdat, 1928.

Tyusin, F. S. *Bor'ba kommunisticheskoi partii za ukreplenie voennogo mogushestva SSSR.* Moscow: Voenizdat, 1955.

Voenno-vozdushnyi sily. Moscow: Voenizdat, 1959.

Voropaev, D. A., and Iovlev, A. M. *Bor'ba KPSS za sozdanie voennykh kadrov.* Moscow: Voenizdat, 1960.

Military Writings and Military Doctrine

Note: There is inevitably a certain overlap between this section and the preceding one.

Bubnov, A. S. *O krasnoi armii.* Moscow: Voenizdat, 1958.

Frunze, M. V. *Izbrannye proizvedeniya.* 2 vols. Moscow: Voenizdat, 1967.

Grechko, A. A. *Vooruzhennye sily sovetskogo gosudarstva*. Moscow: Voenizdat, 1974.

Gusev, S. I. *Grazhdanskaya voina i krasnaya armiya*. Moscow: Voenizdat, 1958.

Shaposhnikov, Boris, *Mozg armii*. 3 vols. Moscow: Voenni Vestnik, 1927-1929.

Sokolovsky, V. D. *Soviet Military Strategy*. Translated by Herbert Dinerstein, Leon Goure, and Thomas Wolfe. Englewood, N.J.: Prentice-Hall, Inc., 1963.

Trotsky, Lev. *Kak vooruzhalas' revoliutsiya*. vols. Moscow: Vyshii Voenni Redaktsionni Soviet, 1924.

Tukhachevsky, M. N. *Izbrannye proizvedeniya*. Moscow: Voenizdat, vol. 1 *(1919-1927)* 1964.

General Works on Aspects of Soviet Development (1921-1940)

Berkhin, I. B. *Istoriya SSSR (1917-1971)*. 2d ed. Moscow: Vyshaya Shkola, 1972.

Daniels, Robert, ed. *A Documentary History of Communism*. 2 vols. New York: Vintage Books, 1962.

Fedyukin, S. A. *Sovetskaya vlast' i burzhuuznye spetsialisty*. Moscow: Mysl', 1965.

Golinkov, David. *Krakh vrazheskogo podpol'ya*. Moscow: Politizdat, 1971.

Gordeyev, Sergei. *Kollektivizatsiya sel'skogo khozyaistva v Smolensk oblast v period 1929-1934*. Unpublished, private manuscript.

Gusev, K. V., and Eritsyan, Kh. A. *Ot soglashatel'stva k kontrrevoliutsii*. Moscow: Mysl' 1968.

Inostrannaya voennaya interventsiya grazhdanskaya voina v Sredneit kazakhstane. Alma Ata: Nauka, 1964.

Iz istorii vserossiiskoi chrezvychainoi komissii 1917-1921. Moscow: Gosizdat, 1958.

Istoriya SSSR—epokha sotsializma. Moscow: Prosveshcheniye, 1973.

Kritsman, Lev. *Geroicheskii period velikoi russkoi revoliutsii*. Moscow: Gosizdat, 1925.

Neuberg, A. *Armed Insurrection*. Translated by Quintin Hoare. London: NLB, 1970. (Note: This book was originally written in the late 1920s in the Soviet Union.)

Ocherki istorii Krasnodarskoi organizatsii KPSS. Krasnodar: Krasnodarskoe Knizdhat, 1966.

Ocherki istorii Pskovskoi organizatskii KPSS. Leningrad: Lenizdat, 1971.

Pashukanis, E. *15 let sovetskogo stroitel'stva.* Moscow: Gosizdat, 1932.
Plotnikov, K. N. *Biudzhet sovetskogo gosudarstva.* Moscow: Gosizdat, 1943.
Polyakov, Yu. A. *Perekhod k NEP y i sovetskoe krest'yanstvo.* Moscow: Nauka, 1967.
Sbornik dokumentov i materialov po istorii SSSR—sovetskogo perioda (1917-1958). Moscow: Moscow University Press, 1966.
Sharapov, G. *Razreshenie agrarnogo voprosa v rossii posle pobedy oktyabr'skoi* revoliutsii. Moscow: Gosizdat, 1961.
Sofinov, P. G. *Ocherkistorii rserossiskoi chreyvychainoi komissii (1917-1920).* Moscow: Gosizdat, 1960.
Spirin, A. M. *Klassy i partii v grazhdanskoi voine v rossii (1917-1920).* Moscow: Mysl, 1968.
Tal', B. *Put' stroitel'stva sozialisma v SSSR.* Moscow: Gosizdat, 1928.
Trifonov, Ilya, *Klassy i klassovaya bor'ba v SSSR v nachale NEPa.* Leningrad: Leningrad University Press, 1964.
Trotsky, Lev. *Khozyaestvennoe stroitel'stvo sovetskoi respubliki.* Moscow: Gosizdat, 1927.
Zverev, A. G. *O gosudarstvennom biudzhete SSSR na 1945.* Moscow: Gosizdat, 1945.

Periodicals and Newspapers

Izvestiya
Krasnaya zvezda
Pravda
Soviet Military Review, translation
Voennaya nauka i revoliutsiya
Voennyi vestnik

Encyclopedias

Bol'shaya sovetskaya entsiklopedia (1930)
Mal'aya sovetskaya entsiklopedia

Articles

Beloborodov, Z. "Nekotorye itogi vyborov v derevne." *Vlast' sovetov* 1 (January 4, 1925).

PERSONAL MEMOIRS AND ACCOUNTS OF SOVIET HISTORY

Abramovitch, Raphael. *The Soviet Revolution—1917-1939*. New York: International Universities Press, Inc., 1962.

Arshinov, P. *Istoriya Makhnovskogo dvizheniya (1918-1921)*. Berlin: Group of Russian Anarchists in Germany, 1923.

Dan, F. I. *Dva goda skitanii*. Berlin, 1922.

Denikin, A. *The White Armies*. Translated by Catherine Zvegintzov. London: Jonathan Cape, 1930.

Ivanovich, St. *VKP, desiat' let kommunisticheskoi monopolii*. Paris, 1928.

Kolchak, Admiral. *The Testimony of Kolchak and Other Siberian Materials*. Stanford, Calif.: Stanford University Press, 1935.

Krivitsky, Walter. *In Stalin's Secret Service*. New York: Harper & Brothers, 1939.

Rudnev, V. V. *Maknovshchina*. Kharkov: Knigospilka, 1928.

Weissberg, Alexander. *The Accused*. Translated by Edward Fitzgerald. New York: Simon and Schuster, 1951.

SELECT BIBLIOGRAPHY OF NON-SOVIET MATERIALS ON THE SOVIET UNION

Note: Although the vast majority of such works are in English, those not in English are also included in this section.

History of Soviet Armed Forces

Note: During the 1918-40 period under study, Soviet armed forces were known as the Red Army.

Andolenka, C. R. *Histoire de L'Armee Russe*. Paris: Flammarion, 1967.

Basseches, Nilolaus. *The Unknown Army*. New York: Viking Press, 1943.

Berchin, Michel, Ben-Horin, Eliahu. *The Red Army*. New York: W. W. Norton and Company, 1942.

Erickson, John. *The Soviet High Command: A Military-Political History, 1918-1941*. London: Macmillan, 1962. (Note: This work is one of the finest studies ever written on the subject and should be read by anyone interested in the history of the Red Army.)

Garder, Michel. *A History of the Soviet Army*. London: Pall Mall Press, 1966.

Garthoff, Raymond. *Soviet Military Policy*. New York: Frederick A. Praeger, 1966.

Hart, B. H. Liddell, ed. *The Red Army*. Gloucester, Mass.: Peter Smith, 1968.

Jackson, Robert. *The Red Falcons: The Soviet Air Force in Action, 1919-1969*. Brighton, England: Clifton Books, 1971.

Kolkowicz, Roman. *The Soviet Military and the Communist Party*. Princeton, N.J.: Princeton University Press, 1967.

Kournakoff, Sergei. *Russia's Fighting Forces*. New York: International Publishers, 1942.

Lee, Asher. *The Soviet Air Force*. New York: John Day Company, 1962.

Mackintosh, Malcolm. *Juggernaut: A History of the Soviet Armed Forces*. New York: The Macmillan Company, 1967.

White, D. Fedotoff. *The Growth of the Red Army*. Princeton, N.J.: Princeton University Press, 1944.

Whiting, Kenneth. *The Development of the Soviet Armed Forces, 1917-1966*. Maxwell Air Force Base, Ala.: Air University, 1966.

Wollenberg, Erich. *The Red Army*. Translated by Claud W. Sykes. London: Secker and Warburg, 1959.

Soviet Armed Forces, Soviet Military

Organization and Soviet Military Doctrine

Brzezinski, Zbigniew, ed. *Political Controls in the Soviet Army*. Ann Arbor, Mich.: Edwards Brothers, Inc., 1954.

Dinerstein, H. S. *War and the Soviet Union*. New York: Frederick A. Praeger, 1962.

Garthoff, Raymond. *How Russia Makes War—Soviet Military Doctrine*. London: George Allen and Unwin, 1954.

Herrick, Robert. *Soviet Naval Strategy*. Annapolis, Md.: U. S. Naval Institute, 1968.

de Sola Pool, Ithiel, et al. *Satellite Generals: A Study of Military Elites in the Soviet Sphere*. Stanford, Calif.: Stanford University Press, 1955.

Soviet Sea Power. Washington, D. C.: Center for Strategic and International Studies, 1969.

Biographies

Deutscher, Issac. *The Prophet Unarmed*. New York: Random House 1959. Vol. 2, *Trotsky: 1921-1929*.

———. *Stalin*. New York: Random House, 1960.

Jacobs, Walter. *Frunze: The Soviet Clausewitz*. The Hague, Netherlands: Martinus Nijhoff, 1969.

Shub, David. *Lenin*. Baltimore, Md.: Penguin Books, Inc., 1970.

Tucker, Robert. *Stalin As Revolutionary 1879-1929*. New York: W. W.
Norton and Company, 1973.

Ulam, Adam. *The Bolsheviks*. New York: The Macmillan Company,
1965.

_____ . *Stalin*. New York: Viking Press, 1973.

Wheatley, Dennis. *Red Eagle—A Story of the Russian Revolution and
of Klementy Efremovitch Voroshilov*. London: Hutchinson and
Company, 1967.

Note: For further biographic material on Soviet officials, especially
military men, see the following works:

Crowley, Edward; Lebed, Andrew; and Schulz, Heinrich, eds. *Party and
Government   Officials   of   the   Soviet   Union   1917-1967*.
Metuchen, N.J.: The Scarecrow Press, 1970.

Institute for the Study of the USSR (Munich). *Who's Who in the USSR
1961/62*. Munich, Germany: Intercontinental Book and Publishing Company, 1962.

_____ . *Who Was Who in the USSR*. Metuchen, N.J.: The Scarecrow
Press, 1972.

Key Officials of the Government. 2d ed. Munich, Germany: A Lebed,
1966. Part 1, *The Soviet Union 1917-1966*.

Levystky, Boris. *The Soviet Political Elite*. Stanford, Calif.: Hoover
Institution, 1969. (Note: This work, including almost 1,000
biographies of members and alternate members of the Central
Committee, is a very useful reference for nearly any attempt at elite
analysis.)

Russian History

Nineteenth Century

Curtis, John. *The Russian Army Under Nicholas I. 1825-1855*.
Durham, N. C.: Duke University Press, 1965.

Mazour, Anatole. *The First Russian Revolution, 1825*. Stanford, Calif.:
Stanford University Press, 1964.

Pares, Bernard. *A History of Russia*. New York: Alfred A. Knopf, 1947.

Vernadsky, George. *A History of Russia*. 4th ed. New Haven, Conn.: Yale
University Press, 1954.

Seton-Watson, Hugh. *The Russian Empire*. New York: Oxford University Press, 1967.

Revolution and Civil War (1917-1921)

Note: A useful introductory work for this period would be Leon Trotsky's *1905*. Translated by Avya Bostock. New York: Random House, 1971. This work, while provocative and controversial, is most interesting as a preview of 1917.

Avrich, Paul. *Kronstadt 1921*. Princeton, N.J.: Princeton University Press, 1970.
Carr, E. H. *The Bolshevik Revolution, 1917-1923*. 3 vols. Baltimore, Md.: Penguin Books, Inc., 1966-1970.
Chamberlin, William. *The Russian Revolution 1917-1921.* 2 vols. New York: Grosset and Dunlap, 1963.
Daniels, Robert. *Red October—The Bolshevik Revolution of 1917*. New York: Charles Scribner's Sons, 1967.
Footman, David. *Civil War in Russia*. New York: Frederick A. Praeger, 1962.
Kenez, Peter. *Civil War in South Russia 1918*. Berkeley and Los Angeles, Calif.: University of California Press, 1971.
Luckett, Richard. *The White Generals*. New York: Viking Press, 1971.
Swettenham, John. *Allied Intervention in Russia 1918-1919*. London: George Allen and Unwin, 1967.

General Works on Aspects of Soviet History (1917-1940)

Avtorkhanov, Abdurakhman. *The Communist Party Apparatus*. Chicago: H. Regnery and Company, 1966.
Barghoorn, Frederick. *Soviet Russian Nationalism*. Wesport, Conn.: Greenwood Press, Inc., 1976.
Baykov, Alexander. *Development of the Soviet Economic System*. Cambridge, England: Cambridge University Press, 1946.
Bialer, Seweryn. "Soviet Political Elite: Concept, Sample, Case Study." Ph. D. dissertation, Columbia University, 1966.
Brzezinski, Zbigniew. *Ideology and Power in Soviet Politics*. New York: Frederick A. Praeger, 1962.
_____ . and Huntington, Samuel. *Political Power: USA/USSR*. New York: Viking Press, 1964.
Conquest, Robert. *The Great Terror*. New York: The Macmillan Company, 1968.

Daniels, Robert. *Conscience of the Revolution.* New York: Simon and Schuster, 1969.

Djilas, Milovan. *Conversations With Stalin.* New York: Harcourt, Brace and Company, 1962.

Fainsod, Merle. *How Russia Is Ruled.* Cambridge, Mass.: Harvard University Press, 1965.

———. *Smolensk Under Soviet Rule.* Cambridge, Mass.: Harvard University Press, 1958.

Hazard, John. *The Soviet System of Government.* Chicago: University of Chicago Press, 1968.

Kassof, Allen, ed. *Prospects for Soviet Society.* New York: Frederick A. Praeger, 1968.

Keefe, Eugene, et al. *Area Handbook for the Soviet Union.* Washington, D. C.: Government Printing Office, 1971.

Leites, Nathan. *A Study of Bolshevism.* Glencoe, Ill. Free Press, 1953.

Lewin, Moshe. *Russian Peasants and Soviet Power.* London: George Allen and Unwin, 1968.

Mavor, James. *The Russian Revolution.* London: George Allen and Unwin, 1928.

Moore, Barrington. *Terror and Progress—USSR.* New York: Harper & Brothers, 1954.

Pipes, Richard. *The Formation of the Soviet Union.* Cambridge, Mass.: Harvard University Press, 1954.

———. *Revolutionary Russia.* Cambridge, Mass.: Harvard University Press, 1968.

Reshetar, John. *A Concise History of the Communist Party of the Soviet Union.* New York: Frederick A. Praeger, 1964.

Rigby, T. H. *Communist Party Membership in the U.S.S.R., 1917-1967.* Princeton, N.J.: Princeton University Press, 1968.

Schapiro, Leonard. *The Communist Party of the Soviet Union.* New York: Random House, 1960. (Note: This is a particularly useful work.)

———. *The Origin of the Communist Autocracy.* New York: Frederick A. Praeger, 1965.

Shanin, Teodor. *The Awkward Class—Political Sociology of Peasantry in a Developing Society: Russia 1910-1925.* London: Oxford University Press, 1972. (Note: This is one of the finest studies extant on the Russian peasantry.)

Treadgold, Donald. *Twentieth Century Russia.* Chicago: Rand McNally, 1964.

von Rauch, Georg. *A History of Soviet Russia*. Translated by Peter and Annette Jacobson. New York: Frederick A. Praeger, 1967.

Wolin, Simon, and Slusser, Robert, eds. *The Soviet Secret Police*. New York: Frederick A. Praeger, 1957.

Zagoria, Janet, ed. *Power and the Soviet Elite*. New York: Frederick A. Praeger, 1965.

Note: While many of the works in this section are not exclusively focused on some part of the 1917-40 period, all contained some material of relevance to this period.

Selected Articles

Berchin-Benedictoff, M. "The High Command of the Red Army." *Russian Review* 1, no. 2 (Autumn 1942).

Carr, E. H. "The Origin and Status of the Cheka." *Soviet Studies* 10, no. 1 (July 1958).

Chamberlin, William. "Russian and American Civil Wars." Russian Review 11, no. 4 (October 1952).

Daniels, Robert. "The Kronstadt Revolt of 1921: A Study in the Dynamics of Revolution." *American Slavic and East European Review* 10, no. 4 (December 1951).

Galay, Nikolai. "The Relationship Between the Structure of Society and the Armed Forces as Illustrated by the USSR," *Bulletin— Institute for the Study of the USSR* 13, no. 1 (November 1966).

———. "The Soviet Armed Forces and the Twenty-Second Party Congress." *Bulletin—Institute for the Study of the USSR* 9, no. 1 (January 1962).

Kolkowicz, Roman. "Interest Groups in Soviet Politics: The Case of the Military." *Comparative Politics* 2, no. 3 (April 1970).

Kruzhin, Peter. "Lenin and the Soviet Armed Forces." *Studies on the Soviet Union* 9 no. 1 (1970).

Narkiewicz, O. A. "Stalin, War Communism and Collectivization." *Soviet Studies* 18, no. 1 (July 1966).

Roberts, Paul. "War Communism: A Re-examination." *Slavic Review* 29, no. 2 (June 1970).

Ruslanov, P. "Marshal Zhukov." *Russian Review* 15, no. 2 (April 1956).

———. "Marshal Zhukov." *Russian Review* 15, no. 3 (July 1956).

Scharndorff, Werner. "The Bukharin Trial and Marshal Tukhachevsky's Rehabilitation." *Bulletin—Institute for the Study of the USSR* 10, no. 6 (June 1963).

Singleton, Seth. "The Tambov Revolt." *Slavic Review* 25, no. 3 (September 1966).

Slusser, Robert. "The Budget of the OGPU and the Special Troops From 1923-4 to 1928-9." *Soviet Studies* 10, no. 4 (April 1959).

Timasheff, N. S. "Overcoming Illiteracy: Public Education in Russia, 1880-1940." *Russian Review* 1, no. 2 (Autumn 1942).

CHINESE MATERIALS

Party Congresses

Eighth National Congress of the Communist Party of China. 3 vols. Peking: Foreign Languages Press, 1956.

Ninth Party Congress of the Communist Party of China, China Pictorial. Special Issue, no. 7 (1969).

Chu Teh. *The Battle Front of the Liberated Areas.* Peking: Foreign Languages Press, 1962. (Note: This speech was originally delivered at the Seventh Party Congress in 1945.)

Lin Piao. "Report to the Ninth National Congress of the Communist Party of China." *Peking Review*, no. 18 (April 30, 1969).

Works of Mao Tse-tung

Mao Tse-tung. *Selected Works. 4 vols. Peking: Foreign Languages* Press, 1967.

Selected Military Writings of Mao Tse-tung. Peking: Foreign Languages Press, 1963.

Party and Army Documents

Pre-1950 Period

Compton, Boyd, ed. and trans. *Mao's China—Party Reform Documents, 1942-1944.* Seattle, Wash.: University of Washington Press, 1966.

1950-1971 Period

Cheng, J. Chester, ed. *The Politics of the Chinese Red Army: A Translation of the Bulletin of Activities of the People's Liberation Army.* Stanford, Calif.: Hoover Institution, 1966.

Union Research Institute (URI). *The Case of P'eng Teh-huai, 1959-1968.* Kowloon, Hong Kong, 1968.

————. *CCP Documents of the Great Proletarian Cultural Revolution, 1966-1967.* Kowloon, Hong Kong, 1968.

────── . *Documents of Chinese Communist Party Central Committee, September, 1956-April, 1969*. Volume 1. Kowloon, Hong Kong, 1971.

Army and Party Publications (1950-1971)

The Chinese People's Liberation Army. Peking: Foreign Languages Press, 1950.

The Diary of Wang Chieh. Peking: Foreign Languages Press, 1967.

Ten Glorious Years. Peking: Foreign Languages Press, 1959. (Note: This is a particularly useful work in its implicit analysis of the faults of the Soviet developmental model.)

Chinese Press

East China Mainland Magazine.

Survey of China Mainland Press. 1950-1972. (Note: Extensive use has been made of this source. It is probably the single best source of information of any work in this section. However, its huge size precludes any significant use except by those who can devote a considerable amount of time.)

Select Bibliography of Non-Chinese Materials on China

Note: While the great majority of books in this section are in English, a few are in Russian. Furthermore, certain books appear in more than one of the following subsections as they cover material which extends beyond the scope of any one subsection.

Imperial China (Pre-1911 Period)

Franke, Wolfgang. *A Century of Chinese Revolution, 1851-1949*. Translated by Stanley Rudman. Columbia, S.C.: University of South Carolina Press, 1970.

Li, Ting-i, ed. *A History of Modern China*. Hanover, N.H.: Oriental Society, 1970.

McAlevay, Henry. *The Modern History of China*. London: Weidenfeld and Nicholson, 1967.

Wright, Mary, ed. *China in Revolution: The First Phase, 1900-1913*. New Haven, Conn.: Yale University Press, 1968.

————. *The Last Stand of Chinese Conservatism—The T'ung-Chih Restoration, 1862-1874.* Stanford Calif.: Stanford University Press, 1962.

1927-1949 Period

Belden, Jack. *China Shakes the World.* New York: Harper & Brothers, 1949.

Bobrow, Davis. "The Political and Economic Role of the Military in the Chinese Communist Movement." Ph. D. dissertation, MIT, 1962.

Bodde, Derk. *Peking Diary—A Year of Revolution.* New York: Henry Schuman, 1950.

Boorman, Scott. *The Protracted Game—A Wei-ch'i Interpretation of Maoist Revolutionary Strategy.* New York: Oxford University Press, 1969.

Chassin, Lionel. *The Communist Conquest of China.* Translated by Timothy Osato, Louis Grelas. Cambridge, Mass.: Harvard University Press, 1965.

Ch'en, Jerome. *Mao and the Chinese Revolution.* New York: Oxford University Press, 1967.

Chi, Hsi-cheng. *The Chinese Warlord System: 1916 to 1928.* Washington, D.C.: American University Press, 1969.

Chiu, Sin-ming. "A History of the Chinese Communist Army." Ph. D. dissertation, University of Southern California, 1958.

Clubb, O. Edmund. *Twentieth Century China.* New York: Columbia University Press, 1964.

Dupuy, Trevor. *The Military History of the Chinese Civil War.* New York: Franklin Watts, 1969.

Ernburg, G. B. *Ocherki natsional'no osvoboditelnoi bor'by kitaiskogo naroda.* Moscow: Voenizdat, 1951.

Fairbank, John K. *The United States and China.* New York: Viking Press, 1962.

Gillin, Donald. *Warlord—Yen Hsi-shan in Shansi Province, 1911-1949.* Princeton, N.J.: Princeton University Press, 1967.

Glunin, V. I. *Tret'ya grazhdanskaya revoliutsionnaya voina v kitae (1946-1949).* Moscow: Izdatel'stvo Vostochnoi Literaturni, 1958.

Guillermaz, Jacques. *A History of the Chinese Communist Party 1921-1949.* Translated by Anne Desternay. New York: Random House, 1972.

Harrison, James. *The Long March to Power—A History of the Chinese Communist Party, 1921-1972.* New York: Frederick A. Praeger, 1972.

Houn, Franklin. *A Short History of Chinese Communism.* Englewood Cliffs, N.J.: Prentice-Hall, Inc., 1967.

Kim, Ilpyong. *The Politics of Chinese Communism—Kiangsi Under the Soviets.* Berkeley and Los Angeles, Calif.: University of California Press, 1974.

Klein, Donald, and Clark, Anne. *Biographic Dictionary of Chinese Communism, 1921-1965.* Cambridge, Mass.: Harvard University Press, 1971.

Liu, F. F. *A Military History of Modern China.* Princeton, N.J.: Princeton University Press, 1956.

Pye, Lucian. *Warlord Politics.* New York: Frederick A. Praeger, 1971.

Rhoads, Edward J. M. *The Chinese Red Army, 1927-1963, An Annotated Bibliography.* Harvard East Asian Monographs. Cambridge, Mass.: Harvard University Press, 1964.

Rigg, Robert. *Red China's Fighting Hordes.* Harrisburg, Pa.: The Military Service Publishing Company, 1952.

Robinson, Thomas. *A Politico-Military Biography of Lin Piao.* Santa Monica, Calif.: RAND Corporation, 1971.

Schram, Stuart. *The Political Thought of Mao Tse-tung.* New York: Frederick A. Praeger, 1963.

Taylor, George. *The Struggle for North China.* New York: Institute of Pacific Relations, 1940.

Thornton, Richard. *China—The Struggle for Power, 1921-1972.* Bloomington, Ind.: Indiana University Press, 1973.

Tret'ya grazhdanskaya revoliutsionnaya viona v kitai. Moscow: Voenizdat, 1958.

United States Department of State. *United States Relations With China.* Washington, D.C.: Government Printing Office, 1949.

Whitson, William. *The Chinese High Command: A History of Communist Military Politics, 1927-1971.* New York: Frederick A. Praeger, 1973.

Communist Period (1950-1971)

Barnett, A. Doak. *Cadres, Bureaucracy and Political Power in Communist China.* New York: Columbia University Press, 1967.

———. ed. *Chinese Communist Politics in Action.* Seattle, Wash.: University of Washington Press, 1971.

_____ . *Communist China: The Early Years, 1949-1955*. New York: Frederick A. Praeger, 1964.

Baum, Richard, ed. *China in Ferment—Perspectives on the Cultural Revolution*. Englewood Cliffs, N.J.: Prentice-Hall, Inc., 1971.

Bobrow, Davis. "The Political and Economic Role of the Military in the Chinese Communist Movement." Ph. D. dissertation, MIT, 1962.

Bradbury, William; Meyers, Samuel; and Biderman, Albert, eds. *Mass Behavior in Battle and Captivity—The Communist Soldier in the Korean War*. Chicago: University of Chicago Press, 1968.

Bueschel, Richard. *Communist Chinese Air Power*. New York: Frederick A. Praeger, 1968.

Clubb, O. Edmund. *Twentieth Century China*. New York: Columbia University Press, 1964.

Daubier, Jean. *A History of the Chinese Cultural Revolution*. Translated by Richard Seaver. New York: Vintage Books, 1974.

Domes, Jurgen. *The Internal Politics of China, 1949-1972*. New York: Frederick A. Praeger 1973.

Elegant, Robert. *Mao's Great Revolution*. New York: World Publishing Company, 1971.

George, Alexander. *The Chinese Communist Army in Action*. New York: Columbia University Press, 1967.

Gillings, John. *The Role of the Chinese Army*. London: Oxford University Press, 1967.

Griffith, Samuel. *The Chinese People's Liberation Army*. New York: McGraw-Hill, 1967.

Harding, Harry, and Gurtov, Melvin. *The Purge of Lo Jui-ching, The Politics of Chinese Strategic Planning*. Santa Monica, Calif.: RAND Corporation, 1971.

Harrison, James. *The Long March to Power—A History of the Chinese Communist Party, 1921-1972*. New York: Frederick A. Praeger, 1972.

Hinton, Harold. *An Introduction to Chinese Politics*. New York: Frederick A. Praeger, 1973.

Ho, Ping-ti, and Tsou, Tang, eds. *China's Heritage and the Communist Political System*. Vol. 1. Chicago: University of Chicago Press, 1968.

Hsieh, Alice Langley. *Communist China's Strategy in the Nuclear Era*. Englewood Cliffs, N.J.: Prentice-Hall, Inc., 1962.

Huck, Arthur. *The Security of China*. New York: Columbia University Press, 1970.

Joffe, Ellis. *Party and Army: Professionalism and Political Control in the Chinese Officer Corps, 1949-1964*. Cambridge, Mass.: Harvard University Press, 1965.

Kau, Ying-mao. *The People's Liberation Army and China's Nation Building*. White Plains, N.Y.: International Arts and Sciences Press, 1972.

————— ; Chancellor, Paul; Ginsberg, Philip; and Perrolle, Pierre. *The Political Work System of the Chinese Communist Military*. Providence, R.I.: Brown University Press, 1971.

Klein, Donald, and Clark, Anne. *Biographic Dictionary of Chinese Communism 1921-1965*. Cambridge, Mass.: Harvard University Press, 1971.

Ping, Ching, and Bloodworth, Dennis. *Heirs Apparent*. New York: Farrar, Straus and Giroux, 1973.

Pye, Lucian. *The Spirit of Chinese Politics*. Cambridge, Mass.: MIT Press, 1968.

Rhoads, Edward J. M. *The Chinese Red Army, 1927-1963. An Annotated Bibliography*. Harvard East Asian Monographs. Cambridge, Mass.: Harvard University Press, 1964.

Schram, Stuart. *The Political Thought of Mao Tse-tung*. New York: Frederick A. Praeger, 1963.

Schurmann, Franz. *Ideology and Organization in Communist China*. Berkeley and Los Angeles, Calif.: University of California Press, 1968.

Thornton, Richard. *China—The Struggle for Power, 1921-1972*. Bloomington, Ind.: Indiana University Press, 1973.

Trager, Frank, and Henderson, William, eds. *Communist China, 1949-1969: A Twenty Year Appraisal*. New York: New York University Press, 1970.

Whiting, Allen. *China Crosses the Yalu*. New York: The Macmillan Company, 1960.

Whitson, William. *The Chinese High Command: A History of Communist Military Politics, 1927-1971*. New York: Frederick A. Praeger, 1973.

————— , ed. *The Military and Political Power in China in the 1970s*. New York: Frederick A. Praeger, 1972.

Selected Articles

Baldwin, Hanson. "China As a Military Power." *Foreign Affairs* 30 (October 1951).

Baum, Richard. "China: Year of the Mangoes." *Asian Survey* 9, no. 1 (January 1969).

Bennett, Gordon. "Military Regions and Provincial Party Secretaries: One Outcome of China's Cultural Revolution." *China Quarterly*, no. 54 (April/June 1973).

Bridgham, Philip. "The Fall of Lin Piao." *China Quarterly*, no. 55 (July/September 1973).

———. "Mao's 'Cultural Revolution': Origin and Development." *China Quarterly*, no. 29 (January/March 1967).

———. "Mao's Cultural Revolution: The Struggle to Consolidate Power," *China Quarterly*, no. 41 (January/March 1970).

Chang, Parris. "The Changing Patterns of Military Participation in Chinese Politics." *Orbis* 16, no. 3 (Fall 1972).

———. "Research Notes on the Changing Loci of Decision in the Chinese Communist Party." *China Quarterly*, no. 44 (October/December 1970).

Charles, David. "The Dismissal of Marshal P'eng Teh-huai." *China Quarterly*, no. 8 (October/December 1961).

Domes, Jurgen. "The Role of the Military in the Formation of Revolutionary Committees, 1967-1968." *China Quarterly*, no. 44 (October/December 1970).

Gittings, John. "The 'Learn From the Army' Campaign." *China Quarterly*, no. 18 (April/June 1964).

———. "Military Control and Leadership, 1949-1964." *China Quarterly*, no. 26 (April/June 1966).

Griffith, Samuel. "Communist China's Capacity to Make War." *Foreign Affairs* 43 (January 1965).

Halperin, Morton, and Lewis, John W. "New Tensions in Army-Party Relations in China (1965-1966)." *China Quarterly*, no. 26 (April/June 1966).

Hsieh, Alice Langley. "China's Secret Military Papers: Military Doctrine and Strategy." *China Quarterly*, no. 18 (April/June 1964).

Joffe, Ellis. "The Chinese Army After the Cultural Revolution: the Effects of Intervention." *China Quarterly*, no. 55 (July/September 1973).

———. "The Chinese Army Under Lin Piao: Prelude to Political Intervention." In *China: Management of a Revolutionary Society*. Edited by John Lindbeck. Seattle, Wash.: University of Washington Press, 1971.

Klein, Donald. "The 'Next Generation' of Chinese Leaders." *China Quarterly*, no. 12 (October/December 1962).

Klein, Sydney. "Capitalism, Socialism and the Economic Thought of Mao Tse-tung." *Political Science Quarterly* 73, no. 1 (March 1958).

Lewis, John W. "China's Secret Military Papers: Continuities and Revelations." *China Quarterly*, no. 18 (April/June 1964).

Nathan, Andrew. "A Factionalism Model for CCP Politics." *China Quarterly*, no. 53 (January/March 1973).

Needham, Joseph. "The Past in China's Present." *The Centennial Review* 4 (1960).

Oksenberg, Michel. "Policy Making Under Mao, 1949-1968: An Overview." In *China: Management of a Revolutionary Society*. Edited by John Lindbeck. Seattle, Wash.: University of Washington Press, 1971.

———, and Goldstein, Steven. "The Chinese Political Spectrum." *Problems of Communism* 23, no. 2 (March/April 1974).

Parish, William L. "Factions in Chinese Military Politics." *China Quarterly*, no. 56 (October/December 1973).

Powell, Ralph. "Commissars in the Economy: 'Learn From the PLA' Movement in China." *Asian Survey* 5, no. 3 (March 1965).

———. "The Military Affairs Committee and Party Control of the Military in China." *Asian Survey* 3, no. 7 (July 1963).

———. The Party, the Government and the Gun." *Asian Survey* 10, no. 6 (June 1970).

———, and Yoon, Chang-Kun. "Public Security and the PLA." *Asian Survey* 12, no. 12 (December 1972).

Robinson, Thomas. "The Wuhan Incident: Local Strife and Provincial Rebellion During the Cultural Revolution." *China Quarterly* no. 47 (July/September 1971).

"Some Perspectives on Chinese Politics." *Problems of Communism* 24, no. 1 (January/February 1975).

Tryon, Carol. "The Role of Demobilized Soldiers in the People's Republic of China, 1955-1965." Certificate essay. Columbia University East Asian Institute, 1969.

Weakland, John. "Chinese Film Images of Invasion and Resistance." *China Quarterly*, no. 47 (July/September 1971).

Whitson, William. "The Field Army in Chinese Communist Military Politics." *China Quarterly*, no. 37 (January/March 1969).

Wilbur, C. Martin. "The Ashes of Defeat." *China Quarterly*, no. 18 (April/June 1964).

SELECT BIBLIOGRAPHY OF WORKS ON KEY AREAS OF RELEVANCE TO THIS STUDY

The Military and Politics

Bienen, Henry, ed. *The Military and Modernization.* Chicago: Aldine-Atherton, 1971.

———, ed. *The Military Intervenes.* New York: Russell Sage Foundation, 1968.

Craig, Gordon. *The Politics of the Prussian Army, 1640-1945.* New York: Oxford University Press, 1955.

Finer, S. E. *The Man on Horseback—The Role of the Military in Politics.* New York: Frederick A. Praeger, 1962.

Janowitz, Morris. *The Military in the Political Development of New Nations.* Chicago: University of Chicago Press, 1964.

Johnson, John. J. *The Military and Society in Latin America.* Stanford, Calif.: Stanford University Press, 1964.

———, ed. *The Role of the Military in Underdeveloped Countries.* Princeton, N.J.: Princeton University Press, 1962.

Kennedy, Gavin. *The Military in the Third World.* New York: Charles Scribner's Sons, 1974.

Lieuwen, Edwin. *Generals vs. Presidents—Neomilitarism in Latin America.* New York: Frederick A. Praeger, 1964.

Ralston, David. *The Army of the Republic—The Development of the Military in the Political Evolution of France, 1871-1914.* Cambridge, Mass.: MIT Press, 1967.

Schmidt, Steffen, and Dorfman, Gerald, eds. *Soldiers in Politics.* Los Altos, Calif.: Geron-X Inc., 1974.

The Military and War

Aron, Raymond. *The Century of Total War.* Boston: Beacon Press, 1954.

Dupuy, R., and Dupuy, Trevor. *The Encyclopedia of Military History.* New York: Harper & Row, 1970.

Earle, Edward, ed. *Makers of Modern Strategy.* Princeton, N.J.: Princeton University Press, 1943.

Eckstein, Harry, ed. *Internal War.* New York: Free Press, 1964.

Fuller, J. F. C. *The Conduct of War, 1789-1961.* New Brunswick, N.J.: Rutgers University Press, 1961.

——— *A Military History of the Western World.* Volume 3. New York: Funk and Wagnalls, 1956.

_____ . *Tanks in the Great War, 1914-1918.* London: John Murray, 1920.

Fulls, Cyril. *The Great War, 1914-1918.* New York: Capricorn Books, 1959.

Higham, Robin. *Air Power: A Concise History.* New York: St. Martin's Press, 1972.

Janowitz, Morris. *The Professional Soldier.* New York: Free Press, 1970.

Jenkins, E. H. *A Study of the French Navy.* London: Macdonald and Jane's 1973.

Kemp, P. K. *A History of the Royal Navy.* New York: G. P. Putnam and Sons, 1969.

Martel, G. LeQ. *Our Armored Forces.* London: Faber and Faber, 1943.

Orgill, Douglas. *The Tank.* London: Morrison and Gibb, 1970.

Ridgway, Matthew. *The Korean War.* Garden City, N.Y.: Doubleday and Company, 1967.

Ropp, Theodore. *War in the Modern World.* Durham, N.C.: Duke University Press, 1959.

Shaul, Moshe Ben. *Generals of Israel.* Translated by I. Hanoch. Tel Aviv, Israel: Hadar Publishing House, 1968.

Sims, Charles, *The Royal Air Force—The First Fifty Years.* London: Adam and Charles Black, 1968.

Speier, Hans. *War and the Social Order: Papers in Political Sociology.* New York: G. W. Stewart, 1942.

Revolution and Modernization

Calvert, Peter. *Revolutions.* New York: Frederick A. Praeger 1970.

Huntington, Samuel. *Political Order in Changing Societies.* New Haven, Conn.: Yale University Press, 1968.

Johnson, Chalmers. *Peasant Nationalism and Communist Power.* Stanford, Calif.: Stanford University Press, 1962.

_____ . *Revolutionary Change.* Boston: Little, Brown and Company, 1966.

_____ . *Revolution and the Social System.* Stanford, Calif.: Hoover Institution, 1964.

Kaplan, Lawrence, ed. *Revolutions: A Comparative Study.* New York: Random House, 1973.

Leys, Colin, ed. *Politics and Change in Developing Countries.* Cambridge, England: Cambridge University Press, 1969.

Moore, Barrington. *Social Origins of Dictatorship and Democracy.* Boston: Beacon Press, 1967.

Tucker, Robert. *The Marxian Revolutionary Idea.* New York: W. W. Norton and Company, 1969.

Wolf, Eric. *Peasant Wars of the Twentieth Century.* New York: Harper & Row, 1969.

Organizations and Conflict

Coser, Lewis. *The Functions of Social Conflict*. Glencoe Ill.: Free Press, 1956.

Etzioni, Amitai. *A Comparative Analysis of Complex Organizations*. New York: Free Press, 1961.

Goffman, Ervin. *Asylums: Essays on the Social Situation of Mental Patients and Other Inmates*. Chicago: Aldine Publishing Company, 1961.

Janowitz, Morris. *Political Conflict: Essays in Political Sociology*. Chicago: Quadrangle Books, 1970.

Katz, Daniel, and Kahn, Robert. *The Social Psychology of Organizations*. New York: John Wiley & Sons, 1966.

Merton, Robert. *Social Theory and Social Structure*. New York: Free Press, 1965.

Selznick, Philip. *Leadership in Administration*. Evanston, Ill.: Row, Peterson and Company, 1957.

Comparative Communism

Bernstein, Thomas. "Leadership and Mobilization in the Collectivization of Agriculture in Russia and China: A Comparison." Ph. D. dissertation, Columbia University, 1970.

Dallin, Alexander, and Breslauer, George. *Political Terror in Communist Systems*. Stanford, Calif.: Stanford University Press, 1970.

Frederick Fleron, ed. *Communist Studies and the Social Sciences*. Chicago: Rand McNally, 1969.

Gripp, Richard. *The Political System of Communism*. New York: Dodd, Mead, 1973.

Ionescu, Ghita. *Comparative Communist Politics*. London: Macmillan, 1972.

Johnson, Chalmers, ed. *Change in Communist Systems*. Stanford, Calif.: Stanford University Press, 1970.

Rubinstein, Alvin, ed. *Communist Political Systems*. Englewood Cliffs, N.J.: Prentice-Hall, Inc., 1966.

Treadgold, Donald, ed. *Soviet and Chinese Communism: Similarities and Differences*. Seattle, Wash.: University of Washington Press, 1967.

Triska, Jan, ed. *Communist Party States: Comparative and International Studies*. Indianapolis, Ind.: Bobbs-Merrill, 1969.

Other Relevant Works

Churchill, Winston. *The World Crisis*. Vol. 5. New York: Charles Scribner's Sons, 1929.

Cipolla, Carlo. *Literacy and Development in the West*. Baltimore, Md.: Penguin Books, Inc., 1959.

Eisenstadt, S. N. *The Political Systems of Empires*. New York: Free Press, 1969.

Pejanovic, Dusan. *The Yugoslav People's Army in the Reconstruction and Development of the Country*. Belgrade, Yugoslavia: Vojnoidavacki Zavod, 1969.

Selected Articles

Barghoorn, Frederick. "Analytic Framework: Soviet Politics in Comparative and Historical Contexts." *Studies in Comparative Communism*. 4, no. 3-4 (July/October 1971).

Blau, Peter. "A Formal Theory of Differentiation in Organizations." *American Sociological Review* 35, no. 2 (April 1970).

Bobrow, Davis. "The Civil Role of the Military: Some Critical Hypotheses." *Western Political Quarterly* 19, no. 1 (March 1966).

Lasswell, Harold. "The Garrison-State Hypothesis Today." In *Changing Patterns of Military Politics*. Edited by Samuel Huntington. New York: Free Press, 1962.

Lissak, Moshe. "Modernization and Role-Expansion of the Military in Developing Countries: A Comparative Analysis." *Comparative Studies in Society and History* 9, no. 3 (April 1967).

Shoup, Paul. "Comparing Communist Nations: Prospects for an Empirical Approach." *American Political Science Review* 62, no. 3 (March 1968).

Tucker, Robert. "On the Comparative Study of Communism." *World Politics* (January 1967).

INDEX

About the Author

JONATHAN R. ADELMAN is an Assistant Professor in the Graduate School of International Studies at the University of Denver, Colorado. His articles have appeared in journals such as *Studies in Comparative Communism, Armed Forces and Society, Survey,* and *Military Affairs.*